DIFFERENTIAL EQUATIONS WITH *MATHEMATICA*™

Kevin R. Coombes
Brian R. Hunt
Ronald L. Lipsman
John E. Osborn
Garrett J. Stuck

University of Maryland at College Park

John Wiley & Sons, Inc.
New York • Chichester • Brisbane • Toronto • Singapore

ISBN 0-471-10874-X

Printed in the United States of America

10 9 8 7 6 5 4 3 2

Printed and bound by Malloy Lithographing, Inc.

Preface

As the subject matter of differential equations continues to grow, as new technologies become commonplace, as old areas of application are expanded, and as new ones appear on the horizon, the content and viewpoint of courses and their textbooks must also evolve.

Boyce & DiPrima, **Elementary Differential Equations**, Fifth Edition.

Traditional introductory courses in ordinary differential equations (ODE) have concentrated on teaching a repertoire of techniques for finding formula solutions of various classes of differential equations. Typically, the result was rote application by students of formula techniques without a serious qualitative understanding of such fundamental aspects of the subject as stability, asymptotics, dependence on parameters, and numerical methods. These fundamental ideas are difficult to teach because they have a great deal of geometrical content and, especially in the case of numerical methods, involve a great deal of computation. Modern mathematical software systems, which are particularly effective for geometrical and numerical analysis, can help to overcome these difficulties. This supplement changes the emphasis in the traditional ODE course by using a mathematical software system to introduce numerical methods, geometric interpretation, symbolic computation, and qualitative analysis into the course in a basic way.

We designed this supplement to accompany the fifth edition of the textbook **Elementary Differential Equations**, by Boyce & DiPrima, the text we use in our own course. It could, however, easily be used in conjunction with most other ODE texts. It addresses most of the standard topics in ODE, but with a strikingly different emphasis.

The mathematical software system we use is *Mathematica*. (The supplement is also available in a forthcoming *Maple* version.) We assume that the user has no prior experience with *Mathematica*. We have included concise instructions for using *Mathematica* on the four most popular computer platforms: *Macintosh*, *Windows*, *NeXT*, and the *X Window System*. This supplement is not a complete introduction or reference manual to either *Mathematica* or any of the computer platforms. Instead, it focuses on the specific features of *Mathematica* that are useful

iii

for analyzing differential equations. It also describes the features of the *Mathematica* "Notebook" interface that are necessary for creating a finished document.

We had two basic goals in mind when we introduced this supplement into our course. First, we wanted to deepen students understanding of differential equations by giving them a new tool, a mathematical software system, for analyzing differential equations. Second, we wanted to bring students to a level of expertise in the mathematical software system that would allow them to use it in other mathematics, engineering, or science courses. These basic goals have guided our project from start to finish. We believe that we have achieved these goals in our own classes. We hope this supplement will be useful to students and instructors on other campuses in achieving the same goals.

Acknowledgements

We thank Peter Olver of the University of Minnesota, and our colleague Jonathan Rosenberg, both of whom contributed material to this book. We are grateful to all of our colleagues who have used earlier versions of this material in their classes at College Park. This published version should make their lives a little easier. We are particularly indebted to the many students who have used these materials, and have communicated to us their comments and suggestions. We are grateful to our departmental administrators for giving us the freedom to experiment in what has been a very stable course. Finally, we thank Barbara Holland, mathematics editor at Wiley, for her enthusiastic and thoughtful support of our project.

Kevin Coombes
Brian Hunt
Ron Lipsman
John Osborn
Garrett Stuck

College Park, Maryland
July 1, 1994

Contents

Chapter 1

Introduction

We begin by describing the philosophy behind our approach to the study of ordinary differential equations. This philosophy has its roots in the way we understand, use, and apply differential equations; it has influenced our teaching and guided the development of this book. This chapter also contains two user's guides, one for students and one for instructors.

Guiding Philosophy

In scientific inquiry, when we are interested in understanding, describing, or predicting some complex phenomenon, we use the technique of *mathematical modeling*. In this approach, we describe the state of a (physical, biological, econometric, or other) system by one or more functions of one or several variables. For example, the position $s = s(t)$ of a particle is a function of the time t; the temperature $T = T(x, y, z, t)$ in a body is a function of the position (x, y, z) and the time t; the gravitational or electromagnetic force on an object is a function of its position; the money supply is a function of time; the populations $x = x(t)$ and $y = y(t)$ of two competing species are functions of time. Next, we attempt to formulate, in mathematical terms, a fundamental law governing the phenomenon. Typically, this formulation results in one or more differential equations; *i.e.*, equations involving derivatives of the functions describing the state of the system with respect to the variables they depend on. Frequently, the functions depend on only one variable, and the differential equation is called *ordinary*. To be specific, if $x = x(t)$ denotes the function describing the state of our system, an *ordinary differential equation* in $x(t)$ might involve $x'(t)$, $x''(t)$, higher derivatives, or other known functions of t. By contrast, in a *partial differential equation*, the functions depend on several variables.

In addition to the fundamental law, we usually describe the initial state of the system. We express this state mathematically by specifying *initial values* $x(0)$, $x'(0)$, etc. In this way, we arrive at an *initial value problem*—an ordinary differential equation together with initial conditions. If we can solve the initial value problem, then the solution is a function $x(t)$ that predicts the future state of the system. Using the solution, we can describe qualitative or quantitative properties of the system.

At this stage, we compare the values predicted by $x(t)$ against experimental data that we accumulate by observing the phenomenon. If the experimental data and the function values match, we congratulate ourselves on a job well done and go on to the next challenge. If they do not match, we go back, refine the model, and start again. Even if we are satisfied with the model, we may later arrive at a time when new technology, new requirements, or newly discovered features of the phenomenon render our old data obsolete. Again, we respond by reexamining the model.

The subject of differential equations consists in large part of building and solving mathematical models. Many results and methods have been developed for this purpose. These results and methods fall within one or more of the following themes:

(1) Existence and uniqueness of solutions

(2) Dependence of solutions on initial values

(3) Derivation of formulas for solutions

(4) Numerical calculation of solutions

(5) Graphical analysis of solutions

(6) Qualitative analysis of differential equations and their solutions.

The basic results on existence and uniqueness (theme 1), and dependence on initial values (theme 2), form the foundation of the subject of differential equations. The derivation of formula solutions (theme 3) is a rich and important part of the subject; a variety of methods have been developed for finding formula solutions to special classes of equations. Although many equations can be solved exactly, many others cannot. However, any equation, solvable or not, can be analyzed using numerical methods (theme 4), graphical methods (theme 5), and qualitative methods (theme 6). The ability to obtain qualitative and quantitative information without the aid of an explicit formula solution is crucial. That information may suffice to analyze and describe the original phenomenon (which led to the model, which gave rise to the differential equation).

Traditionally, introductory courses in differential equations focused on methods for deriving exact solutions to special types of equations, and included some simple numerical and qualitative methods. The human limitations involved in compiling numerical or graphical data were formidable obstacles to implementing more advanced qualitative or quantitative methods. Computer platforms have reduced these obstacles. Sophisticated software and mainframe computers have enhanced the use of quantitative and qualitative methods in the theory and applications of differential equations. With the arrival of comprehensive mathematical software systems on personal computers, this modern approach has become accessible to undergraduates.

In this book, we use the mathematical software system *Mathematica* to implement this new approach. We introduce symbolic, numerical, graphical, and qualitative techniques, and show how to use *Mathematica* to analyze differential equations and their solutions with these techniques. As you encounter each new technique, you should ask: Under which of the six themes listed above does it fit? Answering that question will help you to organize the course material.

In order to take advantage of this modern approach, you must learn to use a computer platform effectively. We give detailed instructions for using *Mathematica* on four specific types of computers. In this way, we minimize the time required to learn to use the computer platform.

Finally, the software system we have chosen provides an additional valuable opportunity: it enables the production of "Notebooks" that combine textual commentary with the numerical, symbolic, and graphical output of the mathematical software system. Engineers and scientists have to develop not only skills in analyzing problems and interpreting solutions, but also the ability to present coherent conclusions in a logical and convincing style. You should use the Notebook capabilities of the software to submit solutions to the computer assignments in such a style. This is excellent preparation for the professional requirements that lie ahead.

Student User's Guide

The chapters of this book can be divided into three classes: descriptions of the computer platform, supplementary material on ordinary differential equations (ODE), and computer problem sets. Here is a brief description of the contents.

The four computer platform chapters require no prior knowledge of computers. Chapter 2 explains how to start *Mathematica* on four kinds of computers: *Macintosh*, *Windows*, *NeXT*, and the *X Window System*. Chapter 3 introduces some basic *Mathematica* commands. You should work through Chapters 2 and 3 while sitting at your computer. Then you should work the problems in Problem Set A. These steps will bring you to a minimal level of competence in the use of *Mathematica*. You should complete these tasks within 1 week after the semester begins. After that, read Chapter 4, which contains detailed instructions for manipulating the *Mathematica* Notebook interface on your computer. Finally, Chapter 8 is an introduction to the more sophisticated *Mathematica* commands that will be useful in later problem sets. It is best to read this chapter after working some problems in Problem Set B, but before starting on Problem Set C.

Keep in mind that the computer platform chapters are intended to teach you enough about *Mathematica* to study ordinary differential equations. If you want to explore the mathematical software system in more depth, then you should consult a book devoted to that topic. The standard reference is: Stephen Wolfram, **Mathematica: A System for Doing Mathematics by Computer**, Second Edition, Addison-Wesley, 1991. Guides to the *Mathematica* interface on various computers are also available from Wolfram Research.

The seven ODE chapters are intended to supplement the material in your text. The emphasis in this book differs from that found in a traditional ODE text. The main difference is less emphasis on the search for exact formula solutions, and greater emphasis on qualitative, graphical, and numerical analysis of the equations and their solutions. Furthermore, the commands for analyzing differential equations with *Mathematica* appear in these chapters.

Although you are expected to devote considerable time to the material in this book, you should remember that it is a *supplement* to your main text. Your instructor should supply a syllabus that explains how to coordinate the chapters in this supplement with the sections of your text. You should keep up with the syllabus, read carefully all the assigned sections in your text, and do many of the problems at the end of those sections. For your information, here is a list of the ODE chapters in this supplement, and the corresponding chapters in the textbook Boyce & DiPrima, **Elementary Differential Equations**, 5th edition.

Title of ODE Chapter	Corresponds to Boyce & DiPrima
Solutions of Differential Equations	Chapter 2
A Qualitative Approach to Differential Equations	Chapter 2
Numerical Methods	Chapter 8
Qualitative Theory of Second Order Linear Equations	Chapter 3
Symbolic Computational Methods	Chapters 5 & 6
Higher Order Equations and Systems of First Order Equations	Chapters 4 & 7
Qualitative Theory for Systems of Differential Equations	Chapter 9

The third collection of documents in this book consists of six sets of computer problems. The problem sets form an integral part of the course. Solving these problems will expose you to the qualitative, graphical, and numerical features of the course. Each set contains about fifteen problems; your instructor will decide which problems to assign, and when and how you are to submit them.

You can most profitably attack the problem sets if you plan to do them in two distinct sessions. Begin by reading the problems and thinking about the issues involved. Jot down some notes about how *Mathematica* can help you solve the problems. Although it is tempting to sit at the computer and start typing immediately, you will find that approach to be inefficient and potentially frustrating. Some preparation with pencil and paper will be useful. Then go to the computer and start solving the problems. If you get stuck, save your work and go on to the next problem. You should expect to spend at least one hour per problem. If there are things you'd like to discuss with your instructor, print out the relevant parts of the Notebook to take with you. Then log out, go home, and try to digest what you've done—decide what's right, what's wrong, what could be done better, what surprises you encountered, etc. Talk to your instructor or your peers about anything you don't understand. This first session should be attempted a week before the assignment is due. After you have reviewed your output and obtained answers to your questions, you are ready for your second session. At this point, you should fill the gaps, correct your mistakes, and polish your Notebook. This will take another hour or so per problem. Although you may find yourself spending extra time on the first few problems, if you read the *Mathematica* chapters carefully, and follow the suggestions above, you should steadily increase your level of competence in using *Mathematica*.

The end of this book contains two useful sections: a Glossary and a collection of Sample Notebook Solutions. The Glossary contains a brief summary of some *Mathematica* commands, options, and built-in functions. The Sample Notebook Solutions show how we solved several problems from this book. These samples will serve as guides when you prepare your own Notebook solutions. Emulate them. Strive to prepare coherent, organized solutions. Combine *Mathematica*'s input, output, and graphics with your own textual commentary and analysis of the problem. Edit the final version of your solution to remove syntax errors and false starts. You will soon take pride in submitting complete, polished solutions to the problems.

Instructor's Guide

The philosophy that guided the writing of this book is explained at the beginning of this chapter. Here is a capsule summary of that philosophy. We seek:

- To guide students into a more interpretive mode of thinking.
- To use a mathematical software system to enhance students' ability to compute symbolic and numerical solutions, and perform qualitative and graphical analysis of differential equations.
- To develop course material that reflects the current state of ODE and emphasizes the mathematical modeling of physical problems.
- To minimize the time required to learn to use the computer platform.

Our material consists of computer platform documents, ODE supplements, and computer problem sets. Here are our recommendations for integrating this material into the course.

Platform Documents. These are discussed in the preceding section. Proper use of these documents will quickly propel students to a reasonable level of proficiency. Students should read Chapters 2 and 3, and work Problem Set A within the first week of the semester. They should read Chapter 4 immediately after that, but they can delay reading Chapter 8 until after they start Problem Set B.

ODE Chapters. These seven chapters supplement the material in a traditional text. We use *Mathematica* to study differential equations using symbolic, numerical, graphical, and qualitative methods. We emphasize the following topics: stability, comparison methods, numerical methods, direction fields, and phase portraits. These topics are not emphasized to the same degree in a traditional text. We suggest that you incorporate this new emphasis into your class discussions. You should devote some class time to each chapter. Specific guidelines are difficult to prescribe, and the required time varies with each chapter, but on average we spend 30–40 minutes per chapter in class discussion. Of course, students will pay greater attention to the chapters if the material appears on quizzes and exams.

The structure of this book requires that numerical methods be discussed early in the course, immediately after the discussion of first order equations. The discussion of numerical methods should be directed toward the use of *Mathematica*'s numerical ODE solver **NDSolve**.

Computer Problem Sets. There are six computer problem sets. The topics addressed in the problem sets are:

(A) Practice with *Mathematica*
(B) First Order Equations
(C) Numerical Solutions of Differential Equations
(D) Second Order Equations
(E) Series Solutions and Laplace Transforms
(F) Systems of Equations

Problem Set A is a practice set designed to acquaint students with the basic symbolic and graphical capabilities of *Mathematica*, and to reacclimate them to calculus. It should be assigned on the first day of class, to be completed within one week. It is best to assign each remaining problem set at least two weeks before the due date. The course material corresponding to the problem set should be covered during those two weeks. It is good practice to set aside a small amount of class time to discuss questions that arise in students' first attempts to work the problems. That should typically be 3–5 days before the due date. (In the student guide, we suggested a two-stage plan of attack for completing the problem sets. Your class discussion should ideally occur after stage 1.)

We recommend that you assign all of Problem Set A and 3–6 problems from the other problem sets. Students should be required not only to analyze the problems critically, but also to present their analysis in coherent English and mathematics, displayed appropriately on their printouts. To accomplish this, students must master the editing features in the Notebook interface of *Mathematica*. These features are discussed in the computer platform chapters. This skill is very important: Engineers and scientists do not just solve problems; they must also present their ideas in cogent and convincing fashion. We expect students to do the same in this course.

It is important to keep in mind that computer files can be copied effortlessly. You should choose a policy regarding student collaboration, and make this policy clear. For example, you might allow students to discuss the assignments, but require them to create the solution Notebooks themselves. Or you might allow students to work jointly and to submit collective solutions. We have found that allowing students to collaborate (in teams of no more than three) can be very beneficial. You should also vary the problems you assign from semester to semester.

Hardware Considerations.   Before using these materials, you should make sure that your institution has enough machines with enough computing power to run *Mathematica*. This determination should be made well before the semester starts. To solve the problems in this book in a reasonable amount of time, you need a computer with 8–12 megabytes of random access memory (RAM). On some platforms, *Mathematica* requires a numeric coprocessor (sometimes called a floating point unit, or FPU); it is recommended for all platforms.

Software Considerations.   New versions of software appear frequently. When a complex system like *Mathematica* changes, many commands work better than they did before, some work differently, and a few may no longer work at all. The version of *Mathematica* that you use affects the problem sets and the chapters that describe the computer interface. Most problems in this book can be solved using *Mathematica* Version 2.0. The exceptions are a few problems in Problem Set E, which require *Mathematica* Version 2.1. You should not expect to be able to solve the problems using a version of *Mathematica* older than 2.0. In principle, you should be able to solve the problems using more recent versions. (One change to watch for: the **Solve** command was modified in Version 2.2 to prevent it from reporting false solutions. Because of the changes, it may fail to find some correct solutions.)   As this book goes to press, the current version of *Mathematica* is Version 2.2. In this book (in Chapters 2 and 4, in particular), we have tried to describe Version 2.2 of *Mathematica*. If you use a different version of the software, then the interface you see may differ slightly from the one we describe.

Generalities.   You do not have to be a *Mathematica* expert to use this course supplement. On the other hand, both you and your students will benefit if you spend some time working with *Mathematica*. We recommend that, in addition to working through Problem Set A, you work through the problems you assign in each set, preferably on the same computers that the students will use.

Our practice is to spend almost no class time discussing *Mathematica* per se. We try not to lose sight of the fact that we are teaching a course in *mathematics*, not *Mathematica*. We expect students to gain expertise in *Mathematica* from this book, from experimentation, from on-line help, from talking to each other, from questions addressed to the instructor after class and in office hours, and by consulting outside literature such as the manual **Mathematica: A System for Doing Mathematics by Computer**, by Stephen Wolfram.

Students often try to establish the following mode in their mathematics courses: "Give me a formula, I will give you a number!" However, we want students to understand the motives and methods behind a formula and its use. In the graphical environment offered by *Mathematica*, students sometimes try to establish a new mode: "Give me a program, I will give you a picture!" We ask not only that students produce a picture, but also that they interpret it, analyze the phenomenon it represents, and describe clearly and coherently the conclusions they derive from it.

Sample Syllabus.   In this section, we assume that the text for the course is the fifth edition of **Elementary Differential Equations** by Boyce & DiPrima. Suitable modifications of these instructions must be made if you use a different text. This supplement contains enough material to address the topics in the first nine chapters of Boyce & DiPrima. This material is more than ample for one semester or two quarters of study. If the course is given in a 15-week semester, then it is likely that some portions of the first nine chapters of Boyce & DiPrima will have to be omitted. For example, at the University of Maryland in College Park, we omit Chapters 5 and 6. Because of the heavy emphasis on *Mathematica*'s numerical ODE solver, it is imperative that numerical methods be treated early in the course.

The following syllabus is for a typical Fall Semester. It assumes a MWF schedule with 38 lectures (14 weeks less one day for Thanksgiving and three days for exams).

Boyce & DiPrima Sections	Material from this book Chapters	Problem Sets	Number of Lectures
2.1–2.8	1–6	A, B	10
8.1–8.4	7, 8	C	3
3.1–3.9	9	D	10
4.1–4.2	11		1
7.1–7.7	11	F	7
9.1–9.5	12	F	7

The following dates indicate where exams and problem set due dates could be placed. Each problem set should be assigned at least two weeks in advance of the due date.

Item	Lecture Number
Problem Set A	5
Exam 1	11
Problem Set B	13
Problem Set C	20
Exam 2	25
Problem Set D	27
Exam 3	38
Problem Set F	40

Here is a sample grading scheme that gives ample weight to the *Mathematica* assignments: 3 Exams (@ 15% each) = 45%; 4 Computer Problem Sets (@ 5% each) = 20%; Quizzes or Standard Homework = 5%; and the Final Exam = 30%.

The culmination of the course is Chapter 12 and Problem Set F, which correspond to Chapter 9 in the text by Boyce & DiPrima. This material unites the numerical, geometric, and qualitative approaches to the study of differential equations, and applies them to systems of equations that model real problems. Many of our students do achieve a synthesis of this material; we believe that they leave the course with a deeper understanding of and a better appreciation for the subject of differential equations.

Instructors have a great deal of flexibility in deciding how to integrate the material from this supplement into a course. By choosing among the ODE chapters (Chapters 5–7 and 9–12), the instructor can decide which aspect of the course to emphasize. In order to emphasize numerical methods, you could stress Chapter 7 and Problem Set C. In order to emphasize symbolic computation, you could stress Chapters 5 and 10 and Problem Set E. In order to emphasize geometric methods, you could stress Chapters 6 and 9 and Problem Sets B and D. Chapter 11 incorporates both symbolic and geometric methods.

By adjusting the number of problems assigned from each problem set, the instructor can adjust the level of intensity. For example, some of our colleagues spread the problems out in a more uniform way during a semester, instead of assigning several substantial problem sets. Although we prefer to assign a few substantial problem sets, the material accommodates either mode.

Chapter 2

Getting Started
with *Mathematica*

In this chapter, we describe the basic skills needed to use *Mathematica* on several different computer platforms. In particular, we describe how to open, save, and print files. These are all features of the *interface* between *Mathematica* and the particular computer operating system that you are using. These instructions are distinct from the actual commands you will use to do mathematics with *Mathematica*. The next chapter introduces the mathematical aspects of *Mathematica*.

This chapter has four parts, one for each of the following user interfaces: *Macintosh*, *Windows*, *NeXTStep*, and the *X Window System*. You should find out what kind of computer and operating system you will be using, and then sit down at the computer with this guide and read the appropriate section. We note that *Windows* is most commonly found on PCs, *NeXTStep* on *NeXT* computers, and the *X Window System* on *UNIX* workstations. If you are using *Windows* or the *Macintosh* operating system on a computer that is networked, some of the features we describe below may be different for your particular installation.

All of the systems we describe are window-based interfaces, which are manipulated using the keyboard and a *mouse* (a small boxy object next to the keyboard). Moving the mouse moves a small arrow on the screen (called a *cursor*). To *click* on an object, place the cursor over the object and click the mouse button (if your mouse has more than one button, use the left button). To *double-click*, position the cursor and press the button twice in rapid succession. To *drag* an object, position the cursor over it, press and hold the mouse button, slide the object to where you want it, and then release the mouse button. A window can be dragged by its titlebar.

Mathematica on a *Macintosh*

When you sit down at a *Macintosh* it may be turned off, or it may be running a screensaver program. If it's off, turn it on and wait until it is finished booting. If a screensaver is running, move the computer's mouse to refresh the display. If all goes well, along the top of the screen you should see the following (from left to right): an Apple icon; a series of menu buttons; the time; a "Balloon Help" icon; and in the upper right-hand corner, an "Application" icon. Click and hold on the Application icon. A menu will appear that will show, among other things, a list of applications running on the *Macintosh*. There will be a check mark on the button corresponding to the current application. Drag the mouse down to the "Finder" button, and then release. Your screen may change, depending on which application was active, and you should see one or more windows or panels on the screen. You are now in the Finder.

The Finder is the *Macintosh* program used for finding, copying, moving, and organizing files. Each of the icons in the Finder represents either a file or a folder; a folder is a group of files bundled together. Clicking on a file or folder icon will *select* the icon, and the icon will be darkened. Double-clicking on a folder icon will cause the Finder to bring up a new window displaying a set of icons representing the files in that folder. Double-clicking on a file icon will open the file. The *Macintosh* tries to open a file using an appropriate *application*, or program. For example, *Mathematica* files will be opened using the *Mathematica* program. Double-clicking on such a file will open it in *Mathematica*. You can usually tell the type of a file by looking at its icon. For example, the icon for *Mathematica* files is a stellated icosahedron (a three-dimensional star).

If a window is partially obscured you can bring it to the front by clicking on any part of it. Clicking in the small box in the upper left-hand corner of a window will make the window disappear.

Moving files from one folder to another is done as follows: find the folder into which you want to move (or copy) a file. This folder can be either in iconic form, or in the form of an open window showing its contents. Then find the file you want to move and drag it to the target folder. An icon representing the file will appear in the target folder. (The file will be moved or copied, depending on who owns the file and folder.) To delete a file, drag its icon into the trash can at the bottom right-hand corner of the screen. Then select **Empty Trashcan** from the **Special** menu at the top of the screen. A warning panel will appear on the screen asking you to confirm that you want to delete the files in the trash can.

On-line Help for the *Macintosh*. If you have never used a *Macintosh* computer before, it is probably a good idea to go through the *Macintosh* tutorial called "Macintosh Basics". You can start this tutorial by double-clicking on its icon. The tutorial will cover the basics of managing files and opening applications and will help you become comfortable using the *Macintosh*. You can also get a rudimentary kind of help by turning on the **Show Balloons** option in the **Balloon Help** menu.

Starting *Mathematica*. The *Mathematica* program uses a lot of memory, so before you start *Mathematica* you should quit any other applications that are running on the *Macintosh*. To do this, use the menu attached to the Application icon in the upper right-hand corner of the screen.

The icon for the *Mathematica* application is a stellated icosahedron with the name "Mathematica" printed below. It should be in a folder called "Mathematica". The location of this folder will depend on your particular machine, so you may have to hunt around in the Finder to locate it. Try looking in folders that have the word "Application" or "Math" in their titles. When you've found the icon, double-click on it to open it. After a brief delay, a new window labeled "Untitled-1'" will appear on the screen, and the menu buttons along the top of the screen will change. This window is a "Notebook". You can now start typing in the Notebook.

Saving your Notebook on a Diskette.   To save your Notebook onto a diskette, you'll need to buy some diskettes for the computer you are using (usually 3.5 inch, 1.44 megabyte High Density (HD) diskettes). These are inexpensive and available in many book stores and computer stores. Insert a diskette in the slot in the front of the *Macintosh*. If the disk is unformatted, or formatted for a different kind of computer, a panel will appear asking you whether you want to format it. If you click **Initialize**, a panel will appear asking whether you really want to erase the diskette. If you click **Erase**, the *Macintosh* will prompt you for a name for the diskette. Type in a name, then hit RETURN. It will take a few minutes to initialize the diskette.

Once you have a properly formatted diskette inserted in the drive, an icon representing the diskette will appear along the right-hand edge of the screen. Make sure that your *Mathematica* window is active by clicking the mouse in it. A darkened titlebar indicates that the window is active. Now select **Save As**... from the **File** menu. A new panel will appear on the screen. Select the button **Desktop** on the right-hand side. In the center of the panel you should see the name of your diskette. Click on the name, and then click **Open**. The panel will change, and there will be a box labeled "Save this document as:". Type the name you'd like to use for the Notebook ("Assignment 1", for example), and then click **Save**. A copy of the file will be saved on the diskette, and the name of the main window will change from "Untitled-1" to the name you typed. To check that the file has been copied, double-click on the diskette icon. A new window will appear containing a list of files on the diskette.

Once a Notebook has a title, you can save further changes by simply selecting **Save** from the **File** menu. *Mathematica* automatically keeps track of where you want to save it. If the diskette on which you originally saved the file is not in the drive, the *Macintosh* will prompt you to insert it. You can get rid of the panel prompting for the diskette by typing "COMMAND-." (see below). If you want to save the Notebook under a different name, you'll have to use the **Save As**... button again. You should save your work frequently.

If the computer you are using is networked, and you have an account on the network, you may be able to save your Notebook on a central file server. Consult your system administrator for instructions.

Opening a Previously Saved Notebook.   There are two ways to open a previously saved Notebook in *Mathematica*. If *Mathematica* is already running, select **Open** from the **File** menu. In the panel that appears, find the name of the file you want to open, and then double-click on it or select **Open**; or, find the icon on your diskette that represents the Notebook you'd like to open. Double-click on the icon. *Mathematica* will start up with the selected Notebook as the active Notebook.

To open a new Notebook, click the **New** button in the "Notebook" submenu. You can open and save as many different Notebooks as you like, using a different name for each one, as long as you don't use up the available disk space.

If you have several Notebooks open, you may want to close one or more. To close a Notebook, make it active by clicking in it, and then select **Close** from the **File** menu. *Mathematica* will prompt you to save the Notebook if the Notebook has changed since the last save. Do not attempt to close a Notebook by selecting **Quit** from the **File** menu; that will terminate your *Mathematica* session entirely.

Printing your Notebook.   To print a Notebook, first make sure the Notebook you want to print is the active window. Then select **Print**. . . from the **File** menu. A new panel will appear offering various options. One option is to print a selected range of pages. You can do this by typing the appropriate page numbers in the "From" and "To" boxes. When you're ready to print, click on the **Print** button.

The COMMAND Key.   On either side of the space bar is a key with both an apple and a cloverleaf-like symbol on it. We will refer to these keys as the COMMAND keys.

We will describe many uses for the COMMAND key in the next few chapters. For now, you should remember one important use. If the *Macintosh* is hung up, or is doing something you don't want it to be doing, you can often free it up by typing "COMMAND-." (*i.e.*, hold down the COMMAND key and type a period). In particular, this usually works if you want to interrupt a *Mathematica* calculation. It also works when the *Macintosh* puts up a panel prompting you to insert a nonexistent or missing diskette.

Ending the *Mathematica* Session.   It is important to quit *Mathematica* when you are done working. First make sure that you have saved your work. Then select the **Quit** button from the **File** menu. If you haven't saved all your work, *Mathematica* will give you one last chance to save it. When you have exited *Mathematica*, its menu and any open Notebooks will disappear. Be sure to quit any other programs you have been using before you leave the machine. (You can check to see which programs are running by using the Application menu in the upper right-hand corner of the screen. You do not have to quit the Finder.)

Don't forget to eject your diskette before you leave. You can eject the diskette by selecting **Eject Disk** from the **Special** menu in the Finder, or by dragging the diskette icon into the trash can.

Mathematica in *Windows*

When you sit down at the computer it may be turned off or it may be running a screensaver program. If it's off, turn it on and wait until it finishes booting. If a screensaver is running, move the computer's mouse to refresh the display. If all goes well, the screen should now contain various windows and/or icons.

In *Windows*, the "Program Manager" is the name of the program that is used to manage other programs, or *applications*. If you do not see a window on the screen with the title "Program Manager", you should try clicking on various things until you find it. (If you are using a networked PC, it's possible that the Program Manager has been replaced on your system by a custom designed application.) Each of the icons in the Program Manager window represents an application, or a window containing several applications. Double-clicking on an application icon will start up the application it represents. Double-clicking on a window icon will open up the window and allow you to view the applications inside it.

Along the top of the Program Manager window you should see a series of buttons labeled **File**, **Options**, **Windows**, and **Help**. If you click on one of these buttons, a menu will appear with a list of various commands and options. You can invoke one of these by clicking on the appropriate button.

If a window is partially obscured you can bring it to the front by clicking on any part of it. Double-clicking in the small box in the upper left-hand corner of a window will make the window disappear.

On-line Help for *Windows*. If you have never used *Windows* before, it's probably a good idea to go through the tutorial called "Windows Tutorial", which is started by selecting the appropriate button in the Program Manager **Help** menu. The tutorial covers the basics of managing windows and applications.

Starting *Mathematica*. The *Mathematica* program uses a lot of memory, so you should close other applications before starting *Mathematica*. An application can be closed by choosing the **Quit** or **Exit** button in the **File** menu belonging to the application.

Once you have closed the other applications, you are ready to start *Mathematica*. The icon for the *Mathematica* application is a stellated icosahedron (a three-dimensional star) with the name "Mathematica" printed on it. The location of this application will depend on your particular machine, so you may have to hunt around to locate it. Try looking in windows that have the word "Application" or "Math" in their titles. When you've found the icon, double-click on it. After a brief delay, a new window labeled "Mathematica for Windows-[Newnb-1]" will appear on the screen. This window is a *Mathematica* "Notebook". You can now start typing in the Notebook.

Saving your Notebook on a Diskette. To save your Notebook onto a diskette, you'll need to buy some diskettes for the computer you are using (usually 3.5 inch,

1.44 megabyte High Density (HD) diskettes). These are inexpensive and available in many book stores and computer stores.

Insert a diskette in the slot in the front of the computer. If the disk is unformatted, or formatted for a different kind of computer, you will have to format it before you can use it. To do this, go back to the Program Manager window, and find the window labeled "Main". (If this window is iconified, you'll have to open it by double-clicking on it.) Now open the application called "File Manager". Then click the button **Format Disk**... in the **Disk** menu of the File Manager window. A dialog panel will appear. In this panel, you should select the proper disk drive if your machine has more than one. You can give a name to the diskette by typing in the **Label** box. Once you have selected the proper drive, and typed in a name, click on the "OK" button. A new panel will appear warning that formatting will erase everything on the diskette. If you click "Yes", the diskette will be formatted. This will take a few minutes.

Once you have a properly formatted diskette inserted in the drive, make sure that your *Mathematica* window is active by clicking in it. A darkened titlebar indicates that the window is active. Now select **Save As/Export**... from the **File** menu. A dialog panel will appear on the screen. Near the bottom of the panel is a box labeled "Drives:". The drive that has your diskette should be either "A:" or "B:", depending on whether you have one or two drives, and depending on which one you're using. Select the proper drive by clicking on its name. (If you don't see the name of the drive, use the arrow button to move around in the list of drives.) Once you have the proper drive selected, click in the box labeled "File Name:" (near the upper left-hand corner) and then type the name you'd like to use for the Notebook ("Assignment 1", for example). Then click "OK". If you get an error message, it is likely that you've inserted the disk incorrectly or in the wrong drive, or the disk is not formatted correctly. If all goes well, a copy of the file will be saved on the diskette, and the name of the *Mathematica* window will change from "Newnb-1" to the name you typed. To verify that the file has been copied, you can use the File Manager application.

Once a Notebook has a title, you can save further changes by simply selecting **Save** from the **File** menu. *Mathematica* automatically keeps track of the filename. If you want to save the Notebook under a different name, you'll have to use the **Save As/Export**... button again. You should save your work frequently.

If the computer you are using is networked, and you have an account on the network, you may be able to save your Notebook on a central file server. Consult your system administrator for instructions.

Opening a Previously Saved Notebook. To open a saved Notebook, click on the **File** button, and then click on the **Open/Import** button. A new dialog panel will appear. This panel is essentially identical to the one that appeared as a consequence of selecting the **Save As/Export**... button. You can navigate in this panel by clicking on drives and/or directories until the file you want appears in the box labeled "File Name:". After selecting the file you want, click on the "OK" button.

Mathematica saves two files for every Notebook. For example, if you saved a Notebook under the name "goodstuff", you will see the entries *goodstuff.ma* and *goodstuff.mb* in your file listing. The former is an ASCII, or text, copy of your Notebook, the latter a binary version. You can open the Notebook by selecting either. The ASCII version of the Notebook is the important one; it contains all the essential information in the Notebook. The binary file is an auxiliary file used by *Mathematica* to open the Notebook more quickly, and to store special formatting information. You can safely delete the ".mb" file if you're running short of disk space.

To open a new Notebook, click the **New** button in the **Notebook** submenu. You can open and save as many Notebooks as you like, using a different name for each one, as long as you don't use up the available disk space.

If you have several Notebooks open, you may want to close one or more. To close a Notebook, make it active by clicking in it or by selecting its name from the menu labeled **Windows**, and then select **Close** from the **File** menu. *Mathematica* will prompt you to save the Notebook if the Notebook has changed since the last save. Do not attempt to close a Notebook by selecting **Quit** from the **File** menu; that will terminate your *Mathematica* session entirely.

Printing your Notebook. To print a Notebook, first make sure the Notebook you want to print is the active window. Then select **Print**... from the **File** menu. A new panel will appear offering various options. One option is to print a selected range of pages. You can do this by typing the appropriate page numbers in the "From" and "To" boxes. When you're ready to print, click on the "OK" button.

The COMMAND and ALT Keys. In the lower left- and right-hand corners of the keyboard are keys labeled "Control", or "Ctrl". We will refer to these keys as the COMMAND keys. Next to the COMMAND keys are keys with the word "Alt" on them. We will refer to these keys as the ALT keys.

We will describe many uses for the COMMAND key (and a few uses for the ALT key) in the next few chapters. For now, you should remember one important use. If *Mathematica* is hung up in a calculation, or is doing something you don't want it to be doing, you can often free it up by typing "ALT-." (*i.e.*, hold down the ALT key and type a period). A panel labeled "Interrupt Kernel" will appear. Clicking on the **Abort** button should cause *Mathematica* to stop whatever it's doing.

Ending the *Mathematica* Session. It is important to quit *Mathematica* when you are done working. First make sure that you have saved your work. Then select the **Quit** button from the **File** menu. If you haven't saved all your work, *Mathematica* will give you one last chance to save it. When you have exited *Mathematica*, its menu and any open Notebooks will disappear. Be sure to quit any other programs you have been using before you leave the machine.

Don't forget to eject your diskette before you leave. On most machines, you eject the diskette by pushing the button just below the slot for the diskette.

Mathematica in *NeXTStep*

We assume in this section that you are using a *NeXT* computer. The same instructions should apply to non-*NeXT* computers running the *NeXTStep* operating system.

When you sit down at a *NeXT* computer its screen may be blank; if so, then move the computer's mouse to refresh the display. There should be a box (called a window or panel) in the middle of the screen with spaces for you to type your account name and password. Type in your account name, and hit the RETURN key (this is the key shaped like a backwards "L"). Then type in your password (which will not be displayed), and hit the RETURN key again. If you make a mistake, the panel will shake briefly, then you will have to try again. If all goes well, the panel will disappear and eventually a large window labeled "File Viewer" will appear near the middle of the screen, a menu labeled "Workspace" will appear in the upper left corner, and a bunch of small icons will appear on the right edge of the screen.

Manipulating Files and Windows. The File Viewer is used for copying, moving, and organizing your files. Each of the icons in the File Viewer represents either a file or a directory (or folder); a directory is a group of files bundled together. Clicking on a file or directory icon will *select* the icon, and the icon will be illuminated. Double-clicking on a directory icon will cause the File Viewer to display a set of icons representing the files in that directory. Double-clicking on a file icon will open the file. The *NeXT* tries to open a file using an appropriate *application*, or program. It does this by looking at a suffix in the file name. For example, *Mathematica* files are stored with the suffix ".ma" or ".mb". Double-clicking on such a file will open it in *Mathematica*.

The area near the top of the File Viewer is called the *shelf*. You can put files or directories on the shelf if you're going to be using them often. There is always at least one icon on the shelf, namely your home directory, which looks like a house with your name under it. Double-clicking on the home directory icon will display the files and subdirectories in your home directory.

To move a copy of a file onto the shelf, drag the appropriate icon to an open space on the shelf. Copying or moving files from one directory to another is done as follows: find the directory into which you want to copy and move its icon onto the shelf. Then find the file you want to copy and drag it to the target directory. The folder icon will open to receive the file (or, if the target is your home directory, the lights in the house will come on). To delete a file, first select its icon. Then select **Destroy** from the **File** submenu of the **Workspace** menu. A warning panel will appear on the screen asking you to confirm that you want to delete the selected file.

You can bring a partially obscured window to the front by clicking on any part of it. Clicking in the small box in the upper left-hand corner of a window will shrink the window to an icon. You can reopen the window by double-clicking on the icon. Clicking in the small box in the upper right-hand corner of a window will make the window disappear.

On-line Help for the *NeXT*. There is some on-line documentation that describes various features of the *NeXTStep* operating system. To access it, click on the **Help** button in the **Info** submenu of the **Workspace** menu. A panel labeled "Workspace Help Panel" will appear. For directions on how to use this panel click the line **Getting help by topic**.

Starting *Mathematica*. The *Mathematica* icon is a stellated icosahedron (three-dimensional star), and should be somewhere along the right-hand column of the screen. Double-click on this icon to start *Mathematica*; the icon will whiten briefly, and soon a new window labeled "Untitled-1" will appear on the screen. Also, the menu in the upper left will change to one labeled "Mathematica". The "Untitled-1" window is a "Notebook". You can now start typing in the Notebook.

Saving your Notebook. To save the Notebook, click on the **Notebook** button in the "Mathematica" menu. A new menu will appear to the right of the original menu. Click on the **Save As**... button. A panel will appear in which you can select a folder or diskette where you want to save the Notebook. Type in a name for your Notebook and hit the RETURN key. The Notebook will be saved and its title will change from "Untitled-1" to the name you typed. If you later want to save your Notebook again using the same name, you simply click on the **Save** button instead of the **Save As**... button. You should save your work frequently.

If you want to save your Notebook on a diskette, you'll need a 1.44 megabyte High Density (HD) diskette. These are inexpensive and available in many book stores and computer stores. Once you have a diskette, insert it in the slot in the right-hand side of the *NeXT*. Bring up the File Viewer window by clicking on it (or double-click on the *NeXT* icon in the upper right-hand corner of the screen). An icon representing the diskette will appear on the shelf. Click on this icon and then select **Initialize** from the **Disk** submenu. A panel labeled "Initialize" will appear on the screen. In this panel, you can type a name for the diskette. Then hit RETURN. After the diskette is initialized, you can save your *Mathematica* Notebooks onto the diskette. You can also make a backup copy of a Notebook by dragging the icon representing the Notebook onto the diskette icon.

Opening a Previously Saved Notebook. To open a saved Notebook, click on the **Notebook** button as before, then click on the **Open** button. A new panel will appear for you to type in the name of the Notebook you want to recall. Alternatively, you can open a *Mathematica* Notebook by double-clicking on the appropriate file in the File Viewer window.

To open a new Notebook, click the **New** button in the **Notebook** submenu. You can open and save as many Notebooks as you like, using a different name for each one, as long as you don't use up the amount of available disk space.

Mathematica saves two files for every Notebook. For example, if you saved a Notebook under the name "goodstuff", you will see the entries *goodstuff.ma* and *goodstuff.mb* in your file listing. The former is an ASCII copy of your Notebook, the latter a binary version. You can open the Notebook by selecting either. The ASCII version of the Notebook is the important one; it contains all the essential information in the Notebook. The binary file is an auxiliary file used by *Mathematica* to open the Notebook more quickly, and to store special formatting information. You can safely delete the ".mb" file if you're running short of disk space.

Printing your Notebook.   To print a Notebook, first make sure the Notebook you want to print is the active window. Then click on **Print** in the menu in the upper left of the screen. Click on the **Print...** button in the submenu that appears. A panel will appear offering several options. Clicking the **Preview** button will produce an image on the screen of what the printed output will be like (although the printed copy generally has better resolution). You move through the pages of the Preview window by typing COMMAND-f and COMMAND-b, *i.e.*, hold down the COMMAND key (see below) and type the letter "b". When you are finished previewing, you can press the **Hide** button in the **Preview** menu. (If you are planning to use an application again, it is better to **Hide** it than to **Quit** because it takes much longer to start an application than it does to unhide it.) To print your document, simply press the RETURN key (or select **Print**) when the print panel appears. You can save a lot of paper by using the **Preview** option to make sure things are just right before you actually print. You can also print a selected range of pages by typing the appropriate page numbers in the "From" and "To" boxes.

The COMMAND Key.   On either side of the space bar is a key with the word COMMAND on it. We will refer to these keys as the COMMAND keys. We will describe many uses for the COMMAND key in the next few chapters. For now, you should remember one important use. If the computer is hung up, or is doing something you don't want it to be doing, you can often free it up by typing "COMMAND-.", *i.e.*, by holding down the COMMAND key and typing a period. In particular, this usually works if you want to interrupt a *Mathematica* calculation.

Logging Out.   When you are done working, it is important to quit *Mathematica* and log out of the *NeXT*. To quit *Mathematica*, click on the **Quit** button. If you haven't saved your work, a new panel will appear giving you a last chance to save it. Click on the button in this panel that indicates how you wish to proceed.

When you have exited *Mathematica*, its menu and any open Notebooks will disappear, and the **Workspace** menu will reappear. (If you have been using another program besides *Mathematica*, a different menu may show up. To get the **Workspace** menu back you can either quit the other programs as you did for *Mathematica*, or you can move the arrow onto the File Viewer window and click the left mouse button. If you can't find the File Viewer, double-clicking on the *NeXT* icon in the upper right-hand corner of the screen will bring it up.) Click on the `Log out` button in the `Workspace` menu. A panel will appear asking you to confirm that you want to log out. Hit the RETURN key if you really do want to log out.

Mathematica in the *X Window System*

We assume that you are using a computer running some version of the *UNIX* operating system and that you are using the *X Window System*. We also assume that you have an account on the computer and know how to log on. The *X Window System* is highly customizable, and you will have to learn the idiosyncrasies of your particular installation. In many installations, windows or panels will appear with a titlebar at the top, with buttons in the right- and left-hand corners. You can bring a partially obscured window to the front by clicking its titlebar. To do much more than this with your windows, you will have to consult site-specific documentation and/or your system manager.

One of the windows on your screen should be a terminal window (probably titled "xterm" or "login"). You can type *UNIX* commands in this window. Here is a list of the basic *UNIX* commands for locating, moving, copying, and deleting files.

UNIX Command	Effect
ls	lists your files
cp file.a file.b	puts a copy of file.a into file.b
mv file.a file.b	renames file.a to file.b
rm file.a	deletes file.a

In fact, you should be able to do most of the necessary file manipulation of your *Mathematica* files from within the *Mathematica* program (to be explained below), but on occasion you may need to maneuver your *Mathematica* files exactly as you would any other files in the *UNIX* environment.

On-line Help for the *X Window System*. The usual way to obtain help in a *UNIX* environment is to consult the *manual* pages using the "man" command. For example, by typing the command "man ls" you can learn about the features of the "ls" command, including options that can be used with it. If you are a *UNIX* novice, you may find it instructive to try the "man" command on some of the basic system commands listed above.

Starting *Mathematica*. *Mathematica* is often started from an xterm window by typing a special command at the *UNIX* prompt. The command may be "math" or "mathematica" or something reasonably close to that. Alternatively, *Mathematica* might be started on your system by clicking on a special menu button. You may need to ask your system administrator for the precise command or start-up procedure. Whatever the procedure, a new window will appear containing a *Mathematica* "Notebook". The Notebook will be labeled "Untitled-1". Near the top of the window will be a row of menu buttons. At the bottom right, the window will be identified as "Mathematica". You can now start typing in the Notebook.

Saving your Notebook. To save a Notebook, click on the **File** button in the menu row. A new menu will appear below the button. Click on the **Save As**... button. A panel with the title "File Browser" will appear in the middle of the screen. This panel has four regions: a Filter region, which displays the current directory; a Directories region, which lists the subdirectories in the current directory; a Files region, which lists the files in the current directory; and a Selection region. There are also four buttons at the bottom of the panel. By double-clicking on a directory name in the Directories region, you cause the selected directory to become the current directory; the Directories and Files regions will change to show the subdirectories and files in the new current directory. The current directory always contains two subdirectories labeled "." and "..". The directory "." is the current directory. The directory ".." is the directory immediately above the current directory (the parent directory). Thus to move back up the directory tree you double-click on the ".." directory in the Directory region. If there are more subdirectories in the current directory than will fit in the Directories region, you can use the mouse to manipulate the slider to the right of the Directories region to scroll up and down through the list of subdirectories. You can also navigate the directory tree by typing a pathname into the Filter region, and then clicking the **Filter** button.

Once you have reached the directory in which you wish to save the Notebook (by double-clicking on successive subdirectories or typing a pathname into the Filter region) you should place the cursor at the end of the pathname in the selection box and click. Then type in the name you wish to give to your Notebook. Then click on the "OK" box in the menu row. The File Browser panel will disappear, the Notebook will be saved, and its title will change from "Untitled-1" to the name you typed. If after working some more you want to save your Notebook again using the same name, all you have to do is click on the **Save** button instead of the **Save As**... button. If you want to save it under a new name, you must repeat the steps above. You should save your work frequently.

Opening a Previously Saved Notebook. To open a saved Notebook, click on the **File** button, and then click on the **Open** button. A new File Browser panel will appear. This panel is essentially identical to the one that appeared as a consequence of selecting the **Save As**... button. You can navigate the directory tree by double-clicking on directories until the file you want appears in the File region of the panel. Then double-click on the name of the appropriate file or click on the name and select "OK". *Mathematica* saves two files for every Notebook. For example if you saved a Notebook under the name "goodstuff", you will see the entries *goodstuff.ma* (or possibly *goodstuff*) and *goodstuff.mb* in your file listing. The former is an ASCII, or text, copy of your Notebook, the latter a binary version. You can open the Notebook by selecting either. The ASCII version of the Notebook is the important one; it contains all the essential information in the Notebook. The binary file is an auxiliary file used by *Mathematica* to open the Notebook more quickly, and to store special formatting information. You can safely delete the ".mb" file if you're running short of disk space.

To open a new Notebook, click the **New** button in the **Notebook** submenu. You can open and save as many Notebooks as you like, using a different name for each one, as long as you don't use up the available disk space.

If you have several Notebooks open, you may want to close one or more. To close a Notebook, make it active by clicking in it, and then select **Close** from the **File** menu. *Mathematica* will prompt you to save the Notebook if the Notebook has changed since the last save. Do not attempt to close a Notebook by selecting **Quit** from the **File** menu; that will terminate your *Mathematica* session entirely.

Printing your Notebook.   To print a Notebook, select **Print** from the **File** menu. A Print panel will appear in the center of the screen. In the region labeled "Print Destination" there are two tiny buttons next to the words **File**. . . and **Printer**. If you click on the button next to **Printer** (the button will appear as a depression when it is on), your Notebook will be directed to the printer. If you click on the button next to **File**. . ., the Notebook will be written to a PostScript file with suffix ".ps". The default filename will be shown to the right of the word **File**. . .. If you want to send the output to a PostScript file with a different filename, you can click on the **File**. . . button to bring up a File Browser panel that you can use to select a new filename. Finally, when you have everything as you want it, click on the "OK" button at the bottom of the panel.

You will notice that there are several other options that you can select in the Print panel. In particular, you can select a range of pages. You do this by typing the appropriate page numbers in the "From" and "To" boxes.

The COMMAND Key.   Somewhere on your keyboard is a key that we refer to as the COMMAND key. On many keyboards it is located next to the space bar, and may have a diamond or other graphic symbol on it. To locate the COMMAND key on your keyboard, click on the **Environment Information** button in the **Help** menu (top right of your Notebook). Then click on **Find Keys and Modifiers** in the panel that appears. You can learn the status of any key by typing it. Press a key that you think might be the COMMAND key and look at the description in the panel. When you find the right key, it will say "Mod1" next to the "Modifiers" label.

We will describe many uses for the COMMAND key in the next few chapters. For now, you should remember one important use. If the computer is hung up in a *Mathematica* calculation, you can often free it up by typing "COMMAND-.", *i.e.*, hold down the COMMAND key and type a period.

Ending the *Mathematica* Session.   When you are done working, it is important to quit *Mathematica*. First make sure that you have saved your work. Then select the **Quit** button from the **File** menu. If you haven't saved all your work, *Mathematica* will give you one last chance to save it. When you exit *Mathematica*, any open Notebooks will disappear. Be sure to quit any other programs you have been using before you log out and leave the machine.

Chapter 3

Doing Mathematics with *Mathematica*

These instructions are designed to get you started doing mathematics with *Mathematica*. The software is fairly easy to use, and with the help of these instructions you should quickly master the basic skills necessary to work with it. Before you read this chapter you should already have read the appropriate section of Chapter 2. After you have read that section, you will know how to get *Mathematica* up and running. Then you should read this chapter, trying out the commands in a *Mathematica* Notebook as you go along. For further practice with these *Mathematica* commands, work the problems in Problem Set A.

Input and Output.   You interact with *Mathematica* using "Notebooks". A Notebook appears on your computer screen as a window with various kinds of text and graphics in it. But *Mathematica* also treats a Notebook as a *document*, and in particular, *Mathematica* knows how to break the Notebook into pages to produce a finished, printed version of the Notebook. A Notebook is divided into *cells*, which are delineated by a bracket in the right-hand margin, and which can be of several different types. We'll discuss this cell structure in detail later, but in this section we discuss only two types of cells: *Input* cells and *Output* cells. An *Input* cell is a place where you type expressions for *Mathematica* to evaluate. An *Output* cell is a place where *Mathematica* gives its response.

The first thing to keep in mind when using *Mathematica* is that there is a difference between typing the RETURN key (just above the SHIFT key on the right-hand side) and typing SHIFT-RETURN (holding down the SHIFT key and pressing RETURN). Typing SHIFT-RETURN tells *Mathematica* to go ahead and evaluate whatever you've typed in. The RETURN key is a simple linefeed; it generates a new line without causing *Mathematica* to evaluate the input. It is useful if you are typing in a long formula, or if you want to group several commands or expressions together in a single *Input* cell. Note that on some systems the ENTER key (in the number pad at the lower right corner of the keyboard) has the same effect as SHIFT-RETURN.

As an example, try typing **1 + 1**. It should appear at the top of the Notebook. To evaluate this expression, press SHIFT-RETURN or ENTER. Notice that while

Mathematica is working, it displays the word "Running..." or "Evaluating..." at the top or bottom of the Notebook. It will take some time for *Mathematica* to answer because *Mathematica* completes its loading process upon the first calculation. From this point, responses to simple inputs should be nearly instantaneous.

Your Notebook should now look something like this:

In[1]:=   **1 + 1**

Out[1]=   2

The symbol *In[1]:=* is an input label in *Mathematica*, and it appears (with a different line number) at the beginning of every *Input* cell after the cell has been evaluated. The output of the command is in an *Output* cell, and has the label *Out[1]=*. Material in the *Output* cells is specially formatted in mathematical notation.

Arithmetic.   As we have just seen, *Mathematica* can do arithmetic like a calculator. You can add with "+", subtract with "−", multiply with "*", divide with "/", and exponentiate with "^". For example,

In[2]:=   **2*5 + 3^2 − 4/2**

Out[2]=   17

In[3]:=   **(5 + 3)(5 − 3)**

Out[3]=   16

Notice in the last example that the "*" for multiplication was left out. You can always use a space instead of "*", even between two numbers: **2 5** would evaluate to 10 just like **2*5**. In some cases, such as between parentheses, or in the case of a number times a variable, even the space can be left out.

Mathematica differs from a calculator in that it prefers to keep track of fractions symbolically rather than give approximate decimal expansions. For example, if you type in **4/7**, *Mathematica* will simply respond "$\frac{4}{7}$". To force *Mathematica* to give you a numerical answer, type **N[4/7]**.

In[4]:=   **N[4/7]**

Out[4]=   0.571429

To get 20 digits rather than 6 in the answer, one would type instead **N[4/7, 20]**. Another way to force *Mathematica* to use decimal approximations rather than exact numbers is to use a decimal point. For example, in *Mathematica*, "**2.**" is different from "**2**". It is important to remember this distinction because approximate, or floating point, arithmetic is usually faster than exact arithmetic. Floating point output is often less complicated as well. To see an example of the difference in speed and appearance between floating point and exact arithmetic, evaluate the following two commands in your Notebook. (Notice that the "2" in the second line has a decimal point after it.)

> **Solve[x^4 − x − 2 == 0, x]**
>
> **Solve[x^4 − x − 2. == 0, x]**

Errors in Input. If you make an error in an input line, *Mathematica* will print an error message. For example,

> *In[5]:=*   **(5 + 3 (5 − 3)**

```
Syntax::sntxi: Incomplete expression.
```

Although *Mathematica* cannot always tell you exactly what is wrong, you should pay attention to error and warning messages. Missing brackets and parentheses are the most common errors on input lines.

    You can edit an input line by using the mouse to position the cursor at the desired insertion point, clicking the button on the mouse, then typing (or using the "delete" or "backspace" keys), and finally pressing SHIFT-RETURN or ENTER to reenter the line. You can also use the arrow keys to move around in the Notebook.

On-line Help. To access the on-line documentation for a *Mathematica* command, type ?<**command**> in an *Input* cell. For example, the input **?FindRoot** will yield information on the **FindRoot** command. To get additional information, including a list of options to the command, use double question marks, as in **??FindRoot**.

Algebra. You can add, subtract, multiply, and divide variables as well as numbers. Consider the following series of examples:

> *In[6]:=*   **(x + y)(x + y)^2**
>
> *Out[6]=* $(x + y)^3$

> *In[7]:=*   **Expand[%]**
>
> *Out[7]=* $x^3 + 3 x^2 y + 3 x y^2 + y^3$

> *In[8]:=*   **Factor[%]**
>
> *Out[8]=* $(x + y)^3$

(The "%" symbol refers to the output of the previous command; see the section *Referring to Previous Output* later in this chapter.) *Mathematica* often makes minor simplifications to the expressions you type in, but does not make any major changes unless you tell it to. The **Expand** command forced *Mathematica* to multiply the expression out, and the **Factor** command told *Mathematica* to put it back in factored form.

Mathematica also has a **Simplify** command, which tries to express a formula as simply as possible. Sometimes this involves factoring, and sometimes multiplying things out. For example,

In[9]:= **Simplify[(x^2 − y^2)/(x − y)]**

Out[9]= x + y

In[10]:= **Simplify[(x + y)(x^2 − x y + y^2)]**

Out[10]= 3 3
x + y

Notice the space between **x** and **y** on the last input line. This space is necessary—*Mathematica* would have interpreted **xy** as a new variable rather than the product of **x** and **y**. Even better, we could put a "***" between **x** and **y**.

Equations and Assignments. In *Mathematica*, a single equal sign is used to assign values to a variable. For instance,

In[11]:= **x = 5**

Out[11]= 5

will give the variable **x** the value 5 from now on. Whenever *Mathematica* sees an **x**, it will substitute the value 5.

In[12]:= **x^2 + 3 x*y + y**

Out[12]= 25 + 16 y

To clear the variable **x**, type either **x = .** or **Clear[x]**.
Assignments can be quite general.

In[13]:= **Clear[x]**

In[14]:= **z = x^2 + 3 x*y + y**

Out[14]= 2
x + y + 3 x y

In[15]:= **z + 7 y**

Out[15]= 2
x + 8 y + 3 x y

In[16]:= **y = 5**

Out[16]= 5

In[17]:= **z**

Out[17]=   2
            5 + 15 x + x

Be careful with assignments like **x = x + 5**. This is not the way to make a recursive assignment in *Mathematica*, and statements like this will often cause errors.

A variable or function name can be any string of letters and digits, as long as it begins with a letter. You should choose names that are both distinctive and easy to remember. For example, you might use **solndampedpend** as the name of the solution of a differential equation that models a damped pendulum.

A common source of puzzling errors in a *Mathematica* session is to forget that you have defined variables. (*Mathematica* never forgets.) You can always check on the current value of a variable by typing a question mark followed by the variable name. For example, to find the current value of the variable **z**, type **?z**.

Equations in *Mathematica* are indicated by a double equal sign. For example, to find the root of the equation $e^x = x + 2$ that is close to $x = 1$, we type

In[18]:= **FindRoot[Exp[x] == x + 2, {x, 1}]**

Out[18]= {x -> 1.14619}

Mathematica can also solve sets of equations.

In[19]:= **Solve[{r + s == 3, r − s == 0}, {r, s}]**

Out[19]=   3   3
            {{r -> -, s -> -}}
                   2   2

Built-in Functions. *Mathematica* has the usual functions from calculus and differential equations already "built-in." These include **Sqrt, Cos, Sin, Tan, Log,** and **Exp**. *Mathematica* has many other built-in functions, including less familiar mathematical functions like **Erf, Gamma,** and **BesselJ**. *Mathematica* also has a few built-in constants, such as **Pi** (the number π), **E** (the base e of the natural logarithm), **I** (the complex number $i = \sqrt{-1}$), and **Infinity** (∞). Some examples:

In[20]:= **Log[E^2]**

Out[20]= 2

$In[21]:=$ **Sin[Pi/3]**

$Out[21]=$ Sqrt[3]
$$\frac{\text{Sqrt}[3]}{2}$$

(To get numerical answers one would use the **N** function.) Notice that **Log** is the natural logarithm, called *ln* in many texts. Note also the use of square brackets instead of parentheses. *Mathematica* would interpret the input **Log(E^2)** as meaning a variable called "Log" times the number e^2. And finally, notice that all of *Mathematica*'s built-in functions and constants begin with a capital letter. This is to avoid confusion with any variables or functions you might define; you should generally stick to lowercase letters for things you define.

User-defined Functions and Expressions.   It is possible to define new functions in *Mathematica*. In the following example, a polynomial function is defined and evaluated at one point.

$In[22]:=$ **f[x_] := x^3 + 7x − 5**

$In[23]:=$ **f[2]**

$Out[23]=$ 17

Notice the underscore after the initial **x**, which means that **x** is a "dummy variable" in the definition, and the colon before the equals sign, which tells *Mathematica* not to evaluate the right-hand side until you actually use the function.

Another kind of object in *Mathematica*, similar to a function, is called simply an *expression*. For example, **x^3 + 7x − 5** is an expression. We can assign an expression to a variable, as follows:

$In[24]:=$ **g := x^3 + 7x − 5**

Although this *expression* looks very much like the *function* we defined above, it is in fact quite different. The function is a rule for changing x into some other quantity, while the expression is merely a quantity involving x. In particular, typing **g[2]** will not give the value of the expression at $x = 2$. (Try it to see what happens!) We can, however, evaluate an expression at a particular point by using the replacement operator "*/.*" and a transformation rule.

$In[25]:=$ **g /. x −> 2**

$Out[25]=$ 17

This input means: replace x by 2 in the expression g.

Referring to Previous Output.   *Mathematica* labels every input and every output; this makes it easy to use previous results in future calculations. The "%" symbol means "the last output", "%%" means "the next-to-last output", and %n refers to the output labeled *Out[n]*. Here is an illustration:

In[26]:=   **2 + 2**

Out[26]=   4

In[27]:=   **%^2**

Out[27]=   16

In[28]:=   **%% * 5**

Out[28]=   20

In[29]:=   **%26/4**

Out[29]=   1

A safer way to refer to past output is to assign the output to a variable. For example, we could type:

In[30]:=   **sum = 2 + 2**

Out[30]=   4

In[31]:=   **sum^2**

Out[31]=   16

The reason this is safer is that in the Notebook, the output that is in the preceding *Output* cell is not necessarily the most recent output generated by *Mathematica*. Even more problematic is the situation in which there are multiple Notebooks open in a single *Mathematica* session. If you switch between Notebooks, the preceding output of *Mathematica* may not even be in the current Notebook. It is a good idea to assign names to any output you expect to use later in a session.

Lists and Tables.   *Mathematica* arranges its data in the form of lists. A list can contain any collection of *Mathematica* objects, including numbers, variables, functions, and equations. Lists are entered in the form {**a, b, c**}, where **a, b,** and **c** are the elements of the list. In many cases, lists can be treated exactly like single objects. For example, we could type

In[32]:=   **v = {1, 2, 3, 4, 5}**

Out[32]=   {1, 2, 3, 4, 5}

In[33]:= **v^2**

Out[33]= {1, 4, 9, 16, 25}

In effect, we instructed *Mathematica* to square the list **v**, and it responded by squaring each element of the list. You can also add, multiply, subtract, and divide lists, plot lists of functions, and solve lists of equations. You can even apply functions to lists, as in **f[v]**.

To extract the *n*th element of a list **v**, type **v[[n]]**. The first element is extracted with either **First[v]** or **v[[1]]**, and the last element with **Last[v]**. As we shall see later, the **First** command is especially useful for extracting solutions to differential equations generated by the *Mathematica* commands **DSolve** and **NDSolve**.

The command **Join** is used for combining lists. For example,

In[34]:= **list1 = {1, 5, 10}**
list2 = {9, 5, 0}
Join[list1, list2]

Out[34]= {1, 5, 10}

Out[35]= {9, 5, 0}

Out[36]= {1, 5, 10, 9, 5, 0}

Note that we have entered three lines in a single *Input* cell by using the RETURN key.

An easy way to generate lists is to use *Mathematica*'s **Table** command. For example, to generate a table of values of the function **f** (defined above) on the even integers from 0 to 10 you would type

In[37]:= **Table[f[x], {x, 0, 10, 2}]**

Out[37]= {-5, 17, 87, 253, 563, 1065}

In this example, the "**0**" represents the starting value of **x**, "**10**" is the ending value, and "**2**" is the increment (so we get only even integers in this case.) The increment is an optional argument, the default increment being 1. The output of the **Table** command can be put in tabular form by appending the command **//TableForm**. In the following example, we make a table of values of **x** together with values of **f[x]**, for integer values of **x** from −1 to 3.

In[38]:= **Table[{x, f[x]}, {x, −1, 3}]//TableForm**

Out[38]=
−1	−13
0	−5
1	3
2	17
3	43

In certain situations you may want to construct lists that depend on two or more parameters. You might do this, for example, if you're solving a second order differential equation in y, and want to study the solutions for various values of the initial conditions $y(x_0) = y_0$, $y'(x_0) = y_0'$. You can do this by using multiple parameters in the **Table** command. Here is an example in which we construct the set of all fractions with numerator and denominator between 1 and 3.

In[39]:= **Table[a/b, {a, 1, 3}], {b, 1, 3}]**

Out[39]= $\left\{\left\{1, \dfrac{1}{2}, \dfrac{1}{3}\right\}, \left\{2, 1, \dfrac{2}{3}\right\}, \left\{3, \dfrac{3}{2}, 1\right\}\right\}$

Note that there are two levels of braces, one for each of the **Table** commands. To remove the extra braces wc can type

In[40]:= **Flatten[%]**

Out[40]= $\left\{1, \dfrac{1}{2}, \dfrac{1}{3}, 2, 1, \dfrac{2}{3}, 3, \dfrac{3}{2}, 1\right\}$

Finally, to eliminate all repetitions from this list we would type

In[41]:= **Union[%]**

Out[41]= $\left\{\dfrac{1}{3}, \dfrac{1}{2}, \dfrac{2}{3}, 1, \dfrac{3}{2}, 2, 3\right\}$

Graphics. Here is the basic command for plotting a function of one variable. (We will encounter several other plotting commands as we go along.)

In[42]:= **Plot[x^3 − x, {x, −1, 1}]**

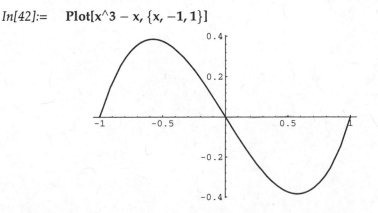

Out[42]= -Graphics-

Plots can be misleading if you do not pay attention to the axes, which are not always what you'd expect. For example, the input **Plot[x^3 − x + 1, {x, −1, 1}]** will produce a plot that looks identical to the previous one, except that the horizontal axis is no longer the x-axis, but rather the horizontal line through $y = 1$.

To produce a plot with a specified range, use the **PlotRange** option, as in: **Plot[x^3 − x + 1, {x, −1, 1}, PlotRange −> {−2, 2}]** (The arrow is typed as a minus sign "−" followed by a greater than sign ">".)

Aborting Calculations.   If *Mathematica* gets hung up in a calculation, or seems to be taking too long, you can usually stop it by pressing "COMMAND-.", *i.e.* hold down the COMMAND key (see Chapter 2) and then press the period key (in *Windows*, you must type "ALT-."). It may take a while for *Mathematica* to abort the calculation, as it tries to clean up the memory it has used during the calculation. If *Mathematica* is hung up, you should try to save your work using the menu button, and then quit *Mathematica* and restart it. It is a good idea when using any computer program to save your work often, as an unexpected crash or power outage can wipe out all your unsaved work.

Problem Set A

Practice with *Mathematica*

In this assignment, you will use *Mathematica* to do some basic calculations, and then to plot, differentiate and integrate various functions. This assignment is the minimum you should do in order to reach a level of proficiency that will enable you to use *Mathematica* throughout the course. In this problem set you should concentrate on the mathematics, but if you wish to try out some of the editing features of the Notebook interface, you can read about them in the next chapter.

1. Evaluate:

   (a) $3 + 9$

   (b) 2^{123}

   (c) π^2 and e to 35 digits

   (d) the fractions $\frac{22}{7}$, $\frac{311}{99}$, and $\frac{355}{113}$, and determine which gives the best approximation to π.

2. Evaluate to ten digits:

   (a) $\dfrac{\sin(0.1)}{0.1}$

   (b) $\dfrac{\sin(0.01)}{0.01}$

   (c) $\dfrac{\sin(0.0001)}{0.0001}$.

3. Factor the polynomial $x^3 - y^3$.

4. *Mathematica*'s **Plot** command plots the graph of one or more functions. Type **?Plot** for a brief explanation of its syntax (or see Chapter 3). Use *Mathematica* to graph the following:

   (a) $y = 3x + 2$ for $-5 \le x \le 5$

   (b) $y = x^2 + x - 1$ for $-5 \le x \le 5$

(c) $y = \sin x$ for $0 \le x \le 4\pi$

(d) $y = \tan x$ for $-\pi/2 \le x \le \pi/2$

(e) $y = e^{-x^2}$ for $-2 \le x \le 2$.

5. Plot the functions x^4 and 2^x on the same graph, and determine how many times their graphs intersect. (*Hint:* You will probably have to make several plots, using intervals of various sizes, in order to find all of the intersection points.) Now find the values of the points of intersection by using the **FindRoot** command.

6. The command **ContourPlot** takes a function of two variables (say $f(x,y)$) and plots several *level curves* of the function (that is, curves of the form $f(x,y) = c$, where c is a constant). For example, **ContourPlot[x^2 + y^2, {x, −5, 5}, {y, −5, 5}]** plots the level curves of the function $f(x,y) = x^2 + y^2$, in the square $-5 \le x \le 5, -5 \le y \le 5$.

(a) Use **ContourPlot** to plot level curves of the function $f(x,y) = 3y + y^3 - x^3$, in the region where x and y are between -1 and 1 (to get an idea of what the curves look like near the origin) and in a larger region (to get the big picture).

(b) A particular level set of a function can be plotted using **ContourPlot** with the options **Contours –> {c}, ContourShading –> False**, where "c" is the value of the constant corresponding to the particular level curve to be plotted. Plot the curve $3y + y^3 - x^3 = 5$.

(c) Plot the level set of the function $f(x,y) = y \ln x + x \ln y$ that contains the point $(1,1)$. (You will have to compute the appropriate value of "c" by evaluating the function at the point $(1,1)$. Note that the logarithm is only defined for positive values of x and y.)

7. The derivative of a function can be found by typing **D[f[x], x]**. Find the derivatives of the following functions. In each case, if it appears that the answer *Mathematica* gives can be simplified, investigate the possibility by using **Simplify**. (The *Mathematica* function for the absolute value of a number is **Abs**.)

(a) $f(x) = 7x^3 + 3x^2 - 2x + 1$

(b) $f(x) = \dfrac{x+1}{x^2+1}$

(c) $f(x) = \cos(x^2 + 1)$

(d) $f(x) = \ln|\sec x + \tan x|$

(e) $f(x) = \sqrt{1 + x^4}$

(f) $f(x) = x^r$

(g) $f(x) = \arctan(x)$.

8. Consider the polynomial $x^6 - 21x^5 + 175x^4 - 735x^3 + 1624x^2 - 1764x + 720$.

   (a) Factor it.

   (b) Find the roots using the *Mathematica* command **Solve**.

   (c) Plot the polynomial for $0.5 \le x \le 6.5$.

   (d) Plot the polynomial and its derivative on the same interval. Explain your plot using calculus.

9. Use the *Mathematica* command **Limit** to evaluate the following limits:

   (a) $\lim\limits_{x \to 0} \dfrac{\sin x}{x}$

   (b) $\lim\limits_{x \to \pi} \dfrac{1 + \cos x}{x - \pi}$

   (c) $\lim\limits_{x \to \infty} x e^{-x}$

   (d) $\lim\limits_{x \to 0^-} \dfrac{1}{x}$

   (e) $\lim\limits_{x \to 0} \sin\left(\dfrac{1}{x}\right)$.

10. The integration command in *Mathematica* is **Integrate**. Type **?Integrate** to see the general syntax for both indefinite and definite integration. As an example, **Integrate[Sin[x], x]** gives the output $-\cos x$. Notice that the constant of integration is left out; *Mathematica* gives you one possible antiderivative of the function you specified. As an example of the definite integral, the command **Integrate[Sin[x], {x, 0, Pi}]** gives the answer 2.

    See if *Mathematica* can do the following integrals. For the indefinite integrals, use *Mathematica* again to check your results by differentiating:

    (a) $\int_0^{\pi/2} \sin x \, dx$

    (b) $\int x \cos(x^2) \, dx$

    (c) $\int \sin(3x) \sqrt{1 - \cos(3x)} \, dx$

    (d) $\int \ln x \, dx$

    (e) $\int x^2 \sqrt{x + 4} \, dx$

    (f) $\int \sqrt{x^4 + 1} \, dx$

    (g) $\int e^{\cos x} \, dx$

    (h) $\int_{-\infty}^{\infty} e^{-x^2} \, dx$.

11. *Mathematica* can also integrate functions numerically, to get an approximate answer. This is useful in cases where *Mathematica* cannot perform the symbolic integration. The command that does this is **NIntegrate**, which has the same syntax as **Integrate**. Find numerical values for the following integrals:

(a) $\int_0^\pi e^{\cos x} dx$

(b) $\int_{-\infty}^\infty e^{-x^2} dx$.

For part (b), figure out how much the numerical answer differs from the exact answer found in the previous problem.

Chapter 4

Using *Mathematica* Notebooks

In this chapter, we describe some aspects of the Notebook feature of *Mathematica* Version 2.2 (some aspects are different in earlier versions). In particular, we describe some of the formatting tools that will help you create an attractive and polished document when you prepare solutions to the problem sets. Most of the Notebook features are the same on all platforms, but there are a few differences; we point out the relevant differences.

Since we refer frequently to menu buttons, we establish the following convention: When referring to a button in a submenu of another menu, we type the name of the button in the top menu, then a colon, then the name of the button in the submenu, and so on. For example, **Action:Prepare Input:Copy Input From Above** means the **Copy Input From Above** button of the **Prepare Input** submenu of the **Action** menu. To get to this button, first click **Action** in the main menu, then **Prepare Input** in the submenu that appears, and then the **Copy Input From Above** button in the next submenu that appears.

Keyboard Equivalents. You may have noticed that some menu buttons have not only a description but also some extra symbols on the right. The symbols on the right consist of a command key symbol followed by a letter. For example, the **Save** button has a command key symbol follow by an "s". This is a *keyboard equivalent*. Holding down the COMMAND key and pressing "s" has the same effect as clicking on the **Save** button. Skilled users often find these keyboard equivalents to be efficient alternatives to using the mouse. You can learn the keyboard equivalents by reading the menu buttons. (If you've forgotten what the COMMAND key is on your computer, look back at Chapter 2. In *Windows*, some of the keyboard equivalents use the ALT key.)

Manipulating Notebooks. Most Notebooks will be longer than the window on the screen. To scroll through the Notebook, drag the slider up and down in the scroll bar at the side of the window.

You can open more than one Notebook at a time by using the **File** menu (the **Notebook** menu on the *NeXT*). The **New** button will open a new untitled Notebook. **Open** can be used to open a previously saved Notebook. Text can be copied and pasted between Notebooks. Note, however, that any definitions of variables, etc., that you make in one Notebook carry over to any other open Notebook, so if you evaluate *Input* cells in two different Notebooks, you may get unexpected results.

The active Notebook is the one with the darkened titlebar, and anything you type will go into that Notebook. You can select a Notebook by clicking anywhere in its window (in the *X Window System* you may need to click on its titlebar to bring it to the front). You can move a Notebook by dragging its titlebar. To close a Notebook without quitting *Mathematica*, use the **Close** button in the **File** menu (**Notebook** menu on the *NeXT*). If you try to close an unsaved Notebook, *Mathematica* will ask whether you want to save it first.

Save your Notebooks often. This is a general principle when working with computers, because a sudden crash of the system could cause your unsaved work to be lost. The simplest way to save is to type COMMAND-s every 10 minutes or so.

Cells. We observed in Chapter 3 that *Mathematica* Notebooks are organized into *cells*. Every cell has a particular style that determines how it is treated by *Mathematica*. In particular, a cell may be either an *Input* cell (one that *Mathematica* can evaluate), an *Output* cell (the result of a *Mathematica* computation), a *Text* cell, a *Title* cell, or any of a number of other types (27 in all!). You can use *Text* cells to insert prose into your Notebooks. For example, if you want to make a plot and then interpret it, you would first type the plot command in an *Input* cell, *Mathematica* would create the graph in a *Graphics* cell, and then you would describe the plot in a *Text* cell.

Each cell type has a particular font, and a particular type of formatting. For example, a *Title* cell has a large boldface font, and text in a *Title* cell is automatically centered. A cell is delineated by a bracket along the right-hand edge of the notebook. If you hit RETURN inside a cell, a new line will be produced and the cell bracket will grow.

The easiest way to change the type of a cell is to select the cell by clicking on its bracket (the bracket will be highlighted), and then type a command equivalent to change the type of the cell. For example, to change a cell to a *Text* cell, click on the cell bracket, and then type COMMAND-7 (in *Windows*, use the ALT key instead of the COMMAND key). The nine most common cell types have command equivalents. Here they are:

COMMAND-1	Title	COMMAND-6	Subsubsection
COMMAND-2	Subtitle	COMMAND-7	Text
COMMAND-3	Subsubtitle	COMMAND-8	Small text
COMMAND-4	Section	COMMAND-9	Input
COMMAND-5	Subsection		

Another way to change the type of a cell is to use the **Cell Style** button. This button is in the **Style** menu (the **Format** menu on the *NeXT*). To see the type of a cell, select the cell, and then select the **Cell Style** button. A list of cell types will pop up, and the style of the current cell will be marked. To change the style of the cell, just drag the cursor to the appropriate button in the `Cell Style` menu. On all of the platforms except the *X Window System*, you can get a copy of the `Cell Style` button at the top of the Notebook by selecting `Style:Show Ruler` on the *Macintosh*; `Format:Show Ruler` on the *NeXT*; and `Options:Tool Bar` in *Windows*. A copy of the `Cell Style` button will appear near the upper left-hand corner of the window.

Cursors. *Mathematica* uses a variety of cursors to indicate the different actions that are available at various places in the Notebook. Move the cursor up and down through a variety of cells and watch how it changes. We will describe the most important cursors. You can experiment with the others.

A horizontal I-bar cursor indicates that the cursor is at the boundary between two cells, or at the end of the Notebook. Clicking the mouse button when the cursor is a horizontal I-bar causes a horizontal line to be inserted into the Notebook. This horizontal line is a *cell insertion point*. To insert a new cell you select a cell insertion point, use the cell style button (or a keyboard equivalent) to select a style, and then start typing. For example, to insert a new *Text* cell at the end of a Notebook you click at the end of the Notebook, type COMMAND-7, and then start typing. (In *Windows*, you must type something into the cell before you can change its type. Remember also that in *Windows* the ALT key is used to change cell type.).

A vertical I-bar cursor appears when pointing at text that can be edited, *e.g.*, text in an *Input* or *Text* cell. Clicking will create a blinking vertical line that indicates a *text insertion point*, where you can add text by typing, or delete text using the backspace or delete key. You can also use the arrow keys on the keyboard to move the insertion point around. Note that the insertion point, *i.e.*, the place where text appears, is independent of the cursor position. The insertion point is always selected by clicking with the mouse, or by using the arrow keys.

In addition, there are several kinds of cursors that appear in graphics cells (see below).

Cell Hierarchy. One of the nicest features of the Notebook is the ability to group cells. One example of this is the automatic grouping of *Input* cells with *Output* cells. A cell grouping is indicated by an extra bracket along the right edge of the Notebook that surrounds one or more cell brackets. On all the systems except *Windows*, cells are automatically grouped according to a *cell hierarchy*. For example, if you create a *Title* cell at the top of your Notebook, there will be an infinitely extendible cell bracket at the far right of the Notebook that will enclose every other cell you create in the Notebook. If you then create a *Section* cell, there will be a new extendible bracket created just inside the first extendible bracket, which will surround all successive cells until you create another *Section* cell. The same is true for *Subsection* and *Subsubsection* cells. In *Windows*, you can accomplish the same thing manually by selecting a range of cells, and then selecting `Cell:Group Cells`.

Here is an example of how this can be useful. When you start the solution to a problem, say Problem 1, create a *Subsection* cell and type "Problem 1". Now create your solution to Problem 1 using *Text* cells, *Input* cells, *Graphics* cells, etc. All of these cells will be grouped together with a bracket along the right-hand side of the Notebook. (You'll have to do this manually in *Windows*.) When you are finished with Problem 1, create a new *Subsection* cell and type "Problem 2". A new grouping bracket for Problem 2 will be created, and subsequent material in the Notebook will be grouped in this bracket until a new sectioning cell is introduced.

These grouping brackets can be used to manipulate entire blocks of cells in the notebook. For example, if you have created a grouping that contains the solution to Problem 1, you can click on the grouping bracket. The bracket will be highlighted and you can move the slider at the side of the panel up and down to verify that all the cells in the solution to Problem 1 are grouped together. If you hit SHIFT-RETURN (or ENTER), then *Mathematica* will evaluate all the cells in this subsection, in order. If you double-click on the grouping bracket, the entire subsection will close up, and only the title will be visible. A small rectangle next to the cell bracket indicates that a cell group is closed. To open the group, just double-click on this rectangle.

If you experiment with this feature, you'll soon see how useful it is for organizing and expediting your work. Note that when you print the Notebook, it will print exactly as it appears on the screen. In particular, closed cell groups will print in closed form.

Manipulating Cells. Occasionally, you will want to combine or divide cells. To divide a cell, first put the insertion point at the place you want the division to occur, and then select `Cell:Divide Cell`. To merge several contiguous cells, first select the cells by dragging the mouse over a range of cell brackets, and then select `Cell:Merge Cell`. The selected cells will merge, and the cell type of the new cell will be the type of the topmost cell in the selection. Formatted cells, including *Graphics* and *Output* cells, cannot be merged or divided.

The command `Action:Prepare Input:Copy Input from Above` is useful for manipulating input. This command places a copy of the contents of the most recent *Input* cell at the current insertion point. This is especially useful if you want to execute several variants of a single input expression.

Editing. The basic editing commands are in the `Edit` menu. The most useful of these are `Cut`, `Copy`, and `Paste`. (Note the keyboard equivalents listed on the menu buttons.) You select text to cut or copy by depressing the mouse button at one end of the selection, and holding it down as you move to the other end. The selected text will be highlighted. While the text is selected, choose either `Cut` or `Copy`. The former will delete the selection and save a temporary copy in a buffer. The latter will save a temporary copy without deleting anything. To paste text that has been cut or copied, move the cursor to the desired insertion point, click to set the insertion point, and choose `Paste`. Note that an entire cell can be selected by clicking on its cell bracket, and the `Cut`, `Copy`, and `Paste` commands work for entire cells.

Printing and Page Breaks.   When you send a *Mathematica* notebook to the printer, *Mathematica* automatically breaks it into pages. You can inspect and adjust the page breaks before you print the Notebook. To do this, select **File:Printing Settings:Show Page Breaks** (on the *NeXT*, **Format:Show Page Breaks**; in *Windows*, **Cell:Page Breaks:Show Page Breaks**). Horizontal dashed lines will appear in the Notebook at the places where *Mathematica* will produce a page break. You should inspect the page breaks to see whether they are satisfactory.

You can fix bad page breaks by forcing or preventing a break above or below a cell. On the *Macintosh* and in the *X Window System*, the options for page breaks are in the menu **Style:Page Breaks**; in *Windows*, in **Cell:Page Breaks**; and on the *NeXT*, in **Format:Style Inspector....** To force a page break just prior to a specific cell, for example, select the cell (by clicking on its cell bracket) and then choose the option **Break above Cell**. When you change the page break near one cell, all the remaining page breaks may change, so it may take some fine tuning to get the page breaks in acceptable places. It is good practice to start at the beginning of your Notebook and set the page breaks in succession as you step through your document. When you're completely satisfied, then you can actually print the Notebook. As you scroll through the Notebook, the page numbers will appear at the bottom of the window. This makes it easy to print selected pages of the Notebook (as described in Chapter 2).

Graphics.   You can use the Notebook interface to adjust and customize graphics. Suppose, for example, that you have a *Graphics* cell with the plot of a function. Click anywhere inside the graphic to select it. You can then move the graph by dragging it with the mouse. You can resize the graph by dragging one of the small squares along the edges that appear after you have selected the graph. If you wish to return your *Graphics* cell to its default size, select the cell (by clicking on its bracket), and choose **Graph:Make Standard Size**. To realign graphics that have been moved, select the appropriate cells, and then choose **Graph:Align Selected Graphics**.

Using the mouse, you can read off coordinates of points in a graph. To do this, hold down the COMMAND key while moving the mouse around in the plot. The cursor will change to crosshairs, and the coordinates of the point in the middle of the crosshairs will appear at the bottom of the Notebook window.

On-line Help.   *Mathematica* has fairly extensive on-line help. First, you can get information about a *Mathematica* command by entering **?command** or **??command** in an *Input* cell. You could try this, for example, by typing **?Plot** to get a description, including the syntax, of the **Plot** command. Second, you can get information about various aspects of the Notebook interface. To do this, click on the **Help** button (**Info** on the *NeXT*). There are several options in this menu, and you should explore each of them. The **Function Browser** button (**Contents** in *Windows*) will open a window that will allow you to use the mouse to browse through a list of *Mathematica* commands and features with short descriptions. On all the systems except *Windows*, selecting the button labeled **On Context** (**Help Pointer** on the *NeXT*) will cause the cursor to change to a question mark; if you position this cursor over a menu button, and then click, a small window will pop up describing the button. (This feature has not been implemented for some of the buttons.)

Most of the pop-up panels also have help buttons. For example, the File Browser panel that pops up when you select **Save As**..., has a help button that will give a brief description of how to use the File Browser.

Quitting the Kernel. Sometimes you may want to quit a *Mathematica* session and start over. This might happen, for example, if you have defined some variables or functions that seem to be causing problems that you can't eradicate. Or you may simply want to reset the In/Out numbering. One way to take care of these problems is to quit and restart the *Mathematica kernel*. When you quit the kernel, the underlying *Mathematica* process will die, along with any variable or function definitions, but your Notebooks will remain on the screen. The next time you hit SHIFT-RETURN (or ENTER), a new kernel will start up, and after a slight delay you can keep working as before. The In/Out numbering will be initialized to 1.

To quit the kernel on the *Macintosh*, simply select **Action:Quit/Disconnect Kernel**. In *NeXTStep* or the *X Window System*, select **Action:Kernels and Tasks**.... In the upper left-hand corner of the panel that appears, there is a region labeled "Kernel Connection Names:". One of the names in this region should be marked. Click on this name to highlight it. Then click on the button **Quit/Disconnect Kernels**. A warning window will pop up asking you to verify that you want to kill the kernel. Click on **Yes**. Then click on the "OK" button in the "Kernels and Tasks" panel.

In *Windows*, you can only quit the kernel during a *Mathematica* evaluation. If *Mathematica* is evaluating, type "ALT-.". In the panel that appears, you can select **Quit Kernel** to quit the kernel.

If Your Notebook Won't Open. You may occasionally find that you are unable to open a previously saved Notebook. On machines running the *X Window System*, *NeXTStep*, or *Windows*, this problem can usually be solved in the following way. First, recall that in these environments, *Mathematica* saves two files for each Notebook, one with the suffix ".ma" and one with the suffix ".mb" (see Chapter 2). All of the information about the Notebook is contained in the ".ma" file, so the ".mb" file can be deleted without compromising the Notebook. On the other hand, the ".mb" file *does not* contain all the information about the Notebook. If you delete the ".ma" file you lose the Notebook.

It sometimes happens that the ".mb" file becomes corrupted, or becomes inconsistent with the ".ma" file. This might happen, for example, if *Mathematica* runs out of memory and/or crashes in the middle of a session. When this happens, *Mathematica* can't open your Notebook because it tries to use the ".mb" file. You can solve the problem by deleting the ".mb" file, and then opening the Notebook. This forces *Mathematica* to use the ".ma" file to open the Notebook, and experience shows that the ".ma" file is much less likely to become corrupted.

Another problem you might encounter, at least in older versions of *Mathematica*, is that *Mathematica* may disappear when you try to type new text into a text cell in a previously saved Notebook. This also seems to be caused by a faulty ".mb" file, and can often be cured by closing the Notebook, deleting the ".mb" file, and then reopening the Notebook.

Setting Defaults. There are many ways to customize *Mathematica* Notebooks and sessions, and once you become comfortable using *Mathematica* you may want to experiment with some of these. For the time being, we suggest that you change the default setting that governs linebreaking of input. This will prevent input from spilling off the right edge of the screen or page. Here are step by step instructions for changing the default setting.

(1) Select **Style:Edit Styles**... (in *Windows*, **Style:Edit Notebook Styles**...; on the *NeXT*, **Format:Style**...). A new window titled "Styles for <notebook>" will appear.

(2) The "Styles for <notebook>" window contains a listing for each cell style. Click on the *Input* cell style.

(3.a) In the *X Window System* and on the *Macintosh*, return to the Notebook window and select **Style:Alignment:Word Wrap**. This option has a mark next to it when it is on.

(3.b) On the *NeXT*, select **Format:Style Inspector**. In the "Style Inspector" panel that pops up, select the **Word Wrap** option in the "Display Attributes" region.

(3.c) In *Windows*, select **Set Format**... in the "Styles for <notebook>" panel. In the "Style Inspector" panel that pops up, select the **Word Wrap** option. Close the "Style Inspector" panel and the "Styles for <notebook>" panel by clicking on the "OK" buttons in those panels. This completes the procedure in *Windows*.

(4) Close the "Styles for <notebook>" window by clicking on the window and then selecting **File:Close**. This finishes the procedure.

The procedure we've described sets the default style for a particular Notebook. You'll have to repeat the procedure in each new Notebook.

Mathematical Typing. When inserting commentary in Notebooks it is often useful to be able to type certain mathematical symbols, including subscripts, superscripts, and special fonts. The Notebook front end has some built-in provisions for special typing. For example, on all the systems except *Windows*, you can create bold text inside a cell: select the appropriate text by dragging the cursor across it, and then select **Style:Face:Bold** (on the *NeXT*, **Format:Font:Bold**). (On all the systems, including *Windows*, you can make a similar change for the entire cell by selecting the cell bracket.) On the *NeXT* and *Macintosh*, you can create superscripts and subscripts in a similar way. If your computer has a "Symbol" font, you may be able to create Greek letters, which are useful in mathematical exposition.

Certain mathematical symbols are available directly from the keyboard on the *NeXT* and the *Macintosh*. Here is a partial list of keystroke combinations that generate mathematical symbols on the *Macintosh*.

Keystrokes	*Symbol*
OPTION-5	∞
OPTION-.	$\geq$
OPTION-,	$\leq$
OPTION-=	$\neq$
OPTION-+	$\pm$
OPTION-p	π
OPTION-b	$\int$

Note that the OPTION key should be held down while the other key is pressed. (The OPTION key is next to the COMMAND key on the *Macintosh* keyboard.)

Here is a partial list of keystroke combinations that generate mathematical symbols on the *NeXT*.

Keystrokes	*Symbol*
ALTERNATE-5	∞
ALTERNATE->	$\geq$
ALTERNATE-<	$\leq$
ALTERNATE-=	$\neq$
ALTERNATE-+	$\pm$
ALTERNATE-p	π
ALTERNATE-B	$\int$
ALTERNATE-X	$\in$

Note that the ALTERNATE key should be held down while the other key is pressed. Note also that some of the characters are uppercase, so "ALTERNATE-<" is really "ALTERNATE-SHIFT-,".

Using the Notebook Effectively.   In preparing solutions to the problem sets in this book, you will use *Mathematica* to analyze various differential equations. You should make use of the editing features of the *Mathematica* Notebook interface to produce a polished document. In particular, material that is not relevant to the final answer (typing errors, trial calculations, etc.) should be deleted from the final printed form of the Notebook. Answers to interpretive questions should appear in a logical place relative to the *Mathematica* output.

You should take special care to make sure that *Input* cells are reevaluated after they are edited. Failure to do this can result in *Input* and *Output* cells that are incompatible, *i.e.*, the output was not generated by the input that appears in the cell. This is confusing and misleading to anyone reading the Notebook.

Rendering Graphics. In some configurations, graphics do not appear automatically in a previously saved notebook when it is reopened, even though the information to generate the graphics is stored in the computer file. To make the graphics appear, you can select a range of cells (or click on **Edit:Select All Cells**), and then click on **Graph:Render PostScript**. You can also use this procedure to redraw a *Graphics* cell that has become garbled.

Evaluating the Notebook. If you save your work and resume it later, you will notice that the "In" and "Out" labels are missing. If you want to get them back, so that you can use the results of your previous work in your current calculation, you must ask *Mathematica* to redo the old calculations. To do this, select **Action:Evaluate:Evaluate Notebook** (in *Windows* and on the *Macintosh*, **Action:Evaluate Notebook**). You may have to wait a while for all the calculations to be redone. Note that the "In/Out" numbering will almost certainly be different than in your previous sessions with the Notebook, so a statement like "%24" will no longer refer to the appropriate output.

Chapter 5

Solutions of
Differential Equations

In this chapter, we show how to solve differential equations with *Mathematica*. For many differential equations, the *Mathematica* command **DSolve** produces the general solution to the differential equation, or the specific solution to an associated initial value problem. These solutions will be called *symbolic solutions*. We also discuss the existence, uniqueness, and stability of solutions of differential equations. These are fundamental issues in the theory and applications of differential equations. An understanding of them helps in interpreting results produced by *Mathematica*.

Finding Symbolic Solutions

Consider the differential equation

$$\frac{dy}{dx} = f(x, y). \tag{1}$$

A solution to this equation is a function $y(x)$ of the independent variable x that satisfies $y'(x) = f(x, y(x))$. It is sometimes possible to find a formula for the solutions to (1); we call such a formula a *symbolic solution*. In *Mathematica*, the command that finds symbolic solutions is **DSolve**. To find a symbolic solution of the differential equation (1), type

> **DSolve[y'[x] == f[x, y[x]], y[x], x]**

Notice that you must type **y[x]** instead of **y** to let *Mathematica* know that y is the dependent variable and x is the independent variable. Notice also that the equation is typed with a double equal sign. *Mathematica* produces the answer in terms of an arbitrary constant C[1]. (For higher order equations, there will be several arbitrary constants.) For example, consider the differential equation

$$\frac{dy}{dx} = x + y.$$

You can solve this equation in *Mathematica* by typing

> **DSolve[y'[x] == x + y[x], y[x], x]**

The output from this command is

$$\{\{y[x] \rightarrow -1 - x + E^x\, C[1]\}\}$$

You can then obtain specific solutions by choosing specific values for C[1]. For example, the solution satisfying a given initial condition can be obtained by choosing C[1] appropriately. This value of C[1] can be found by imposing the initial condition on the general solution and solving for C[1]. Alternatively, you can specify the initial condition as well as the differential equation when you use **DSolve**. To solve the initial value problem

$$\frac{dy}{dx} = f(x,y), \qquad y(x_0) = y_0, \tag{2}$$

you would type

DSolve[{y'[x] == f[x,y[x]], y[x0] == y0}, y[x], x]

For example, the command

sol1 = DSolve[{y'[x] == x + y[x], y[0] == 2}, y[x], x]

produces the output

$$\{\{y[x] \rightarrow -1 + 3\, E^x - x\}\}$$

The solution of the differential equation is the expression following the arrow. In this example, we have given the name **sol1** to the output.

Next, suppose you want to plot the solution, or find its value at a particular value of x. You can't just tell *Mathematica* to plot **y[x]** or evaluate **y[x]** at $x = 5$, say, because **DSolve** presents the solution in the form of a *transformation rule*, not a function. The most straightforward way to plot or evaluate the solution is to define a function equal to the expression following the arrow,

y1[x_] = -1 + 3 Exp[x] - x

and then plot or evaluate **y1[x]**. You can also use the *Mathematica* replacement operator (/.) to extract the function automatically from **sol1**. The command

y1[x_] = y[x] /. First[sol1]

does the job. This command is equivalent to the previous explicit definition of **y1[x]**. Transformation rules, the replacement operator, and the **First** command are explained in Chapter 8.

We often want to look at a family of solutions obtained by varying the initial condition. Here is a natural way to do this in *Mathematica*. Begin by solving the differential equation with a generic initial value. For example,

sol2 = DSolve[{y'[x] == x + y[x], y[0] == c}, y[x], x]

produces a solution formula in terms of the initial value c. The result of this command is

$$\{\{y[x] \rightarrow -1 + (1 + c)\, E^x - x\}\}$$

Next, view the right-hand side as a function of both x and c. To define such a function in *Mathematica*, type

y2[x_, c_] = y[x] /. First[sol2]

Now suppose we want to plot a family of solution curves with initial values $y(0) = -2, -1, \ldots, 4$ on the interval $0 \le x \le 3$. We can type

Plot[Evaluate[Table[y2[x,c], {c, –2, 4}]], {x, 0, 3}]

The result of this command is shown in Figure 1. The **Evaluate** command is explained in Chapter 8; the **Table** command, in Chapter 3.

Figure 1

DSolve is a robust command that can solve many differential equations. In fact, it can solve most of the differential equations that can be solved with the standard solution methods one learns in an introductory course. However, there are many other equations, some of which can be solved by more advanced solution methods, that *Mathematica* cannot solve.

Existence and Uniqueness

The fundamental existence and uniqueness theorems for differential equations guarantee that every initial condition $y(x_0) = y_0$ leads to a unique solution near x_0, provided that the right-hand side of the differential equation (1) is a "nice" function (to be specific, provided that f and $\partial f / \partial y$ are continuous functions). Thus, initial value problems have exactly one solution, but, since there are an infinite number of initial conditions, differential equations have an infinite number of solutions. This principle is implicit in the results obtained above with **DSolve**; when we do not specify an initial condition, the solution depends on an arbitrary constant; when we specify an initial condition, the solution is completely determined.

It is important to remember that the existence and uniqueness theorems only guarantee the existence of a solution *near* the initial point x_0. Consider the initial value problem

$$\frac{dy}{dx} = y^2, \qquad y(0) = 1.$$

From the *Mathematica* command

sol3 = DSolve[{y'[x] == y[x]^2, y[0] == 1}, y[x], x]

we get the output

$$\{\{y[x] \to \frac{1}{1-x}\}\}$$

To understand where the solution exists, we can graph the expression given by **DSolve** in Figure 2.

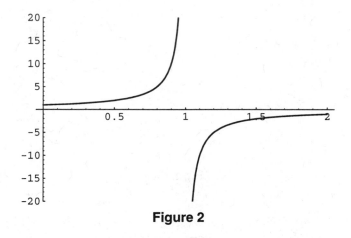

Figure 2

We see that the graph has two branches. Since the left branch passes through the initial data point $(0, 1)$, it is the desired solution. Furthermore, we see that the solution exists from $-\infty$ to 1, but does not extend beyond 1. In fact, it becomes unbounded as x approaches 1 from the left.

Stability of Differential Equations

In addition to existence and uniqueness, the sensitivity of the solution of an initial value problem to the initial value is a fundamental issue in the theory and application of differential equations. We introduce this issue through the following examples.

EXAMPLE 1.   Consider the initial value problem

$$\frac{dy}{dx} + 2y = e^{-x}, \qquad y(0) = y_0.$$

We ask: How does the solution $y(x)$ depend on the initial value y_0? More specifically: Does the solution depend continuously on y_0? Do small variations in y_0 lead to small, or large, variations in the solution? Since the solution is

$$y(x) = e^{-x} + (y_0 - 1)e^{-2x},$$

we immediately see that, for any fixed x, the solution $y(x)$ depends continuously on y_0. We can say more. If we let $\tilde{y}(x)$ be the solution of the same equation, but with the initial condition $\tilde{y}(0) = \tilde{y}_0$, then $\tilde{y}(x) = e^{-x} + (\tilde{y}_0 - 1)e^{-2x}$. So, we have

$$|y(x) - \tilde{y}(x)| = |y_0 - \tilde{y}_0|e^{-2x}.$$

Thus for $x \geq 0$ we see that $|y(x) - \tilde{y}(x)|$ is never larger than $|y_0 - \tilde{y}_0|$. In fact, $|y(x) - \tilde{y}(x)|$ decreases as x increases. For $x \leq 0$ the situation is different. When x is a large negative number, the initial difference $|y_0 - \tilde{y}_0|$ is magnified by the large factor e^{-2x}. Even though $y(x)$ depends continuously on y_0, small changes in y_0 lead to large changes in $y(x)$. For example, if $|y_0 - \tilde{y}_0| = 10^{-3}$, then $|y(-7) - \tilde{y}(-7)| = 10^{-3}e^{14} \approx 1203$. These observations are confirmed by Figure 3, a plot of the solutions corresponding to initial values $y(0) = 0.97, 1, 1.03$ for $-3 \leq x \leq 3$.

Figure 3

EXAMPLE 2.   The solution of the initial value problem

$$\frac{dy}{dx} - 2y = -3e^{-x}, \qquad y(0) = y_0$$

is $y(x) = e^{-x} + (y_0 - 1)e^{2x}$. Again, $y(x)$ depends continuously on y_0 for fixed x. Letting $\tilde{y}(x)$ be the solution with initial value $\tilde{y}_0$, we see that

$$|y(x) - \tilde{y}(x)| = |y_0 - \tilde{y}_0|e^{2x}.$$

Now we see that $y(x)$ is very sensitive to changes in the initial value for x large and positive, but insensitive for x negative. These observations are confirmed by

Figure 4, a plot of the solutions corresponding to initial values $y(0) = 0.97, 1, 1.03$ for $-2 \le x \le 2$.

Figure 4

Often, we are primarily interested in positive values of x, such as when x corresponds to time in a physical problem. If an initial value problem is to predict the future of a physical system effectively, the solution for positive x should be fairly insensitive to the initial value, *i.e.*, small changes in the initial value should lead to small changes in the solution for positive time. To see the importance of this principle, note that for a physical system the initial value y_0 is typically not known exactly, but is found by measurement. When measuring y_0, we usually get only an approximate value $\tilde{y}_0$. Then, if $\tilde{y}(x)$ is the solution corresponding to $\tilde{y}_0$ and the solution is very sensitive to the initial value, $\tilde{y}(x)$ will have little relation to the actual state y (x) of the system as x increases.

A differential equation (like the equation in Example 1) whose solution is fairly insensitive to the initial value as x increases is called *stable*, while a differential equation (like the equation in Example 2) whose solution is very sensitive to the initial value as x increases is called *unstable*. As we have seen, if an equation is unstable and is used over a long time interval, a small error in the initial value can result in a large error later on. Caution should be exercised when using an unstable equation to model a physical problem.

REMARK. We have considered stability as x increases, *i.e.*, stability to the right. We can also consider stability to the left. We note that there are equations that are stable both to the left and to the right, and equations that are unstable both to the left and right.

The following theorem, which we state without proof, is often useful in assessing stability.

THEOREM. *Suppose $f(x, y)$ has continuous first order partial derivatives in the vertical strip*

$$R = \{(x, y) \; : \; x_0 \leq x \leq x_1, -\infty < y < \infty\},$$

and suppose there are numbers K and L such that

$$K \leq \frac{\partial f}{\partial y}(x, y) \leq L, \quad \text{for all } (x, y) \in R.$$

If $y(x)$ and $\tilde{y}(x)$ are solutions of $dy/dx = f(x, y)$ on the interval $x_0 \leq x \leq x_1$ with initial values $y(x_0) = y_0$ and $\tilde{y}(x_0) = \tilde{y}_0$, respectively, then

$$|y_0 - \tilde{y}_0|e^{K(x-x_0)} \leq |y(x) - \tilde{y}(x)| \leq |y_0 - \tilde{y}_0|e^{L(x-x_0)},$$

for all $x_0 \leq x \leq x_1$.

If $L \leq 0$, then the right-hand inequality in the theorem shows that

$$|y(x) - \tilde{y}(x)| \leq |y_0 - \tilde{y}_0|, \quad \text{for all } x_0 \leq x \leq x_1.$$

Thus the solutions differ by no more than the initial values differ, and the differential equation is stable. Moreover, if $L > 0$, but not too large, and $x_1 - x_0$ is not too large, then

$$|y(x) - \tilde{y}(x)| \leq M|y_0 - \tilde{y}_0|, \quad \text{for all } x_0 \leq x \leq x_1,$$

where $M = e^{L(x_1-x_0)}$ is a moderate sized constant. Thus the equation is only mildly sensitive to changes in the initial value, and the equation is only mildly unstable. On the other hand, if $K > 0$, then the left-hand inequality in the theorem shows that the solution is sensitive to changes in the initial value, especially over long intervals. We can briefly summarize these results by saying that if $\partial f/\partial y \leq 0$, then the differential equation is stable; but if $\partial f/\partial y > 0$, then the equation is unstable.

REMARK. The right-hand inequality in the theorem is an example of a continuous dependence result.

Let us examine our examples in light of these observations. Rewriting the equation in Example 1 as $dy/dx = -2y + e^{-x}$, we see that $f(x, y) = -2y + e^{-x}$ and $\partial f/\partial y = -2$. We can apply the theorem with $x_0 = 0, x_1 = \infty$, and $L = K = -2$ to find that

$$|y(x) - \tilde{y}(x)| = |y_0 - \tilde{y}_0|e^{-2x}, \quad \text{for all } x_0 \leq x \leq x_1,$$

as we found above from the solution formula. Thus the equation is stable. We could also conclude this just by noting that $\partial f/\partial y < 0$. Likewise, for the equation of Example 2, $f(x, y) = 2y - 3e^{-x}$ and $\partial f/\partial y = 2 > 0$, so the equation is unstable.

Of course, we can understand the stability of the differential equations in these two examples by examining the solution formulas. But $\partial f/\partial y$ can be calculated and its sign and size found, even if a solution formula cannot be found. For example, we can immediately tell that the differential equation $dy/dx + x^2 y^3 = \cos x$ is stable because

$$f(x, y) = -x^2 y^3 + \cos x$$

and $\partial f / \partial y = -3x^2 y^2 \leq 0$. Yet neither **DSolve** nor any other standard technique enables us to find a formula solution to this differential equation.

Throughout the course we will see many examples that illustrate the dependence (either sensitive or insensitive) of the solution to an initial value problem on the initial value.

Caveat.   It is important to realize that *Mathematica*, like any software system, may occasionally produce misleading results. Consider, for example, the initial value problem

$$\frac{dy}{dx} = -\frac{x}{y}, \qquad y(0) = -1.$$

In Versions 2.0 and 2.1 of *Mathematica*, the command

DSolve[{y'[x] == −x/y[x], y[0] == −1}, y[x], x]

gives the output

$$\{\{y[x] \rightarrow \text{Sqrt}[1 - x^2]\}, \{y[x] \rightarrow -\text{Sqrt}[1 - x^2]\}\}$$

suggesting that there are two solutions, in violation of uniqueness. However, it is easily seen that only the second function satisfies the initial condition. (Both functions satisfy the differential equation.) This example shows that a good theoretical understanding is a valuable guide in interpreting computer generated results, and therefore in identifying situations in which *Mathematica* has produced a misleading result. We note that Version 2.2 of *Mathematica* does solve this initial value problem correctly.

Chapter 6

A Qualitative Approach to Differential Equations

In this chapter, we discuss a qualitative approach to the study of differential equations. With this approach, we obtain qualitative information about the solutions directly from the differential equation, without the use of a solution formula.

Consider the general first order differential equation

$$\frac{dx}{dt} = f(t, x). \tag{1}$$

We can obtain qualitative information about the solutions $x(t)$ by viewing (1) geometrically. Specifically, we can obtain this information from the direction field of (1). Recall that the direction field is obtained by drawing through each point (t, x) in the (t, x)-plane a short line segment with slope $f(t, x)$. Solutions, or integral curves, of (1) have the property that at each of their points they are tangent to the direction field at that point, and therefore the general *qualitative* nature of the solutions can be determined from the direction field. Direction fields can be drawn by hand for some simple differential equations, but *Mathematica* can draw them for any first order equation. We illustrate the qualitative approach with two examples.

EXAMPLE 1. Consider the equation

$$\frac{dx}{dt} = e^{-t} - 2x. \tag{2}$$

Mathematica has a package to plot direction fields. To load this package, type <<**Graphics`PlotField`** (note that these are backward single quotes). After doing this, you can plot the direction field of (2) on the rectangle $-2 \le t \le 3$, $-1 \le x \le 2$ by typing

```
PlotVectorField[{1, Exp[−t] − 2 x}, {t, −2, 3}, {x, −1, 2},
    ScaleFunction −> (1&), Axes −> True, Ticks −> None,
    Frame −> True, AspectRatio −> 1]
```

Note that the **ScaleFunction** option ensures that the arrows have equal length (see Chapter 8). The resulting direction field is shown in Figure 1.

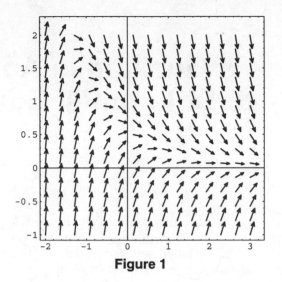

Figure 1

The direction field strongly suggests that if a solution is negative at some point, then it is increasing at that point, and that all solutions approach zero as $t \to \infty$. The general solution of equation (2) is $e^{-x} + ce^{-2x}$. Figure 2 shows the direction field together with several of these solutions.

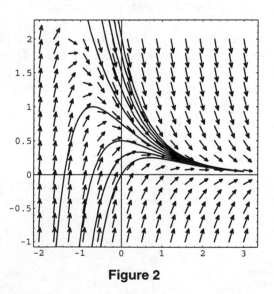

Figure 2

We can also deduce from the differential equation itself that the maximum points on the solution curves depicted in Figure 2 will occur along the curve $2x = e^{-t}$, since that is where $x' = 0$.

EXERCISE. Pursue this idea further by differentiating (2) and showing that the inflection points on the solution curves lie along the curve $4x = 3e^{-t}$.

Equation (2) can be solved explicitly because it is linear. Now let us consider an example that cannot be solved explicitly by any of the standard solution methods.

EXAMPLE 2. Consider the equation

$$\frac{dx}{dt} = x^2 + t. \tag{3}$$

Its direction field is obtained by the the *Mathematica* command

**PlotVectorField[{1, x^2 + t}, {t, −2, 2}, {x, −2, 2}, Axes −> True,
    ScaleFunction −> (1&), Ticks −> None, Frame −> True]**

and is shown in Figure 3.

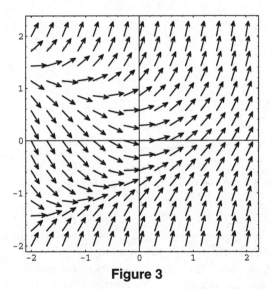

Figure 3

From the direction field, it appears that all solutions are increasing for $t > 0$, and that all solutions eventually become positive. Figure 3 also suggests that all solutions approach infinity. Does this happen at a finite value of t or only at $t = \infty$? It is not easy to decide on the basis of Figure 3, but in fact for each solution $x(t)$ there is a finite value t^* such that $\lim_{t \to t^*} x(t) = \infty$. Later, we will again encounter equations that cannot be solved explicitly by formula techniques. We will apply a combination of qualitative and numerical tools to analyze such equations, and in particular establish the fact just asserted about the solutions to equation (3) approaching infinity in finite time.

EXERCISE. Use the *Mathematica* command **PlotVectorField** to duplicate some of the direction fields in your textbook.

Autonomous Equations

Equations of the form

$$\frac{dx}{dt} = f(x), \tag{4}$$

that do not involve t in the right-hand side, are called *autonomous* equations. Autonomous equations represent physical laws that do not change with time, and are particularly susceptible to qualitative analysis.

Consider equation (4); to be concrete, suppose $f(x)$ has two zeros x_1 and x_2, called *critical points* of the differential equation. Furthermore, suppose the graph of $f(x)$ is as shown in Figure 4.

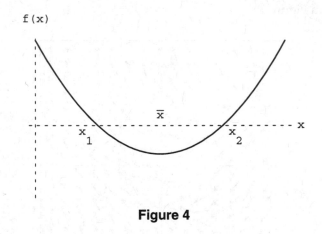

Figure 4

Then by considering the properties of $f(x)$, the direction field of (4) can be easily understood and drawn by hand. At the points $(0, x_1)$ and $(0, x_2)$ the slope is zero; at points $(0, x)$ with $x < x_1$, the slope is positive and increases from 0 to ∞ as x decreases from x_1 to $-\infty$; at points $(0, x)$ with $x_1 < x < x_2$, the slope is negative, first decreases and then increases as x increases from x_1 to x_2; at points $(0, x)$ with $x > x_2$ the slope is positive and increases from 0 to ∞ as x increases from x_2 to ∞; finally, the slopes along any horizontal line are constant (since f does not depend on t). The direction field thus has the general appearance shown in Figure 5. Note that the graph above depicts $f(x)$ vs. x, while the graph below shows x vs. t.

Several facts are suggested by the direction field, namely that: (i) there are two constant solutions $x = x_1$ and $x = x_2$; (ii) solutions starting above x_2 tend to ∞; and (iii) all other solutions tend to x_1 as $t \to \infty$. In fact, we can derive these properties of the solutions $x(t)$ directly from the graph of $f(x)$ as follows.

(a) The constant functions $x(t) = x_1$ and $x(t) = x_2$ are solutions, called the *equilibrium solutions*. They are the unique solutions that satisfy the initial conditions $x(0) = x_1$ and $x(0) = x_2$, respectively.

x(t)

Figure 5

(b) Consider a solution $x(t)$ with $x(0) < x_1$. Then, because of the uniqueness of solutions, it must be that $x(t) < x_1$ for all t and

$$x'(t) = f(x(t)) > 0.$$

Hence $x(t)$ is an increasing function. Since it is also bounded, it has a limit at infinity

$$\lim_{t \to \infty} x(t) = b \le x_1. \tag{5}$$

Could it happen that $b < x_1$? The answer is no, because if $b < x_1$, then

$$x'(t) = f(x(t)) \to f(b) > 0. \tag{6}$$

But equations (5) and (6) say that $x(t)$ approaches a horizontal asymptote at the same time that its slope is "permanently" bigger than a positive number. The resulting contradiction guarantees that

$$\lim_{t \to \infty} x(t) = x_1.$$

(c) If $x(t)$ is a solution with $x(0) > x_2$, then $x(t) > x_2$ for all t. Also

$$x'(t) = f(x(t)) > 0.$$

Hence $x(t)$ is once again increasing. In fact $x(t) \to \infty$. This can be shown by an argument similar to that used in part (b). Sometimes, as we shall see from the example below, $x(t)$ actually reaches ∞ in finite time.

(d) Now consider $x_1 < x_0 < x_2$. Then if $x(t)$ is a solution with $x(0) = x_0$, we must have $x_1 < x(t) < x_2$ for all t. Also, $x'(t) = f(x(t)) < 0$. Hence $x(t)$ is a decreasing function. Exactly as in part (b), it is not difficult to show that $\lim_{t \to \infty} x(t) = x_1$.

Note that in this analysis the properties of $x(t)$ are determined solely from the sign of $f(x)$.

We call the critical point $x_1 = 0$ *asymptotically stable* and call the critical point $x_2 = 1$ *unstable*, since solutions that start near x_1 converge to x_1, and those that start near x_2 not only do not converge to x_2, but eventually move away from x_2.

EXERCISE.   Let $\bar{x}$ be the value between x_1 and x_2 where f takes on its minimum. Show that if $\bar{x} < x(0) < x_2$, then $x(t)$ has an inflection point where $x(t) = \bar{x}$.

Now we examine a more specific example.

EXAMPLE 3.   Consider the equation

$$\frac{dx}{dt} = x^2 - x. \tag{7}$$

Its direction field has the general appearance of Figure 5, with $x_1 = 0$ and $x_2 = 1$. But we can actually derive an explicit formula solution. If $x \neq 0$ and $x \neq 1$, we can solve by separating variables:

$$
\begin{aligned}
t + C = \int dt = \int \frac{dx}{x^2 - x} \\
= \int \left(\frac{1}{x - 1} - \frac{1}{x} \right) dx \\
= \ln|x - 1| - \ln|x| \\
= \ln \left| \frac{x - 1}{x} \right| \\
= \ln \left| 1 - \frac{1}{x} \right|.
\end{aligned}
$$

Exponentiating both sides, we obtain

$$1 - \frac{1}{x} = ke^t,$$

where $k = \pm e^C$. Solving for x, we find that $x(t) = 1/(1 - ke^t)$. Noting that $x_0 = x(0) = 1/(1 - k)$ we have

$$x(t) = \frac{x_0}{(1 - x_0)e^t + x_0}. \tag{8}$$

Although formula (8) was derived under the assumption that $x_0 \neq 0, 1$, it is easily seen to be valid for all values of x_0.

Figure 6 contains the actual solution curves for the differential equation—as drawn by *Mathematica*.

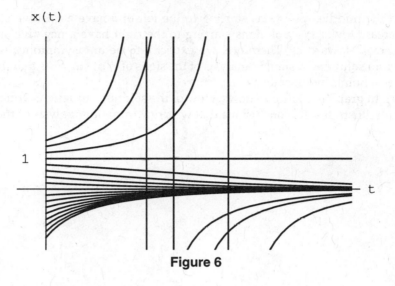

Figure 6

EXERCISES.

(a) Use formula (8) to verify the properties of $x(t)$ obtained above by the qualitative method. Check where the solutions are increasing or decreasing; and whether there are limits as $t \to \infty$.

(b) Suppose $x_0 > 1$. Use formula (8) to show that $x(t) \to \infty$ in finite time. Find the time t^* at which this happens.

(c) Show that $x(t) = 0$ and $x(t) = 1$ are the equilibrium solutions. Does formula (8) yield these solutions?

Here is another example of an autonomous equation.

Figure 7

The left graph in Figure 7 shows a function $f(x)$ with three zeros; thus, the differential equation $x' = f(x)$ has three critical points. Let's look at the critical point in the middle. Solutions starting to the left of b have a positive slope, so they increase toward b. Solutions starting to the right have a negative slope, so they decrease toward b. Therefore, we expect b to be an asymptotically stable equilibrium solution. A similar analysis of the signs of $f(x)$ suggests that the other two critical points are unstable.

The right graph in Figure 7 shows a few of the solution curves. As you can see, this graph illustrates the conclusions that we drew from our analysis of the graph of $f(x)$.

Problem Set B

First Order Equations

1. The initial value problem

$$xy' + 2y = \sin x, \qquad y(\pi/2) = 1$$

has the solution

$$y(x) = x^{-2} \left(\frac{\pi^2}{4} - 1 - x \cos x + \sin x \right).$$

Define this function in *Mathematica* and then

(a) Make a table of the values of $y(x)$ at $x = 0.5, 1, 1.5, 2, \ldots, 5$. This can be done with the commands **Table** and **TableForm** (see Chapter 3). (Remember to use the **N** command to get numerical values.)

(b) Graph $y(x)$ on the intervals $0 < x \le 2$, $1 \le x \le 10$, and $10 \le x \le 100$. Describe the behavior of the solution near $x = 0$ and for large values of x.

(c) Find the solutions $y_j(x)$ of the differential equation corresponding to the initial conditions

$$y_j(\pi/2) = 0.2j, \qquad j = 1, \ldots, 5.$$

Plot the functions $y_j(x)$, $j = 1, \ldots, 5$, on the same graph.

(d) What do the solutions have in common near $x = 0$? for large values of x? Can you find a solution to the differential equation that has no singularity at $x = 0$?

2. Solve the initial value problem

$$xy' + y = 2x, \qquad y(1) = c.$$

Use *Mathematica* to graph the solutions for $c = 0.8, 0.9, 1, 1.1, 1.2$. Evaluate these solutions at $x = 0.01, 0.1, 1, 10$. How do changes in the initial data affect the solution locally, say on the interval $(0.75, 1.25)$; and globally, say on the interval $(0, 2.5)$?

3. Solve the initial value problem

$$y' - y = \cos x, \qquad y(0) = c.$$

Use *Mathematica* to graph solutions for $c = -0.9, -0.8, \ldots, -0.1, 0$. Display all the solutions on the same interval between $x = 0$ and an appropriately chosen right endpoint. Explain what happens to the solution curves for large values of x. (*Hint*: You should identify three distinct types of behavior.) Now, based on this problem, and the material in Chapters 5 and 6, discuss what effect small changes in initial data can have on the global behavior of solution curves.

4. Solve the differential equation

$$\frac{dy}{dx} = \frac{x - e^{-x}}{y + e^y}$$

(*cf.* Problem 7, Section 2.3 in Boyce & DiPrima). The solution is given implicitly in the form

$$f(x, y) = c.$$

(a) Use **ContourPlot** (*cf.* Problem Set A) to see what the solution curves look like. For your x and y ranges, you might use $\{x, -1, 3\}$ and $\{y, -2, 2\}$.

(b) Plot the solution satisfying the initial condition $y(1.5) = 0.5$. Your plot should show two curves. Indicate which one corresponds to the solution.

(c) Given a value x_1, to find $y(x_1)$ you need to find the solution of

$$f(x_1, y) = f(1.5, 0.5)$$

(viewed as an equation in y) near $y = 0.5$. This can be done with the **FindRoot** command. Find $y(0), y(1), y(1.8), y(2.1)$. Mark these values on your plot.

5. Solve the differential equation

$$(e^x \sin y - 2y \sin x)\, dx + (e^x \cos y + 2 \cos x)\, dy = 0,$$

(*cf.* Problem 7, Section 2.8 in Boyce & DiPrima). The solution is given implicitly in the form

$$f(x, y) = c.$$

(a) Use **ContourPlot** to see what the solution curves look like. For your x and y ranges, you might use $\{x, -3, 3\}$ and $\{y, -3, 3\}$.

(b) Plot the solution satisfying the initial condition $y(0) = 0.5$. Your plot may show several curves. Indicate which one corresponds to the solution.

(c) Given a value x_1, to find $y(x_1)$ you need to find the solution of

$$f(x_1, y) = f(0, 0.5)$$

(viewed as an equation in y) near $y = 0.5$. This can be done with the **FindRoot** command. Find $y(-1), y(1), y(2)$. Mark these values on your plot.

6. In this problem, we study continuous dependence of solutions on initial data.

   (a) Solve the initial value problem

   $$y' = y/(1+x^2), \qquad y(0) = c.$$

   (b) Let y_c denote the solution in part (a). Use *Mathematica* to plot the solutions y_c for $c = -10, -9, \ldots, -1, 0, 1, \ldots, 10$ on one graph. Display all the solutions on the interval $-20 \le x \le 20$. You may need to employ the **PlotRange** option to ensure that all the graphs are fully displayed.

   (c) Compute $\lim_{x \to \pm\infty} y_1(x)$.

   (d) Now find a single constant L such that for all real x, we have

   $$|y_a(x) - y_b(x)| \le L|a - b|,$$

   for any pair of numbers a and b. Show that $L = 1$ will work if we consider only negative values of x.

7. Use **DSolve** to solve the following differential equations or initial value problems from Boyce & DiPrima. In some cases, *Mathematica* will not be able to solve the equation (but before moving on to the next equation, make sure you haven't mistyped something). In other cases, *Mathematica* may give extraneous solutions (sometimes these correspond to imaginary roots of the equation it solves to get y in terms of x). If so, you should indicate which solution or solutions are valid. You also might try entering alternate forms of an equation, for example, $M + Ny' = 0$ instead of $y' = -M/N$, or vice versa.

   (a) $x^3 y' + 4x^2 y = e^{-x}, y(-1) = 0$ (Sect. 2.1, Prob. 15)

   (b) $y' = ry - ky^2, r > 0$ and $k > 0$ (Sect. 2.2, Prob. 29)

   (c) $y' = x(x^2 + 1)/4y^3, y(0) = -1/\sqrt{2}$ (Sect. 2.3, Prob. 14)

   (d) $(2x - y)\,dx + (2y - x)\,dy = 0, y(1) = 3$ (Sect. 2.8, Prob. 13)

   (e) $dy/dx = (2y - x)/(2x - y)$ (Sect. 2.9, Prob. 9(a))

   (f) $dy/dx = (2x + y)/(3 + 3y^2 - x), y(0) = 0$ (Sect. 2.10, Prob. 3).

8. Use **DSolve** to solve the following differential equations or initial value problems from Boyce & DiPrima. See Problem 7 for additional instructions.

   (a) $xy' + (x + 1)y = x, y(\ln 2) = 1$ (Sect. 2.1, Prob. 16)

   (b) $y' - (1/x)y = x^{1/2}$ (Sect. 2.2, Prob. 15)

   (c) $y' = 2(1 + x)(1 + y^2), y(0) = 0$ (Sect. 2.3, Prob. 16)

   (d) $(x \ln y + xy)\,dx + (y \ln x + xy)\,dy = 0; x > 0, y > 0$ (Sect. 2.8, Prob. 11)

   (e) $(x^2 + 3xy + y^2)\,dx - x^2\,dy = 0$ (Sect. 2.9, Prob. 8)

   (f) $dy/dx = -(2xy + y^2 + 1)/(x^2 + 2xy)$ (Sect. 2.10, Prob. 5).

9. Chapter 6 describes how to plot the direction field for a first order equation. For each equation below, plot the direction field on a rectangle large enough (but not too large) to show clearly all of its equilibrium points. Find the equilibria in each case and state whether each one is stable or unstable.

   (a) $y' = -y(y - 2)(y - 4)/10$

   (b) $y' = y^2 - 3y + 1.$

10. In this problem, we use the direction field capabilities of *Mathematica* to study two nonlinear equations, one autonomous and one nonautonomous.

    (a) Plot the direction field for the equation

    $$\frac{dy}{dx} = 3\sin y + y - 2$$

    on a rectangle large enough (but not too large) to show all possible limiting behaviors of solutions as $x \to \infty$. Find approximate values for all the equilibria of the system (you should be able to do this with **FindRoot** using guesses based on the direction field picture), and state whether each one is stable or unstable.

    (b) Plot the direction field for the equation

    $$\frac{dy}{dx} = y^2 - xy,$$

    again using a rectangle large enough to show the possible limiting behaviors. Describe qualitatively how the limiting behavior of the solution depends on the initial point in the (x, y) plane.

11. The solution of the differential equation

    $$y' = \frac{2y - x}{2x - y} \qquad (i)$$

    is given implicitly by $|x-y| = c|x+y|^3$ (Boyce &DiPrima, Problem 9, Section 2.9). However, it is difficult to understand the solutions directly from this algebraic information.

    (a) Use **PlotVectorField** to plot the direction field in several different rectangles. Note that *Mathematica* plots the direction field by computing vectors at the points of a regularly spaced grid. In this problem, if the grid contains a point on the line $y = 2x$ (where the denominator of (i) vanishes and the equation is singular), then an error message ensues. You can avoid this problem by choosing the endpoints of your rectangles so that the grid does not contain any points on the singular line. One way to achieve this is by selecting irrational endpoints, as in the following example:

    PlotVectorField[{1, 1/(x + y)}, {x, −1, Sqrt[2]}, {y, −1, Sqrt[2]}]

(b) Use **ContourPlot** to plot the solutions with initial conditions $y(2) = 1$ and $y(0) = -3$. Use the **Show** command to put these plots and the vector field plot together on the same graph.

(c) For the two different initial conditions in part (b), estimate the largest interval on which the unique solution function is defined.

12. Consider the differential equation

$$x' = -tx^2.$$

(a) Use *Mathematica* to plot the direction field of the differential equation. Is there a constant solution? If $x(0) > 0$, what happens as t increases? If $x(0) < 0$, what happens as t increases?

(b) Use **DSolve** to solve the differential equation, thereby obtaining a solution of the form

$$x(t) = \frac{2}{t^2 + 2c}$$

(where c stands for either C[1] or $-$C[1] depending on your version of *Mathematica*). In graphing $x(t)$, it helps to consider three separate cases: (i) $c > 0$, (ii) $c = 0$, and (iii) $c < 0$. In each case, graph the solution for several specific values of c, and identify important features of the curves. In particular, in case (iii), compute the location of the asymptotes in terms of c.

(c) Do the curves in case (i) lie below the curve in case (ii)? What is the interval of existence for the solutions in case (i)? In case (iii), your graphs should have three branches. Consider these branches as separate solutions; what are their intervals of existence?

(d) Use the **Show** command to combine the direction field plotted in (a) with the plot of a solution in case (iii). (Two plots can be combined with the **Show** command; see Chapter 8.)

13. Consider the following logistic-with-threshold model for population growth:

$$x' = -x(1 - x)(3 - x) = x(1 - x)(x - 3).$$

(a) Find the equilibrium solutions of the differential equation. Now draw the direction field, and use it to decide which equilibrium solutions are stable and which are unstable.

(b) Next replace the logistic law by the Gompertz model, but retain the threshold feature. The equation becomes

$$x' = x(1 - \ln x)(x - 3).$$

Once again, find the equilibrium solutions and draw the direction field. You may have trouble near $x = 0$ (because of the logarithm). Use a range like $\{x, 0.01, 4\}$

to circumvent that problem. But you will also have difficulty "reading the field" between 2.5 and 3. There appears to be a continuum of equilibrium solutions.

(c) Plot the function $f(x) = x(1 - \ln x)(x - 3)$ on the interval $0.01 \leq x \leq 4$, and then use *Mathematica's* **Limit** command to evaluate $\lim_{x \to 0} f(x)$.

(d) Use these plots and the discussion in Chapter 6 to decide which equilibrium solutions are stable and which are unstable. Now use the last plot to explain why the direction field appears so inconclusive on the interval $2.5 \leq x \leq 3$, regarding the stability of the equilibrium solutions.

14. This problem is based on Example 3 in Section 2.5 of Boyce & DiPrima: "A tank contains Q_0 lb of salt dissolved in 100 gal of water. Water containing $\frac{1}{4}$ lb of salt per gallon enters the tank at a rate of 3 gal/min, and the well-stirred solution leaves the tank at the same rate. Find an expression for the amount of salt $Q(t)$ in the tank at time t."

The differential equation

$$Q'(t) = 0.75 - 0.03Q(t)$$

models the problem (*cf.* equation (17) in Section 2.5).

(a) Plot the right-hand side of the differential equation as a function of Q, and identify the critical point.

(b) Analyze the long-term behavior of the solution curves by examining the sign of the right-hand side of the differential equation, in a similar fashion to the discussion in Chapter 6.

(c) Use *Mathematica* to plot the direction field of the differential equation. In choosing the rectangle for the direction field be sure to include the point $(0,0)$ and the critical value of Q. It is also helpful if the rectangle is nearly a square.

(d) Use the direction field to determine the limiting amount of salt, and to determine how the amount of salt approaches this limit. Does it increase to it? decrease to it?

(e) Use **DSolve** to find the solution $Q(t)$ and plot it for several specific values of Q_0. Do the solutions behave as indicated in parts (b) and (d)? (You might try combining a direction field plot with that of the solution curves.)

15. A 10-gallon tank contains a mixture consisting of 1 gallon of water and an undetermined number $S(0)$ of pounds of salt in the solution. Water containing 1 lb/gal of salt begins flowing into the tank at the rate of 2 gal/min. The well-mixed solution flows out at a rate of 1 gal/min. Derive the differential equation for $S(t)$, the number of pounds of salt in the tank after t minutes, that models this physical situation. (Note: At time $t = 0$ there is 1 gallon of solution, but the volume increases with time.) Now draw the direction field of the differential equation on the rectangle $0 \leq t \leq 10$, $0 \leq S \leq 10$. From your plot,

(a) find the value S_0 of $S(0)$ below which the amount of salt is a constantly increasing function; but above which, the amount of salt will temporarily decrease before increasing;

(b) indicate how the nature of the solution function in case $S(0) = 1$ differs from all other solutions.

Now use **DSolve** to solve the differential equation. Reinforce your conclusions above by

(c) algebraically computing the value of S_0;

(d) giving the formula for the solution function when $S(0) = 1$;

(e) giving the amount of salt in the tank (in terms of $S(0)$) when it is at the point of overflowing;

(f) computing, for $S(0) > S_0$, the minimum amount of salt in the tank, and the time it occurs;

(g) explaining what principle guarantees the truth of the following statement: if two solutions S_1, S_2 correspond to initial data $S_1(0)$, $S_2(0)$ with $S_1(0) < S_0 < S_2(0)$, then for any $t \geq 0$, it must be that $S_1(t) < S_2(t)$.

16. In this problem we'll use **FindRoot** and **DSolve** to model some population data. The procedure will be:

   (i) Assume a model differential equation involving unknown parameters.
   (ii) Use **DSolve** to find the solution of the differential equation in terms of the parameters.
   (iii) Use **FindRoot** to find the values of the parameters that fit the given data.
   (iv) Make predictions based on the results of the previous steps.

(a) Let's use the model

$$\frac{dp}{dt} = ap + b, \quad p(0) = c,$$

where p represents the population at time t. Check to see that **DSolve** can solve this initial value problem in terms of the unknown constants a, b, c. Then define a function that expresses the solution at time t in terms of a, b, c, and t.

(b) Next, let's try to model the population of Nevada, currently the fastest growing state in the U.S. Here is a table of census data:

Year	Population in thousands
1950	160.1
1960	285.3
1970	488.7
1980	800.5
1990	1201.8

We would like to find the values of a, b, and c that fit the data. However, with 3 unknown constants we will not be able to fit 5 data points. Use **FindRoot** to find the values of a, b, and c that give the correct population for the years 1960, 1970, and 1980. We will later use the data from 1950 and 1990 to check the accuracy of the model. *Important:* In this part let t represent the time in years since 1960, because *Mathematica* may get stuck if you ask it to fit the data at such high values of t as 1960–1980. You may have to experiment with your initial guesses for a, b, and c, and/or increase the option **MaxIterations** beyond its default value of 15 in order to get **FindRoot** to work.

(c) Now define a function of t that expresses the predicted population in year t using the values of a, b, c found in part (b). Find the population this model gives for 1950 and 1990, and compare with the values in the table above. Use the model to predict the population of Nevada in the year 2000, and to predict when the population will reach 3 million. How would you adjust these predictions based on the 1950 and 1990 data? Finally, graph the population the model gives from 1950 to 2050, and describe the predicted future of the population of Nevada, including the limiting population (if any) as $t \to \infty$.

17. Consider $x' = (\alpha - 1)x - x^3$.

(a) Use **Solve** to find the roots of $(\alpha - 1)x - x^3$. Explain why $x = 0$ is the only real root when $\alpha \leq 1$, and why there are three distinct real roots when $\alpha > 1$.

(b) For $\alpha = -2, -1, 0$, draw a direction field for the differential equation and deduce that there is only one equilibrium solution. What is it? Is it stable?

(c) Do the same for $\alpha = 1$.

(d) For $\alpha = 1.5, 2$, draw the direction field. Identify all equilibrium solutions, and describe their stability.

(e) Explain the following statement: "As α increases through 1, the stable solution $x = 0$ *bifurcates* into two stable solutions."

Chapter 7

Numerical Methods

Even though many differential equations can be solved explicitly in terms of the elementary functions of calculus, many others cannot. Consider, for example, the equation

$$\frac{dy}{dx} = e^{-x^2}.$$

Its solutions are the integrals or antiderivatives of e^{-x^2},

$$y(x) = \int e^{-x^2}\, dx + C,$$

but it is known that these integrals cannot be expressed in terms of the elementary functions of calculus. Likewise the solution to the associated initial value problem

$$\frac{dy}{dx} = e^{-x^2}, \qquad y(x_0) = y_0$$

can be written as

$$y(x) = y_0 + \int_{x_0}^{x} e^{-s^2}\, ds,$$

but this formula cannot be simplified further; specifically, it is not an elementary function. (An *elementary function* is defined to be a polynomial, power, trigonometric, inverse trigonometric, exponential, or logarithmic function, or any combination of them via the processes of algebra and of composition and inversion.) More dramatic is the "simple" equation

$$\frac{dy}{dx} = x + y^2.$$

It is known that the solutions to this equation cannot be written in terms of elementary functions, or even in terms of repeated integrals of elementary functions!

Just as we turn to numerical methods (*e.g.*, the trapezoidal or Simpson's rule) to evaluate definite integrals when we cannot find an antiderivative in terms of elementary functions, we also turn to numerical methods to solve initial value problems for differential equations that cannot be solved explicitly in terms of

73

elementary functions. Even if the differential equation can be solved, the resulting formula may be so complicated (*e.g.*, it may be implicit) that a numerical method may be preferable.

Numerical Solutions Using *Mathematica*

Suppose we are interested in determining the solution to the initial value problem

$$\frac{dy}{dx} = f(x, y), \qquad y(x_0) = y_0$$

on an interval $a \leq x \leq b$ containing x_0. Suppose further that we have no formula for $y(x)$. Then we have no obvious way to calculate $y(x)$ for particular values of $x \in [a, b]$. In such a situation, our strategy will be to produce a function $y_a(x)$ that satisfies:

   (i) $y_a(x)$ is a good approximation to $y(x)$ for $x \in [a, b]$; and
   (ii) $y_a(x)$ can be calculated for any $x \in [a, b]$.

The subscript a on y_a stands for *approximate solution*. Such a function $y_a(x)$ can be found with the *Mathematica* command **NDSolve**.

   We illustrate the use of **NDSolve** by considering the simple initial value problem

$$\frac{dy}{dx} = \frac{x}{y}, \qquad y(0) = 1. \tag{1}$$

The equation in (1) is separable, and its solution is

$$y(x) = \sqrt{x^2 + 1}.$$

Since we have an explicit formula for the solution in this example, we will be able to compare the approximate solution $y_a(x)$ and the exact solution $y(x)$. Suppose we want an approximate solution on the interval $[a, b] = [0, 2]$. To obtain $y_a(x)$ we first use the command

   sol1 = NDSolve[{y′[x] == x/y[x], y[0] == 1}, y[x], {x, 0, 2}]

NDSolve requires three arguments. In this example, they are

   (i) **{y′[x] == x/y[x], y[0] == 1}**, a list consisting of the differential equation and the initial condition,
   (ii) **y[x]**, the dependent variable; and
   (iii) **{x, 0, 2}**, a list consisting of the independent variable and the endpoints of the interval on which we wish to calculate the approximate solution.

The command produces the output

$$\{\{y[x] \rightarrow \text{InterpolatingFunction}[\{0., 2.\}, <>][x]\}\}$$

This is not quite the desired form of the approximate solution. To get the desired form, we use the replacement operator and the **First** command (exactly as we did when introducing **DSolve** in Chapter 5). We type

> **ya1[x_] = y[x] /. First[sol1]**

which yields the output

$$\text{InterpolatingFunction}[\{0., 2.\}, <>][x]$$

Now the approximate solution **ya1[x]** can be evaluated for any particular $x \in [0, 2]$, and hence can be graphed on the interval $0 \le x \le 2$. We find, for example, that

$$\text{ya1}[1.5] = 1.80277.$$

Note that the exact value is $y(1.5) = \sqrt{13}/2 = 1.802775637\ldots$, so that **ya1[1.5]** is an approximate value with 6 correct digits. The command

> **TableForm[Table[{x, ya1[x], N[Sqrt[x^2 + 1], 10]}, {x, 0, 2, 0.2}]]**

produces a table of numerical solution values and exact solution values at the points $0, 0.2, \ldots, 1.8, 2$. The result is shown in Table 1.

$\underline{x}$	**ya1[x]**	$y(x)$
0	1.	1.
0.2	1.0198	1.019803903
0.4	1.07703	1.077032961
0.6	1.16619	1.166190379
0.8	1.28062	1.280624847
1.0	1.41422	1.414213562
1.2	1.56205	1.562049935
1.4	1.72046	1.720465053
1.6	1.88679	1.886796226
1.8	2.05912	2.059126028
2.0	2.23607	2.236067977

Table 1

We see that we have at least 5 correct digits in all cases. So **ya1[x]** is indeed a very good approximation to $y(x)$.

A graph of the approximate solution can be obtained with the command

> **Plot[ya1[x], {x, 0, 2}]**

The result is shown in Figure 1.

Figure 1

EXERCISE.   Display both **ya1[x]** and the exact solution $y(x) = \sqrt{x^2 + 1}$ on the same graph. Can you distinguish between the two curves?

REMARK.   If you use a delayed evaluation

   ya[x_] := y[x] /. First[sol1]

for **ya[x]**, then you need to use **Evaluate[ya[x]]** instead of **ya[x]** in the **Plot** command, since **Plot** doesn't automatically evaluate its arguments. (See Chapter 8 for an explanation of delayed evaluation and the **Evaluate** command.)

   We have illustrated **NDSolve** on the initial value problem (1), which can easily be solved explicitly. We can just as readily apply **NDSolve** to any first order initial value problem. Consider, for example,

$$\frac{dy}{dx} = x + y^2, \qquad y(0) = 1, \tag{2}$$

which, as we have noted, cannot be solved with an explicit formula.

   The commands

   sol2 = NDSolve[{y'[x] == x + y[x]^2, y[0] == 1}, y[x], {x, 0, 1}]
   ya2[x_] = y[x] /. First[sol2]

will produce an approximate solution.

EXERCISE.   The solution $y(x)$ to (2) is increasing for x positive and there is a finite value x^* such that $\lim_{x \to x^*} y(x) = \infty$; the interval of existence of the solution is $(-\infty, x^*)$. Execute the previous two commands and then graph **ya2[x]**. Does **NDSolve** reveal the value of x^*?

   The numerical differential equation solver **NDSolve** attempts to produce an approximate solution $y_a(x)$ satisfying the accuracy requirement

$$\text{Error} = |y(x) - y_a(x)| \text{ is approximately} \leq 10^{-6}.$$

Greater accuracy can be achieved by using some options that modify the behavior of the numerical solver. (See the sections *Controlling the Error in NDSolve* and *Reliability of Numerical Methods* later in this chapter.) Note that when using **NDSolve**, the interval on which we calculate an approximate solution does not have to be of the form $[x_0, b]$; in particular, a can be less than x_0.

REMARK.   Although we have focused on first order equations in this chapter and in Chapter 5, both **NDSolve** and **DSolve** work on higher order equations. See Chapter 8 and the sample solutions for examples.

Some Elementary Numerical Methods

In order to explain how **NDSolve** calculates approximate values, we now discuss three elementary numerical methods. Each method will be applied to problem (1). The three methods provide better and better approximations.

   We want to approximate the solution of the initial value problem

$$\frac{dy}{dx} = f(x, y), \qquad y(x_0) = y_0$$

on an interval $x_0 \le x \le b$. For n a positive integer, we divide the interval into n equal parts using points

$$x_0 < x_1 < x_2 < \cdots < x_n = b.$$

Each part has the same width, or *step size*, $h = x_{i+1} - x_i = (b - x_0)/n$; therefore $x_i = x_0 + ih$. At each point x_i we seek an approximation, which we call y_i, to the true solution $y(x_i)$ at x_i:

$$y_i \approx y(x_i).$$

Euler's Method.   The simplest numerical solution method goes back to Euler, and is based on the tangent line approximation to a function. Given the initial value y_0, we define y_i recursively by

$$y_{i+1} = y_i + h\, f(x_i, y_i), \qquad i = 0, 1, \ldots, n-1.$$

This formula is derived as follows:

$$\begin{aligned}
y(x_{i+1}) &\approx y(x_i) + hy'(x_i), && \text{by the tangent line approximation} \\
&= y(x_i) + hf(x_i, y(x_i)), && \text{using the differential equation} \\
&\approx y_i + hf(x_i, y_i), && \text{since } y_i \approx y(x_i) \\
&= y_{i+1}.
\end{aligned}$$

The approximations $y(x_i) \approx y_i$ should become better and better as h is taken smaller and smaller.

EXAMPLE.   Consider the initial value problem

$$\frac{dy}{dx} = \frac{x}{y}, \qquad y(0) = 1.$$

We wish to approximate $y(0.3)$ using Euler's Method with step size $h = 0.1$ and three steps. We find

$$x_0 = 0, \quad x_1 = 0.1, \quad x_2 = 0.2, \quad x_3 = 0.3$$
$$y_0 = 1$$
$$y_1 = y_0 + hf(x_0, y_0) = y_0 + hx_0/y_0 = 1$$
$$y_2 = y_1 + hx_1/y_1 = 1.01$$
$$y_3 = 1.0298.$$

Thus

$$y(0.3) = \sqrt{1.09} = 1.044030... \approx y_3 = 1.0298$$

$$\text{Error} = |y(0.3) - y_3| = 0.0142....$$

Next use $h = 0.05$ and 6 steps:

$$y_0 = 1$$
$$y_1 = 1$$
$$y_2 = 1.0025$$
$$y_3 = 1.0075$$
$$y_4 = 1.0149$$
$$y_5 = 1.0248$$
$$y_6 = 1.0370$$

$$\text{Error} = |y(0.3) - y_6| = 0.0070....$$

Note that cutting the step size in half has the effect of cutting the error approximately in half. One can prove that Euler's Method is a *first order method*, which means that at each point in the interval $[x_0, b]$,

$$\text{Error} \leq Ch$$

for some constant C (depending on $f(x, y)$, the initial condition, and the interval, but not on h). Thus, to gain an additional digit of accuracy, one would reduce the step size by a factor of $1/10$.

Euler's Method can be implemented using *Mathematica* as follows:

```
EulerMethod[f_, {x0_, y0_}, h_, n_] :=
    (EMStep[{x_, y_}] := N[{x + h, y + h*f[x, y]}];
        NestList[EMStep, {x0, y0}, n])
```

To apply this program to the initial value problem (1), we begin by defining the function $f(x, y) = x/y$, and then run the routine. So,

```
f[x_,y_] := x/y;
em = EulerMethod[f,{0,1},0.1,10]
```

will produce a list of approximate solution values at $x = 0, 0.1, 0.2, \ldots, 1$. These can be displayed using the command **TableForm[em]**. Note that the routine **Euler-Method** begins by defining a new function, called **EMStep**, that performs a single Euler Method step. The second line uses the *Mathematica* command **NestList** to iterate the Euler step function **EMStep**.

To evaluate the solution at a point x that is not one of the x_i's, one must *interpolate* the approximate solution. The simplest way to do this is to "connect the dots" by drawing straight line segments from each point (x_i, y_i) to the next point (x_{i+1}, y_{i+1}); thus $y_a(x)$ would be the piecewise linear function connecting the computed points (x_i, y_i). To graph $y_a(x)$, we can use the *Mathematica* command

ListPlot[em, PlotJoined -> True]

See Chapter 8 for an explanation of **ListPlot**.

The Improved Euler Method. We again start with the tangent line approximation, replacing the slope $y'(x_i)$ by the average of the two slopes $y'(x_i)$ and $y'(x_{i+1})$. This yields

$$y(x_{i+1}) \approx y(x_i) + h \, \frac{y'(x_i) + y'(x_{i+1})}{2}$$
$$= y(x_i) + h \, \frac{f(x_i, y(x_i)) + f(x_{i+1}, y(x_{i+1}))}{2}.$$

We now combine the approximation $y(x_i) \approx y_i$ with the previous Euler approximation $y(x_{i+1}) \approx y_i + hf(x_i, y_i)$, to get

$$y(x_{i+1}) \approx y_i + h \, \frac{f(x_i, y_i) + f(x_{i+1}, y_i + hf(x_i, y_i))}{2}$$
$$= y_i + h \, \frac{y_i' + f(x_{i+1}, y_i + hy_i')}{2}$$
$$= y_{i+1},$$

where $y_i' = f(x_i, y_i)$. Given the initial value y_0, this analysis leads to the recursive method

$$y_{i+1} = y_i + h \, \frac{y_i' + f(x_{i+1}, y_i + hy_i')}{2}, \qquad i = 0, 1, \ldots, n.$$

EXAMPLE. We again consider problem (1) and find an approximation to $y(0.3)$ with $h = 0.1$. We obtain

$$y_1 = y_0 + h \, \frac{y_0' + f(x_1, y_0 + hy_0')}{2}$$
$$= y_0 + \frac{h}{2} \left(\frac{x_0}{y_0} + \frac{x_1}{y_0 + hx_0/y_0} \right)$$
$$= 1.1005$$
$$y_2 = 1.019828$$
$$y_3 = 1.044064.$$

So Error = $|y(0.3) - y_3| = 0.000033....$ Note that the error in the Improved Euler Method with $h = 0.1$ is considerably less than the error in Euler's Method with $h = 0.05$.

The Improved Euler Method is a *second order method*, which means that

$$\text{Error} \leq Ch^2.$$

Thus, to gain one more digit of accuracy in the approximation, one would reduce the step size by a factor of $1/\sqrt{10} \approx 0.32$. Equivalently, reducing the step size by a factor of $1/10$ will produce 2 more digits of accuracy.

The Runge-Kutta Method.   Given the initial value y_0, this method is defined recursively by

$$y_{i+1} = y_i + \frac{h}{6}(k_1 + 2k_2 + 2k_3 + k_4),$$

where

$$k_1 = f(x_i, y_i)$$

$$k_2 = f(x_i + \frac{h}{2}, y_i + \frac{h}{2}k_1)$$

$$k_3 = f(x_i + \frac{h}{2}, y_i + \frac{h}{2}k_2)$$

$$k_4 = f(x_{i+1}, y_i + hk_3).$$

Note that a weighted average of the "slopes" k_1, k_2, k_3, k_4 is used in the formula for y_{i+1}.

EXAMPLE.   Consider problem (1) and again find an approximation to $y(0.3)$, but now let $h = 0.3$ and take just one step. Then

$$k_1 = f(0, 1) = 0$$

$$k_2 = f(0 + 0.15, 1 + 0.15(0)) = 0.15$$

$$k_3 = f(0.15, 1 + 0.15(0.15)) = 0.146699$$

$$k_4 = f(0.3, 1 + 0.3(0.146699)) = 0.287354$$

$$y_1 = 1 + \frac{0.3}{6}(0 + 2(0.15 + 0.146699) + 0.287354)$$

$$= 1.044038 \approx y(0.3).$$

So Error = $|y(0.3) - y_1| = 0.000007....$ We see that the error in the Runge-Kutta Method with $h = 0.3$ is less than the error in the Improved Euler Method with $h = 0.1$.

The Runge-Kutta Method is a *fourth order method*, which means that

$$\text{Error} \leq Ch^4.$$

Reducing the step size by a factor of $1/10$ will produce 4 more digits of accuracy.

We have illustrated these methods on problem (1). They can be applied in exactly the same manner to any first order equation.

There are many other numerical methods for differential equations in addition to the ones we have presented here. The method used in **NDSolve** is based on two of these: the Adams Predictor-Corrector Method and Gear's Method. It uses *variable step sizes*, choosing the step size at each step to try to ensure that the desired accuracy is achieved. It produces approximate solution values y_i at the points $x_1 = x_0 +$ (1st step), $x_2 = x_1 +$ (2nd step), ... Then **NDSolve** interpolates the points it has computed, not by straight lines, but by cubic polynomials, thereby producing a smooth approximate solution $y_a(x)$. **NDSolve** attempts to perform both approximation processes—the calculation of the approximate solution values y_i and the interpolation process—in such a way that the total error (in both processes) does not exceed the desired level:

$$\text{Error } = |y(x) - y_a(x)| \text{ is approximately } \leq 10^{-6}.$$

The type of error we have mentioned here is called *truncation error*. In addition there is *round-off error*, which arises because the computer uses a fixed, finite number of digits. Letting $\tilde{y}_a(x)$ denote the actual computed approximate solution, which includes round-off error, the total error can be written

$$y(x) - \tilde{y}_a(x) = (y(x) - y_a(x)) + (y_a(x) - \tilde{y}_a(x))$$
$$= \text{Truncation Error} + \text{Round-off Error}.$$

Since most computers that run *Mathematica* carry 16 digits, the major portion of the error will be the truncation error. Thus, for most problems, round-off error can be safely ignored. For this reason we will not distinguish between $y_a(x)$ and $\tilde{y}_a(x)$.

REMARK. With numerical methods as with qualitative methods, we obtain information on the solution—quantitative in the one case and qualitative in the other—without the use of a solution formula.

Controlling the Error in NDSolve

As indicated above, **NDSolve** attempts to provide an approximate solution with error approximately $\leq 10^{-6}$. More accurate approximate solutions can be obtained by using some of the options to **NDSolve**. For example,

> **sol3 = NDSolve[{y′[x]==x/y[x], y[0]==1}, y[x], {x, 0, 2},**
> **AccuracyGoal −> 15, PrecisionGoal −> 15, WorkingPrecision −> 25]**

and

> **ya3[x_] = y[x] /. First[sol3]**

produce a more accurate approximate solution. To see this, note that

> **N[ya3[1.5],16] = 1.802775637731999,**

which is a 15-digit approximation to $\sqrt{13}/2$, the value of the exact solution at $x = 1.5$. We have used **N[ya3[1.5],16]** here in order to print out 16 digits from **ya3[1.5]**.

The setting **AccuracyGoal** $\rightarrow$ **d**, where **d** is a positive integer, attempts to control the absolute error, *i.e.*, to ensure that

$$\text{Absolute Error } = |y(x) - y_a(x)| \text{ is approximately } \leq 10^{-d}.$$

The setting **PrecisionGoal** $\rightarrow$ **p**, where **p** is a positive integer, attempts to control the relative error, *i.e.*, to ensure that

$$\text{Relative Error } = \frac{|y(x) - y_a(x)|}{|y(x)|} \text{ is approximately } \leq 10^{-p}.$$

Actually, **NDSolve** only tries to satisfy the easier of these two goals. For this reason both d and p may have to be increased to get the desired accuracy.

The setting **WorkingPrecision** $\rightarrow$ **e** determines the number of digits **NDSolve** uses in its calculations. If these options are not used, *Mathematica* employs the default settings:

WorkingPrecision = Normal machine precision of the computer
AccuracyGoal = **PrecisionGoal** = **WorkingPrecision** $-$ 10 (digits).

So for any computer that has a machine precision of 16 digits, the default options lead to approximately 6 digit accuracy. This will be satisfactory for most of the calculations in this course; but see the section *Reliability of Numerical Methods* below.

When you use *Mathematica* to calculate an approximate numerical solution to an initial value problem on an interval $[a, b]$, you should be aware that the solution may not exist over the entire interval. Naturally, *Mathematica* can only calculate the solution over the largest subinterval of $[a, b]$ on which it exists. See the second exercise in this chapter to learn how **NDSolve** reports the answer in this situation.

Now suppose the solution does exist over the entire interval $[a, b]$. In attempting to calculate the solution with the desired accuracy, **NDSolve** will use up to 500 steps. On certain problems this limit will be reached before the solution has been calculated over the entire interval, and **NDSolve** will return a message indicating this. You can then change the default setting to a higher number, say 700, with the option **MaxSteps** $\rightarrow$ **700**, and obtain the solution on a (possibly) larger interval.

EXERCISE.   Attempt to calculate the solution to

$$\frac{dy}{dx} = y \sin(x^2), \qquad y(0) = 1$$

over the interval $[0, 15]$, first using the default option (**MaxSteps** $\rightarrow$ **500**), and then using **MaxSteps** $\rightarrow$ **700**. What difference do you observe? Find a value for **MaxSteps** that allows the solution to be calculated over the entire interval $[0, 15]$. Graph the solution.

Reliability of Numerical Methods

We have claimed that **NDSolve**, when used with the default options, leads to approximately 6 digit accuracy. More precisely, the default options ensure that the *local error* is approximately 10^{-6}, *i.e.*, that the error made in a step of length h is approximately $10^{-6} \times h$. One is generally more interested in the *global error*, *i.e.*, in the error committed in going from x_0 to b. This error cannot be controlled completely by the numerical method because it depends on the differential equation as well as on the numerical method. The key issue is whether the differential equation is stable or unstable; these terms were defined in Chapter 5.

You have seen equations for which **NDSolve** gives very accurate results (*cf.* the initial value problem (1) above). Now we will look at an example where **NDSolve** gives very poor results.

EXAMPLE. Consider the initial value problem

$$\frac{dy}{dx} - y = -3e^{-2x}, \qquad y(0) = 1.$$

The exact solution is $y(x) = e^{-2x}$; we plot it in Figure 2.

Figure 2

Next we find the numerical solution using **NDSolve**, and plot it together with the exact solution:

```
sol4 = NDSolve[{y'[x] − y[x] == −3Exp[−2x], y[0] == 1}, y[x], {x, 0, 12}]
ya4[x_] = y[x] /. First[sol4]
Plot[{Exp[−2x], ya4[x]}, {x, 0, 12}, PlotRange −> {0,1}]
```

Figure 3

We see from Figure 3 that the graphs of **ya4** and y are indistinguishable from 0 to about 6, but then the curves separate sharply. Their values at $x = 12$, for instance, are very different (**ya4[12]**≈ 0.76 and $y(12) = e^{-24} \approx 3.77 \times 10^{-11}$).

How can this failure be explained? The solution to our differential equation with initial condition $y(0) = 1 + \epsilon$ is $y(x) = e^{-2x} + \epsilon e^x$. Figure 4 shows a plot of the solutions corresponding to initial values $1 - (0.5 \times 10^{-5}), 1 - (0.5 \times 10^{-5}), 1, 1 + (0.25 \times 10^{-5}), 1 + (0.5 \times 10^{-5})$.

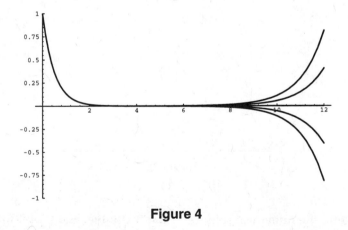

Figure 4

We see that solutions with initial values slightly different from 1 separate very sharply from the solution with initial value exactly 1 after about 6; those with initial values greater than 1 approach $+\infty$, and those with initial values less than 1 approach $-\infty$. Now **NDSolve**, like any numerical method, introduces errors. These errors—whether truncation errors or round-off errors—have caused the numerical solution to jump to a solution that started just above 1. Once on such a solution, the numerical solution will follow it or another such solution. Since these solutions approach $+\infty$, the numerical solution will do likewise.

Could we have anticipated this failure? Recall the discussion of stable and unstable differential equations in Chapter 5. The solutions of unstable equations are very sensitive to their initial values, and hence a numerical method will have trouble following the solution it is attempting to calculate. Recall also that an equation is unstable if $\partial f/\partial y > 0$, and stable if $\partial f/\partial y \leq 0$. For our example, $f(x,y) = y - 3e^{-2x}$ and $\partial f/\partial y = 1 > 0$. So we are trying to approximate the solution of an unstable differential equation, and we should not be surprised that we have trouble, especially over long intervals (beyond about 6 for this example). By contrast, note that for the initial value problem (1) above, $\partial f/\partial y = -x/y^2 < 0$ for $x > 0$. All this suggests caution when dealing with unstable equations. In fact, caution is always recommended when modeling physical problems with unstable equations, especially over long intervals (*cf.* the discussion in Chapter 5).

In assessing the reliability of a numerically computed solution there is another test one can make. Suppose we have made a calculation using the default options, as we have done with our example. Then one can do another calculation, using more stringent accuracy requirements, and compare the results. If they are nearly the same, one can have confidence that they are fairly accurate; but if they differ substantially, then one should suspect that the first calculation is not accurate.

Let's do this with our example:

sol5 = NDSolve[{y'[x] − y[x] == −3Exp[−2x], y[0] == 1}, y[x], {x, 0, 14},
    AccuracyGoal −> 8, PrecisionGoal −> 8, WorkingPrecision −> 18]
ya5[x_] = y[x] /. First[sol5]

Next we plot both numerical solutions together with the exact solution:

Plot[{Exp[−2x], ya4[x], ya5[x]}, {x, 0, 14}, PlotRange −> {0,1}]

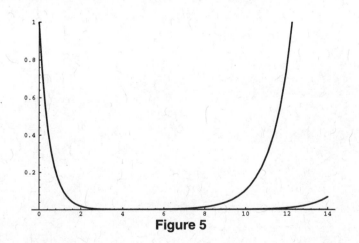

Figure 5

We see from Figure 5 that the second numerical solution is accurate over a longer interval, out to about 10, whereas the first was accurate out to about 6. In particular, the two numerical solutions differ after about 6. Even if we didn't know the exact solution we could have concluded that the first numerical solution is accurate out to, but not beyond, about 6.

In summary, we have learned that local accuracy—the accuracy that a numerical method can control—leads to reasonable global accuracy if the differential equation is stable, and that the reliability of a numerical solution can also be checked by computing another numerical solution with more stringent accuracy requirements.

Chapter 8

Features of *Mathematica*

This chapter is a continuation of Chapter 3, *Doing Mathematics with Mathematica*. We describe some of the more advanced features of *Mathematica*, focusing on the *Mathematica* commands and techniques that are most useful for studying differential equations. We also describe some aspects of *Mathematica*'s internal structure that should help in working with complicated expressions and commands.

Functions.   *Mathematica* distinguishes between a *function* of a variable, and an *expression* involving the variable. In order to use *Mathematica* effectively, you must learn to make the same distinction. You should review the section *Functions and Expressions* in Chapter 3 to refresh your memory on the difference between functions and expressions.

The simplest way to define a function is via the assignment method. For example, to define $f(x)$ to be the cubic polynomial $x^3 - 2x^2 + 1$, type

```
In[1]:=     f[x_] = x^3 - 2x^2 + 1
Out[1]=            2     3
            1 - 2 x  + x
```

The argument of the function must be enclosed in square brackets, and on the left-hand side of the equal sign the argument must be followed by an underscore.

A function can be evaluated with either a numeric or a symbolic argument:

```
In[2]:=     f[-1]
Out[2]=     -2
```

```
In[3]:=     f[u^2]
Out[3]=            4     6
            1 - 2 u  + u
```

The result of this evaluation is the expression $1 - 2u^4 + u^6$. This is a subtle point: the symbol **f** is the name of a *function*; the symbol **f[u]** is the name of an *expression* involving **u**.

An alternative way of defining a function is to use the "colon-equal" sign. For example,

In[4]:=   **f[x_] := x^3 − 2x^2 + 1**

The difference between the two methods is the following. In the first (without the colon), the right-hand side of the definition is evaluated at the time the definition is made. In the second (with the colon), the right-hand side of the definition is evaluated only when the value of the function is requested. This is illustrated by *Mathematica's* lack of response to the second definition, which indicates that *Mathematica* is holding the definition in reserve for evaluation at a later time. Here is an example to illustrate this distinction.

In[5]:=   **expr = x^2 + 3**

Out[5]=
$$3 + x^2$$

In[6]:=   **g[x_] = expr**

Out[6]=
$$3 + x^2$$

In[7]:=   **h[x_] := expr**

In[8]:=   **g[2]**

Out[8]=   7

In[9]:=   **h[2]**

Out[9]=
$$3 + x^2$$

What happens here is that when *Mathematica* evaluates a function defined with the := notation, it *first* substitutes the argument (in this case x) into the expression on the right-hand side, and *then* evaluates the right-hand side. Since x does not appear explicitly as a variable on the right-hand side in the definition of h, the function we define this way is actually independent of x. Thus h has been defined to be a function that returns as its *constant* value the expression *expr*. The point of this discussion is that the distinction between = and := can be important depending upon when you actually want evaluation to occur. A crucial example appears later when we discuss the command **NDSolve**.

Finally, we note that functions of several variables can also be defined. For example, we could define **phi[x_,y_] = x^2 + y^2**.

Pure Functions. In the examples above, each of the functions we defined was given a name—f, g, h, or *phi*. *Mathematica* provides a way to define functions that are unnamed, or *pure*. There are two types of syntax for pure functions. Here are the two ways to define the pure function $x \mapsto x^3 - 2x^2 + 1$.

> Function[x, x^3 − 2x^2 + 1]

> #^3 − 2 #^2 + 1 &

In the latter syntax, the number sign (#) is a stand-in for the variable, and the ampersand (&) indicates that the expression is a pure function. The only time we will use pure functions in this book is as scale functions for the **PlotVectorField** command, but *Mathematica* occasionally reports its answers in pure function form. For example, if **f** has been defined as in the preceding section, then *Mathematica* reports the derivative in pure function format if you type

> *In[10]:=*   **f′**
> *Out[10]=*   2
>   −4 #1 + 3 #1   &

The "1" after the number sign is there to indicate the first variable. There is only one variable here, but the syntax allows for functions of several variables. You can, however, avoid the pure function format in this case by typing

> *In[11]:=*   **f′ [x]**
> *Out[11]=*   2
>   −4 x + 3 x

Suppressing Output. Certain commands produce output that might be considered superfluous. For example, when you assign a value to a variable, *Mathematica* will echo the value. The output of a *Mathematica* command can be suppressed by putting a *semicolon* after the command. Semicolons can also be used to separate a string of *Mathematica* commands when you are only interested in the output of the final command. Ending a statement with a semicolon has no effect on what *Mathematica* does internally; it only affects what you see in the Notebook. A semicolon after a graphics command will not suppress the graphic, but it will suppress the superfluous *Output* cell that ordinarily follows a graphic.

Clearing Values. One of the most common sources of errors in using *Mathematica* is the failure to keep track of variable or function definitions. For example, suppose that during the course of a *Mathematica* session you type

> *In[12]:=*   **k = 1;**

You keep working, and twenty minutes later you try to define a function of two variables by typing

In[13]:=   **g[x_, k_] = x + k; g[3, 4]**

Out[13]=   4

The answer should have been $3 + 4 = 7$. But the function **g[x, k]** is not really **x + k**, rather it's **x + 1** since **k** has previously been set to 1. In this simple case you might have noticed that **g** wasn't what it should have been, but in a complicated expression this type of error is difficult to detect.

The best way to avoid this problem is to clear a variable either before using it or immediately after using it. For example, you can avoid errors like the one in the preceding example by typing

In[14]:=   **Clear[g, x, k]; g[x_, k_] = x + k**

Out[14]=   x + k

Another way to avoid the error is by using **:=** instead of **=**.

In[15]:=   **k = 1; g[x_, k_] := x + k; g[3, 4]**

Out[15]=   7

In this example, because we have used **:=** to define the function, *Mathematica* does not evaluate the right-hand side until the function is actually invoked, at which time it uses the value of the variable specified in the function call rather than the previously defined value. In the earlier case, *Mathematica* evaluates the right-hand expression immediately, and substitutes, once and for all, the value 1 for **k**. For this reason, it is often safer to use **:=** rather than **=** when defining functions.

The command **Clear[h]** will clear *all* definitions of the function **h**. (A function may have more than one definition!) Another way to clear values of functions or variables is to use a command like "**h[x_] = .**". This is not as reliable since it only clears a single definition of **h**, but sometimes it seems to be the only thing that works. For example, if you've typed **q´ [t] = t^2** (which is easy to do accidentally when using **DSolve**), then **Clear** won't work on **q´** , but **q´ [t] = .** does work.

You can always find out the current value of a function or variable by typing a question mark before the function or variable name. For example, **?f** will show you the current value or definition of **f**.

You should be aware that if you have several Notebooks open in a single *Mathematica* session, the definitions you make in one Notebook will carry over to the other Notebooks. This happens because the underlying *Mathematica* process, or *kernel*, is the same for all the Notebooks. This also accounts for the fact that In/Out numbering carries over from Notebook to Notebook in a single *Mathematica* session, so if you enter input in one Notebook and the input is labeled *In[n]*, then the next input will be labeled *In[n+1]*, even if it is in a different Notebook.

Managing Memory.   We have noted that *Mathematica* stores in computer memory *every* input statement and *every* output (that's what it's doing when it assigns those labels *In[n]* and *Out[n]*). In a long *Mathematica* session, this uses a tremendous amount of computer memory, and might lead to a crash if the available memory is exhausted. The simplest way to ameliorate this problem is to reset the line numbering to zero. To do this, simply type **$Line=0**. The In/Out numbering will be reset, and subsequent inputs and outputs will be written over the old ones instead of using new memory space.

Another way to free up memory is to quit and restart the kernel. We described how to do this in Chapter 4. You should probably quit and restart the kernel each time you start a new problem.

The Replacement Operator and Transformation Rules. We have seen that a function can be evaluated at various values of the independent variable. A similar effect can be accomplished with expressions by using the *replacement operator (/.)*, together with a *transformation rule*. For example,

In[16]:=   **(x^2 − 1) /. x −> 5**

Out[16]= 24

This input means: in the expression $x^2 - 1$, replace x by 5. The notation **x −> 5** is an example of a transformation rule.

The replacement operator is extremely useful and versatile. What it does is to substitute for one or more variables in an expression using one or more transformation rules. Here is another example:

In[17]:=   **((x^2− 3*y)/z) /. {x −> a, y −> b, z −> c}**

Out[17]=   2
            a   - 3 b
           ----
               c

A general feature of *Mathematica*'s various "solve" routines is that the solutions are reported in the form of transformation rules. For example, the simple quadratic equation $x^2 - 1 = 0$ has the two solutions $x = 1$ and $x = -1$.

In[18]:=   **sol = Solve[x^2 − 1 == 0, x]**

Out[18]= {{x -> 1}, {x -> -1}}

Mathematica's response is a list consisting of two transformation rules. (We have named this list **sol** so we can use it later.) Note that *Mathematica* could not possibly report these solutions in the form "$x = 1$" and "$x = -1$" because these two assignments would be in conflict. In fact, *Mathematica* *never* assigns values to variables unless specifically directed to do so. Transformation rules are *Mathematica*'s elegant way of steering clear of assigning values to variables.

Now let us use the transformation rules that we generated with the **Solve** command. To do this, we have to extract the transformation rules from the list. If we want to use the rule **x −> 1** on the expression $x^2 + x$, we type

In[19]:=   **x^2 + x /. First[sol]**

Out[19]=   2

To use the rule **x −> −1**, we type

In[20]:=   **x^2 + x /. Last[sol]**

Out[20]=   0

The most common use of the replacement operator is to transform expressions that have been previously typed by the user or generated by *Mathematica*. Here is a more complicated example, in which we find the function that solves the initial value problem $y' = xy$, $y(0) = 1$.

In[21]:=   **sol1 = DSolve[{y´ [x] == x*y[x], y[0] == 1} y[x], x]**

Out[21]=
```
                       2
                     x /2
        {{y[x]  -> E      }}
```

In[22]:=   **Clear[f]; f[x_] = y[x] /. First[sol1]**

Out[22]=
```
          2
        x /2
      E
```

DSolve reports its result as a transformation rule. We have used this transformation rule to define a function f, which is the solution to the initial value problem.

Equations vs. Assignments.   In *Mathematica*, an *equation* is different from an *assignment*. For example, **x==2** is an equation, whereas **x=2** or **x:=2** is an assignment. Compare the effects of entering an equation and an assignment.

In[23]:=   **x == 2**

Out[23]=   x == 2

In[24]:=   **x = 2**

Out[24]=   2

Note that an equation has no effect on the value of the variables in the equation. Names can even be assigned to equations.

In[25]:=   **niceeqn = energy == m*c^2**

Out[25]=   2
            energy == c   m

Differentiation.   The distinction between functions and expressions becomes important when differentiating. *Mathematica* has two different commands that perform differentiation. The **D** command operates on expressions.

In[26]:=   **Clear[g, x]; g[x_] := x^2; D[g[x], x]**

Out[26]= 2x

Notice that the output of **D** is another expression. The syntax for second derivatives is **D[g[x], {x, 2}]**, and for *n*th derivatives, **D[g[x], {x, n}]**.

As we observed in the section on pure functions, the *prime* operator differentiates functions, and returns a pure function. When differentiating an expression with **D**, you must state explicitly which variable should be used. When differentiating a function with the *prime* operator, you must not mention the name of the variable.

One place where you must use the *prime* format is to specify initial values for derivatives in **DSolve** or **NDSolve**. So, to solve the second order initial value problem $y'' = 9y + 2x$, $y(0) = 1$, $y'(0) = 0$, you could type

In[27]:=   **diffeqn = D[y[x], {x, 2}] == 9*y[x] + 2*x**

Out[27]= y''[x] == 2 x + 9 y[x]

In[28]:=   **initialpos = y[0] == 1; initialvel = y'[0] == 0;**

In[29]:=   **DSolve[{diffeqn, initialpos, initialvel}, y[x], x]**

Out[29]=   3 x
                      25   29 E   2 x
            {{y[x] -> -------- + ------- - ---}}
                      3 x   54   9
              54 E

Packages.   The *Mathematica* system actually consists of several distinct parts. The part that reads input, displays output, and manipulates Notebooks is called the *interface*, or *front end*. The computational engine, the part that actually evaluates the input, is called the *kernel*. The kernel contains the core parts of *Mathematica* that must always be available. A third part consists of *Mathematica packages*, which contain additional commands. To use commands in packages, you must explicitly tell *Mathematica* to load the commands. For example, the command **PlotVectorField** is part of the **Graphics`PlotField`** package, and must be loaded explicitly before it can be used. To load this package, type

In[30]:=   **<<Graphics` PlotField`**

(Note that the word **PlotField** is surrounded by *backwards* quotes.) If you use a package command without explicitly loading it, *Mathematica* will not recognize the command and will simply echo the input line in the output area. If you do make this mistake, you can recover by typing **Remove[<command>]** and then loading the package properly. For example, if we had tried to use the **PlotVectorField** command before loading it, we would have to type **Remove[PlotVectorField]** before we could properly load the command and use it.

The two packages you will need most often in doing the problem sets are called **Graphics`PlotField`** and **Calculus`LaplaceTransform`**. The former contains a collection of specialized plotting routines including **PlotVectorField**. The latter contains routines for working with Laplace Transforms.

Graphics.   We will encounter at least six different plotting commands in this book. These include: **Plot, ListPlot, ContourPlot, PlotVectorField, Show,** and **ParametricPlot**. We briefly describe each of them.

The most important thing to keep in mind for the various plotting commands is the type of *Mathematica* objects that the command is designed to plot. For example, the **Plot** command plots expressions involving a single variable. On the other hand, **PlotVectorField** is designed to plot a list of two expressions involving two variables. If *Mathematica* gives you an error message or an implausible plot when you enter a plot command, the first thing to check is whether you are plotting the right kind of object for that particular command, and whether you are using precisely the right syntax for that object and that command.

Plot is the simplest and most versatile plotting command; it plots an expression or list of expressions involving a single variable over a specified interval. The vertical range of the plot can also be specified using the option **PlotRange**. For example, to plot the two functions $e^x \cos x$ and $x^3 - 3x + 2$ over the interval $[-3, 3]$ with range $[-10, 10]$, we type

In[31]:=   **plot1 = Plot[{Exp[x]Cos[x], x^3 − 3x + 2}, {x, −3, 3},**
            PlotRange −> {−10, 10}];

We have named this plot for future reference.

When *Mathematica* responds to a **Plot** command (or any of the plotting commands described below), it samples points according to a default setting. If curves are exceptionally oscillatory, or there are many curves to be generated by the command, the default setting may be inadequate. You can adjust it with the option **PlotPoints** –> **n**. The default setting is $n = 25$. Higher settings will improve your graphs at the cost of an increase in computation time.

ListPlot takes a list of points (given as pairs of (x,y) coordinates) and plots them. The list may be given explicitly or it may be generated by the **Table** command. With the option **PlotJoined** –> **True**, **ListPlot** will connect the plotted points with line segments.

In[32]:= **plot2 = ListPlot[{{−3, 1}, {−1, 2}, {0.5, 8}, {2, 3}, {3, 2}},
PlotJoined –> True];**

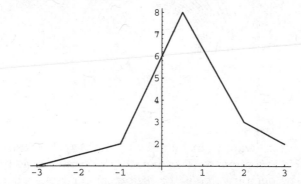

ContourPlot plots level curves of an expression involving two variables, *i.e.*, sets of points on which the expression is constant.

In[33]:= **ContourPlot[x^2/2 + y^2, {x, −5, 5}, {y, −5, 5}];**

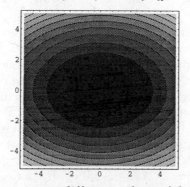

The shading in the plot represents different values of the function: the larger the value of the function, the lighter the color. Shading can be turned off using the option **ContourShading** –> **False**. The option **Contours** –> **n** produces *n* contours.

The option **Contours** −> {**a, b,** ... } produces contours at levels $a, b, \ldots$.

Note that if you have defined a function **f[x,y]** to which you want to apply **ContourPlot**, you must type **f[x,y]** rather than just **f**. The same holds for all the plotting commands. (Another way of saying this is that the plotting routines plot *expressions*, and not *functions*.)

ParametricPlot is used to plot the trajectory traced out by a pair of expressions {**f[t], g[t]**} as the parameter **t** varies. It is useful for graphing solutions of systems of differential equations.

In[34]:=   **ParametricPlot[{Exp[−t/100] Cos[t], Exp[−t/100] Sin[t]},**
         {t, 0, 100}, AspectRatio −> Automatic];

You may sometimes want to include the option **AspectRatio −> Automatic** in the **ParametricPlot** command. The **AspectRatio** controls the height-to-width ratio for plots. The default value is the reciprocal of the so-called *Golden Ratio*, approximately 0.618, which is considered to be a ratio that is "pleasing" to the eye. The **Automatic** option instructs *Mathematica* to set the ratio based on the actual coordinates used in the plot. The **PlotRange** option can be used to adjust both the horizontal and vertical range of the plot. The syntax is **PlotRange −> {{a, b}, {c, d}}**. This will restrict the plot to the rectangle $a \le x \le b, c \le y \le d$.

PlotVectorField is used for plotting vector or direction fields, and was described in Chapter 6. It is in the package **Graphics`PlotField`**. The **ScaleFunction** option to the **PlotVectorField** command can be used to rescale the length of vectors in the plot. The default setting causes the vector field to be displayed with vectors having length proportional to the magnitude of the actual vectors. But often one is interested in the behavior of a vector field near critical points, where the vectors are very short. The default setting produces a plot that is relatively uninformative near critical points, because the vectors are so short that it is impossible to discern their direction. The simplest solution is to make all the vectors the same size. The option **ScaleFunction −> (1&)** does this. The ampersand is present because **ScaleFunction** expects a *pure function* as its argument; we have used the constant function 1. Note also that in Version 2.2 of *Mathematica*, the default setting of **AspectRatio** is **Automatic** for **PlotVectorField**; this can produce a thin graph if the

x and y ranges of the plot have different lengths. In such cases you should use the option **AspectRatio** $\rightarrow$ **1** to obtain a square graph.

The **Show** command is used to superimpose several graphs. We named two of the graphs above **plot1** and **plot2** so that we could use the **Show** command on them.

In[35]:=   **Show[plot1,plot2];**

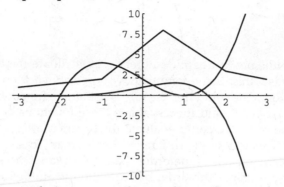

The **Show** command always puts the graphs on the same horizontal and vertical scales, so if you are going to use the **Show** command to superimpose two graphs, you may want to make sure that the plotting ranges of the two graphs are comparable.

Various other options are available for improving the quality of the pictures generated by the plotting commands. For example,

    Plot[x^3 − 3, x, 0, 2, AxesLabel −> { "x", "y" }]

will cause the axes to be labeled. You can learn about many other options by typing **??Plot**. Some of the most useful are: **Axes** $\rightarrow$ **False** (hides the axes), **Ticks** $\rightarrow$ **None** (turns off the tick marks on the axes), **Frame** $\rightarrow$ **True** (encloses the plot in a box), and **PlotStyle** $\rightarrow$ **{GrayLevel[0.5]}** (causes the curve to be plotted in gray).

Finally, you can locate coordinates on your graphs much as you would on a graphics calculator. This is explained in the *Graphics* section of Chapter 4.

The Evaluate Command. Each of the plotting commands just described can be applied to lists of arguments rather than to a single argument. For example, in the preceding section we applied the **Plot** command to a list of two functions. It is also possible to pass a list of functions to a plotting command using the **Table** command, or some other *Mathematica* command. However, when you use a command inside of a plotting routine, you must use **Evaluate** to force evaluation of the command. For example, we could type

In[36]:=   **Plot[Evaluate[Table[x^c, {c, 1, 5}]], {x, −5, 5}];**

The reason *Mathematica* doesn't automatically evaluate the arguments to the plotting commands is this: In the command we typed above, there are two possible orders of evaluation. One could first create the list of five functions corresponding to the values $c = 1, \ldots, 5$, and then evaluate these functions at each value of x. Or, for each value of x, one could evaluate the function at (x, c), for each of the five values of c. This is a subtle difference, but in many cases the first order of evaluation is easier, and this is the order that *Mathematica* uses when you type the command above. Since the order of evaluation is ambiguous, *Mathematica* requires that you tell it explicitly what to do by using the evaluate command.

Here is another example of the **Evaluate** command. Suppose we define

f[t_] := { {f1[t], g1[t]}, {f2[t], g2[t]}, {f3[t], g3[t]} };

where the functions **f1[t]**, ..., **g3[t]** have been previously defined. If we want to apply **ParametricPlot** to the list **f[t]** then we must use **Evaluate** inside of the plotting routine:

ParametricPlot[Evaluate[f[t]], {t, −3, 3}, AspectRatio −> Automatic]

It is sometimes hard to tell whether **Evaluate** is necessary, but if you're having trouble getting your plots to work, you should try it. In our experience, it never hurts to include **Evaluate**, even when it is not necessary.

DSolve.   We have discussed the command **DSolve**, *Mathematica*'s symbolic ODE solver, in Chapter 5. Here we present some additional remarks concerning this command.

Here is an application of **DSolve** to find the general solution of a second order equation.

In[37]:=   **gensol = DSolve[x^2*y"[x] + x*y'[x] − y[x] == 0, y[x], x]**

Out[37]=
```
                  C[1]
          {{y[x] -> ---- + x C[2]}}
                   x
```

You should recognize from the discussion earlier in this chapter that *Mathematica* has reported the solution as a *list* of transformation rules, even though there is only one element in the list. The output is a general solution, and the expressions **C[1]** and **C[2]** are arbitrary constants. These constants are "protected" variables, so we can't actually assign values to them. But we can replace them with particular values by using a transformation rule.

In[38]:=   **ygen[x_] = y[x] /. First[gensol];**
             y0[x_] = ygen[x] /. {C[1] -> 1, C[2] -> -1}

Out[38]=   1
             - - x
             x

Mathematica Version 2.2 has an enhanced **DSolve** command that can be loaded by typing <<**Calculus`DSolve`**. The enhanced command has exactly the same syntax as the ordinary **DSolve** command, and can solve some classes of equations that the ordinary command can't solve. You might try it if you encounter an equation that the ordinary **DSolve** command can't handle.

NDSolve. The function **DSolve** yields *symbolic* solutions of differential equations, *i.e.*, algebraic expressions that satisfy the original differential equation. **NDSolve**, on the other hand, generates approximate *numerical* solutions of differential equations. These solutions are really just lists of numbers corresponding to approximate values of the solution at particular values of the independent variable. The output of **NDSolve** can generally be treated as a function, however, because *Mathematica* can interpolate between values in the list. In fact, the only essential difference you have to keep in mind when using **NDSolve** (as opposed to **DSolve**) is that **NDSolve** requires actual *numbers*, whereas **DSolve** can work with variables. In particular, you must specify a numerical initial condition when using **NDSolve**.

In[39]:=   **approxsol = NDSolve[{y'[x] == Sqrt[y[x] + x], y[1] == 3},**
             y[x], {x, 1, 10}]

Out[39]=   {{y[x] -> InterpolatingFunction[{1.,10.},<>][x]}}

The output is different from that of **DSolve**—the transformation rule specifies an interpolating function rather than a specific algebraic expression. But we can manipulate the output in exactly the same way as we did for **DSolve**.

In[40]:=   **ya[x_] = y[x] /. First[approxsol]**

Out[40]=   InterpolatingFunction[{1., 10.}, <>][x]

This defines a function **ya[x]**, which is an approximation to the actual solution of the initial value problem. Note that this function is defined on the interval [1, 10], which is the interval we specified when we executed the **NDSolve** command. We can plot it (via a command like **Plot[ya[x], {x, 1, 10}]**), or evaluate it at specific points (*e.g.*, **ya[3.45]** or **Table[ya[1+i], {i, 0, 9}]**).

It is possible to have the function depend on the initial data, but here the difference between **NDSolve** and **DSolve** becomes important. Since **NDSolve** works numerically rather than symbolically, and therefore cannot compute its interpolation function unless specific data is supplied for its initial value, you must type

In[41]:=   **f[x_,c_] := y[x] /. First[NDSolve[{y'[x] == Sqrt[y[x] + x],**
y[1] == c}, y[x], {x, 1, 10}]];

Note the switch to ":=" usage. This is necessary to prevent *Mathematica* from evaluating **NDSolve** before specific initial data is supplied. Now to plot several solution curves corresponding to different initial data you can type

In[42]:=   **Plot[Evaluate[Table[f[x, c], {c, 1, 5}]], {x, 1, 10}];**

If you want to compute values of **f** for specific choices of the initial data, *e.g.*, to evaluate the value of the solution function at $x = 2$ for initial data $c = 5$, you cannot type **f[2, 5]** (because the order of evaluation causes **NDSolve** to fail). Instead, you can type **f[x, 5] /. x –> 2**. Alternatively, you could type:

g[c_] := (v[x_] = y[x] /. First[NDSolve[{y'[x] == Sqrt[y[x] + x], y[1] == c},
y[x], {x, 1, 10}]])

After that, typing **g[5]; v[2]** would tell *Mathematica* to find the solution with initial value $c = 5$ and then to give its value at $x = 2$. See also the end of Chapter 11.

Troubleshooting

In this section, we list some advice for avoiding mistakes that users of *Mathematica* commonly make. We also discuss the warning messages that *Mathematica* produces, and describe some techniques for recovering from errors.

The Most Common Mistakes.   Here are some of the most common mistakes in using *Mathematica*.

(1) Failure to clear values. See the section *Clearing Values* above.

(2) Failure to keep track of In/Out numbering. This mistake occurs if you use the expression % to refer to the output of the previous command. The previous command is the one most recently executed, not necessarily the preceding command in the Notebook. See the section *Referring to Previous Output* in Chapter 3.

(3) Using a command from a *Mathematica* package before the package has been loaded. See the section *Packages* in this chapter.

(4) Typing the wrong kind of "=" sign. The worst instance is typing "=" when you intend "==". This causes a value to be assigned to an expression and this value must be explicitly cleared before you can proceed. Be particularly wary of this mistake when using the commands **Solve**, **DSolve**, and **NDSolve**, all of which require an equation as one of the arguments.

(5) Mismatched braces or brackets. *Mathematica* usually catches this kind of mistake.

(6) Improper use of built-in functions. For example, to use the natural logarithm function in *Mathematica* you type **Log[x]** and not **Log x** or **Log(x)**.

(7) Improperly concatenating variables. For example, **xy** is a variable named xy, whereas **x y** or **x*y** means x *times* y.

(8) Using **y** instead of **y[x]** in **DSolve** and **NDSolve**.

(9) Typing past the edge of the page in an input cell—the extra text gets lost in printing. One should use RETURN liberally, or change the default settings to force line breaking. See *Setting Defaults* in Chapter 4.

(10) Omitting the **Evaluate** command when using **Table** inside a plotting command. See the section *The Evaluate Command* in this chapter.

Error and Warning Messages. You should pay close attention to the error and warning messages that *Mathematica* generates. Although these messages may seem cryptic at first, you will find that they give valuable clues to locating mistakes in input. For example, suppose that we execute the following command without first defining a function $u(x)$.

In[43]:=   **Plot[u[x], {x, 0, 3}]**

```
Plot::plnr: CompiledFunction[{x}, <<1>>, -CompiledCode-][x]
    is not a machine-size real number at x = 0..

Plot::plnr: CompiledFunction[{x}, <<1>>, -CompiledCode-][x]
    is not a machine-size real number at x = 0.125.

Plot::plnr: CompiledFunction[{x}, <<1>>, -CompiledCode-][x]
    is not a machine-size real number at x = 0.25.

General::stop:
   Further output of Plot::plnr
     will be suppressed during this calculation.
```

This imposing error message is *Mathematica*'s way of telling you that whatever it is that you're trying to plot is not evaluating to a real number. In this case, we tried to plot a function that hadn't been defined, so of course it didn't evaluate to a real number.

It is important to distinguish between *error* messages and *warning* messages. An error message means that something is really wrong, and *Mathematica* will probably not be able to produce any output. A warning message is an indication that something might be wrong, or that *Mathematica* can't do exactly what you've instructed it to do. Examples of warning messages are:

```
NDSolve::mxst:
   Maximum number of 500 steps reached at the point
     0.999981.

InterpolatingFunction::dmval:
   Input value lies outside domain of the interpolating
     function.
```

The first of these was generated by a call to **NDSolve** and is probably due to a vertical asymptote of the solution. The second message was generated when we tried to plot the solution generated by **NDSolve** on the interval $[0, 3]$, and is due to fact that the solution is not defined past 0.999981. In both of these cases, *Mathematica* produces the proper output, but warns us that something unusual is going on.

As you become comfortable using *Mathematica*, you may occasionally want to turn off certain warning messages. To do this you use the **Off** command. For example, to turn off the warning message "NDSolve::mxst" you would enter **Off[NDSolve::mxst]**. To turn it on again, enter **On[NDSolve::mxst]**.

Recovering from Errors.   From time to time you may experience certain problems using *Mathematica*. This is an unavoidable aspect of any complicated software product. We have tried to alert you to the most common and frustrating problems. More suggestions appear in the *On-line Help* sections of Chapters 2–4; the *Aborting Calculations* section of Chapter 3; and the *Quitting the Kernel*, *If Your Notebook Won't Open*, and *Rendering Graphics* sections of Chapter 4. The three most common crises and their remedies are:

(1) Notebooks won't open, or disappear unexpectedly. Solution: Delete the ".mb" file, as explained in *If Your Notebook Won't Open* in Chapter 4.

(2) Computer is hung up and won't respond. Solution: Type "COMMAND-." (in *Windows*, "ALT-.") to abort the calculation. If all else fails, reboot the computer.

(3) *Mathematica* input produces unexpected results. Solution: Clear variables; go through the list of common mistakes given above.

Above all, remember to save your work often.

Problem Set C

Numerical Solutions
of Differential Equations

In this problem set you will use **NDSolve**, *Mathematica's* numerical solver for ordinary differential equations. Chapters 7 and 8 explain how to use **NDSolve**.

1. We are interested in the solution $y = \phi(x)$ to the Initial Value Problem (IVP)

$$y' = x^2 + y^2, \qquad y(0) = 1.$$

Observe that on the interval $0 \le x \le 1$, we have the inequalities

$$y^2 \le x^2 + y^2 \le 1 + y^2.$$

Therefore we must have $\phi_0(x) \le \phi(x) \le \phi_1(x)$, where ϕ_0, ϕ_1 are the solutions to the respective IVP's

$$\begin{cases} y' = y^2 \\ y(0) = 1, \end{cases} \qquad \begin{cases} y' = 1 + y^2 \\ y(0) = 1. \end{cases}$$

Solve these IVP's explicitly and conclude that $\phi(x) \to \infty$ as $x \to x_*$, where $\pi/4 \le x_* \le 1$. Then use *Mathematica* to approximate the value of x_*.

2. We are interested in the solution $y = \phi(x)$ to the IVP

$$y' = y^2 - x, \qquad y(0) = 2$$

on the interval $0 \le x \le 1$. Observe that on this interval, we have the inequalities

$$y^2 \ge y^2 - x \ge y^2 - 1.$$

Therefore we must have $\phi_0(x) \ge \phi(x) \ge \phi_1(x)$, where ϕ_0, ϕ_1 are the solutions to the respective IVP's

$$\begin{cases} y' = y^2 \\ y(0) = 2, \end{cases} \qquad \begin{cases} y' = y^2 - 1 \\ y(0) = 2. \end{cases}$$

Solve these IVP's explicitly and conclude that $\phi(x) \to \infty$ as $x \to x_*$, where $0.5 \le x_* \le 0.5 \ln 3$. Use *Mathematica* to approximate the value of x_*.

3. We shall study solutions $y = \phi_b(x)$ to the IVP

$$y' = (y - x)(1 - y^3), \qquad y(0) = b.$$

(a) Use **NDSolve** to generate approximate solutions $\phi_b(x)$ for several values of b. Plot these solutions. Make sure to include values of b that are less than 1, equal to 1, and greater than 1.

(b) Now, based on these plots, describe the behavior of the solution curves $\phi_b(x)$ for positive x, when $b < 1$, $b = 1$, and $b > 1$. Explain how the long-term behavior of the solution curves differs according as b is less than or greater than 1.

(c) Show that the solution curves for $b > 1$ are asymptotic to the line $y = x$. Explain from the differential equation why that is plausible. Plot the direction field of the differential equation to confirm your analysis.

4. We shall study solutions $y = \phi_b(x)$ to the IVP

$$y' = (y - x^2)(1 - y^2), \qquad y(0) = b$$

for nonnegative values of x.

(a) Use **NDSolve** to generate approximate solutions $\phi_b(x)$ for several values of b. Plot these solutions. Make sure to include values of b that are: less than -1, equal to -1, between -1 and 1, equal to 1, and greater than 1.

(b) Now, based on these plots, describe the behavior of the solution curves $\phi_b(x)$ for large positive x, when $b < -1$, $b = -1$, $-1 < b < 1$, $b = 1$, and $b > 1$. For $-1 < b < 1$, explain how the initial behavior of the solution curves differs according as b is positive or negative.

(c) Finally, by combining your plots with a plot of the parabola $y = x^2$, show that the solution curves for $b > 1$ are asymptotic to the parabola. Explain from the differential equation why that is plausible.

5. Use **NDSolve** to analyze the Gompertz-threshold model from Problem 13 of Problem Set B. That is, consider the differential equation

$$y' = y(1 - \ln y)(y - 3).$$

Solve it using **NDSolve** for various values of $y(0)$. Plot several solution curves on the interval $0 \leq t \leq 10$. (The option **PlotRange** may be helpful here.) By examining the differential equation and analyzing your plots, identify the equilibrium solutions and discuss their stability.

6. Consider the IVP

$$\frac{dy}{dx} = \frac{x - e^{-x}}{y + e^y}, \qquad y(1.5) = 0.5.$$

(a) Use **NDSolve** to find approximate values of the solution at $x = 0, 1, 1.8$, and 2.1. Then plot the solution.

(b) If you did Problem 4 in Problem Set B, recall your results—either by reloading the file or redoing the problem. Compare the values of the actual solution and the numerical solution at the 4 points. Plot the actual solution and the numerical solution on the same graph.

(c) Now plot the numerical solution on several large intervals (*e.g.*, $0 \leq x \leq 10$ or $0 \leq x \leq 100$). Make a guess about the nature of the solution function as $x \to \infty$. Try to justify your guess on the basis of the differential equation.

7. Consider the IVP

$$e^x \sin y - 2y \sin x + (e^x \cos y + 2 \cos x) \frac{dy}{dx} = 0, \qquad y(0) = 0.5.$$

(a) Use **NDSolve** to find approximate values of the solution at $x = -1, 1$, and 2. Then plot the solution.

(b) If you did Problem 5 in Problem Set B, recall your results—either by reloading the file or redoing the problem. Compare the values of the actual solution and the numerical solution at the 3 points. Plot the actual solution and the numerical solution on the same graph.

(c) Now plot the solution on several large intervals (*e.g.*, $0 \leq x \leq 10$ or $0 \leq x \leq 100$). Make a guess about the nature of the solution function as $x \to \infty$. Try to justify your guess on the basis of the differential equation.

8. We know that the differential equations

$$y' = e^{-x^2}, \qquad y' = e^{x^2}$$

cannot be solved in terms of elementary functions (Chapter 7).

(a) Use **DSolve** to solve these two equations.

(b) Note the occurrence of the built-in functions **Erf** and **Erfi**. Mathematics texts refer to the function **Erf** as the *error function*, which is usually written $\mathrm{erf}(x)$. The function **Erfi** is the real-valued function defined by $\mathrm{erfi}(x) = -i \cdot \mathrm{erf}(ix)$, where $i = \sqrt{-1}$. Use the *Mathematica* differentiation operator **D** to see that

$$\frac{d}{dx}(\mathrm{erf}(x)) = \frac{2}{\sqrt{\pi}} e^{-x^2} \quad \text{and} \quad \frac{d}{dx}(\mathrm{erfi}(x)) = \frac{2}{\sqrt{\pi}} e^{x^2}.$$

In fact,

$$\mathrm{erf}(x) = \frac{2}{\sqrt{\pi}} \int_0^x e^{-t^2}\, dt \qquad \mathrm{erfi}(x) = \frac{2}{\sqrt{\pi}} \int_0^x e^{t^2}\, dt.$$

(c) Although one does not have elementary formulas for these functions, the numerical capabilities of *Mathematica* mean that we "know" these functions as well as we "know" elementary functions like $\tan x$. To illustrate this, evaluate $\lim_{x \to \infty} \mathrm{erf}(x)$, and compute $\int_{-\infty}^{\infty} e^{-t^2}\, dt$.

(d) Plot erf(x). Discuss the features of the graph.

(e) Next solve the IVP

$$y' = 1 - 2xy, \qquad y(0) = 0,$$

using the *Mathematica* command **DSolve**. What does the solution do for large x? Find the value x at which the solution takes its maximum. What is the maximum value?

(f) Compute $\dfrac{\partial f}{\partial y}$ for the function $f(x,y) = 1 - 2xy$. Discuss stability of the equation in (e). Illustrate your conclusions about stability by graphing solutions with different initial conditions on the interval $[-5, 5]$.

9. Consider the IVP
$$xy' + (\sin x)y = 0, \qquad y(0) = 1.$$

(a) Use **DSolve** to solve the IVP.

(b) Note the occurrence of the built-in function **SinIntegral**. Mathematics texts usually refer to this function by the symbol $Si(x)$. Check that this function is an antiderivative of $\sin x/x$ by differentiating it. Evaluate $\lim_{x \to \infty} Si(x)$. (You may have to do this indirectly.)

(c) Plot $Si(x)$. Discuss the features of the graph.

(d) Do the same with the solution function to the IVP.

(e) Now try to solve the IVP using **NDSolve**. You will find that *Mathematica* fails. It refuses to deal with $\sin x/x$ at $x = 0$, even though the singularity is removable. One way to get around this is to give the initial condition $y = 1$ at a value of x extremely close to, but not equal to, zero. Since we are only finding an approximate solution with **NDSolve** anyhow, there shouldn't be much harm done as long as the amount by which we move the initial condition is small compared with the error we expect from the numerical procedure.

Alternatively, you could try redefining the differential equation to be $y' + f(x)y = 0$ with
$$f(x) = \begin{cases} \sin x/x, & x \neq 0 \\ 1, & x = 0. \end{cases}$$

(f) Discuss stability of the differential equation. Illustrate your conclusions by graphing solutions with different initial conditions on the interval $[-10, 10]$.

10. Use **NDSolve** to solve the following equations numerically, then plot the solutions. On the basis of your plots, predict what happens to the solution as x increases. (In particular, if there is a limiting value for y, either finite or infinite, then find it.) If it is unclear from the plot you've made, try redoing **NDSolve** and replotting on a larger interval. Another possibility is that the solution blows

up in finite time. If so, estimate the time. If your solution curves appear jagged, use the **PlotPoints** option to the **Plot** command.

(a) $y' = e^{-2x} + \dfrac{1}{1+y^2}$, $\quad y(0) = -1$

(b) $y' = e^{-2x} + y^2$, $\quad y(0) = -1$

(c) $y' = \cos x - y^3$, $\quad y(0) = 0$

(d) $y' = (\sin x)y - y^2$, $\quad y(0) = 1$.

11. Use **NDSolve** to solve the following equations numerically, then plot the solutions. On the basis of your plots, predict what happens to the solution as x increases. See Problem 10 for more instructions.

(a) $y' = 5x - 3\sqrt{y}$, $\quad y(0) = 2$

(b) $y' = (x^2 - y^2)\sin y$, $\quad y(0) = -1$

(c) $y' = \dfrac{y^2 + 2xy}{x^2 + 3}$, $\quad y(1) = 2$

(d) $y' = -2x + e^{-xy}$, $\quad y(0) = 1$.

12. This problem illustrates one of the possible pitfalls of blindly applying numerical methods without paying attention to the theoretical aspects of the differential equation itself. Consider the equation

$$-4\,x^2 + 2\,y(x) + x\,y'(x) = 0.$$

(a) Use the *Mathematica* program in Chapter 7 to compute the Euler approximations to this equation with initial condition $y(-0.5) = 4.25$, step size $h = 0.2$, and $n = 10$ iterations. The program will generate a list of ordered pairs of numbers representing the (x, y) coordinates of points of the approximate solution. Use the function **ListPlot** with the option **PlotJoined -> True** to obtain a piecewise linear graph of the approximate solution.

(b) Now repeat part (a) with step size $h = 0.1$ and $n = 20$. Compare the values of the two approximations at $x = 0.1$.

(c) Now modify the program to implement the Improved Euler Method. Repeat parts (a) and (b) using the Improved Euler Method. Compare the approximations at $x = 0.1$. Can you make sense of your answers?

(d) Next try to use **NDSolve** to find an approximate solution on the interval $(-0.5, 1.5)$. Note the warning message *Mathematica* gives you. What is the interval on which the approximate solution has been defined? Now plot the solution on an appropriate interval.

(e) Solve the equation explicitly and graph the solutions for the initial conditions $y(0) = 0$, $y(-0.5) = 4.25$, $y(0.5) = 4.25$, $y(-0.5) = -3.75$, and $y(0.5) = -3.75$.

Now explain your results in (a)–(d). Could we have known, without solving the equation, whether to expect meaningful results in parts (a)–(c)? Why? Can you guess how **NDSolve** avoids making the same "mistake"?

13. Consider the IVP

$$\frac{dy}{dx} = e^{-x} - 2y, \qquad y(-1) = 0.$$

(a) Use the *Mathematica* program in Chapter 7 to compute the Euler approximation to $y(x)$ with step size $h = 0.5$ and number of steps $n = 4$. The program will generate a list of ordered pairs (x_i, y_i). Use the **ListPlot** command with the option **PlotJoined –> True** to display the piecewise linear function connecting the points (x_i, y_i). Repeat with $h = 0.2$ and $n = 10$.

(b) Now modify the program to implement the Improved Euler Method, and repeat part (a) using the Improved Euler Method.

(c) Find the exact solution of the IVP and plot the solution, the two Euler approximations, and the two Improved Euler approximations on the same graph. Label the five curves.

(d) Now use the Euler's Method program with $h = 0.5$ to approximate the solution on the interval $[-1, 9]$. Plot both the approximate and the exact solutions on this interval. How close is the approximation to the exact solution as x increases? Recall the discussion of stability at the end of Chapters 5 and 7. By computing the partial derivative of the right side of the equation with respect to y, can you explain your results?

14. Consider the IVP

$$\frac{dy}{dx} = y - 4e^{-3x}, \qquad y(0) = 1.$$

(a) Use the *Mathematica* program in Chapter 7, with step size $h = 0.5$ and $n = 6$ steps, to find approximate values, using Euler's Method, for the solution of the IVP on the interval from $x = 0$ to $x = 3$. Then plot the approximate solution on this interval using the **ListPlot** command with the option **PlotJoined –> True**. What appears to be happening to y as x increases?

(b) Repeat part (a) with $h = 0.2$ and $n = 15$, and then with $h = 0.1$ and $n = 30$. How are the approximate solutions changing as the step size decreases? Can you make a reliable prediction about the long-term behavior of the solution?

(c) Use **NDSolve** to find an approximate solution and plot it on the same interval. Now what does it look like y is doing as x increases? Next plot the solution from **NDSolve** on a larger interval (going at least to $x = 10$). Again, what is happening to y as x increases?

(d) Solve the IVP explicitly and compare the actual solution to the approximations found above. Now compute the partial derivative of the right side of the equation with respect to y. In light of the discussion of stability at the ends of Chapters 5 and 7, explain your results in parts (a)–(c).

15. Consider the IVP

$$\frac{dy}{dx} = 2y - 2 + 3e^{-x}, \qquad y(0) = 0.$$

(a) Use the *Mathematica* program in Chapter 7, with step size $h = 0.2$ and $n = 10$ steps, to find approximate values, using Euler's Method, for the solution of the IVP on the interval from $x = 0$ to $x = 2$. Then plot the approximate solution on this interval using the **ListPlot** command with the option **PlotJoined** $\rightarrow$ **True**. What appears to be happening to y as x increases?

(b) Repeat part (a) with $h = 0.1$ and $n = 20$, and then with $h = 0.05$ and $n = 40$. How are the approximate solutions changing as the step size decreases? Can you make a reliable prediction about the long-term behavior of the solution?

(c) Use **NDSolve** to find an approximate solution and plot it on the same interval. Now what does it look like y is doing as x increases? Next plot the solution from **NDSolve** on a larger interval (going at least to $x = 5$). Again, what is happening to y as x increases?

(d) Solve the IVP explicitly and compare the actual solution to the approximations found above. Now compute the partial derivative of the right side of the equation with respect to y. In light of the discussion of stability at the ends of Chapters 5 and 7, explain your results in parts (a)–(c).

16. We know that e^x is the solution to the IVP

$$\frac{dy}{dx} = y, \qquad y(0) = 1, \tag{i}$$

so if we solve (i) numerically we will be getting approximate values for e^x. Use **NDSolve**, employing the accuracy options discussed in Chapter 7, to calculate values for $e^{0.1}, e^{0.2}, \ldots, e$ that have 10 correct digits. Present your results in a table. In a second column print the values of e^x for $x = 0.1, 0.2, \ldots, 1$, obtained by using built-in function **Exp**. Show at least 10 digits. Compare the two columns of values.

Chapter 9

Qualitative Theory of Second Order Linear Equations

In this course, we spend a great deal of time learning how to solve second order linear differential equations with *constant coefficients*:

$$ay'' + by' + cy = g(x).$$

This is in part because such equations model a wide variety of physical situations. It is also because we usually cannot find solution formulas for more general second order equations. Nevertheless, general second order equations are important in many applications.

In this chapter, we study second order linear differential equations with *variable coefficients*. The general form of such an equation is:

$$y'' + p(x)y' + q(x)y = g(x).$$

Airy's equation,

$$y'' - xy = 0, \tag{1}$$

and Bessel's equation,

$$y'' + \frac{1}{x}y' + y = 0, \tag{2}$$

are examples of variable coefficient equations. Both equations have important applications in physics. For example, Airy's equation arises in diffraction problems in optics, and Bessel's equation occurs in the study of vibrations of a circular membrane and of water waves with circular symmetry.

In this chapter, we introduce comparison methods and a geometric method for analyzing second order linear equations with variable coefficients. These qualitative methods are important because they do not require explicit solution formulas.

Comparison methods provide information on the solutions of a variable coefficient equation by comparing the equation with an appropriate constant coefficient equation. This possibility is suggested by the following example. For large x, the coefficient $1/x$ in Bessel's equation (2) is close to 0. So, Bessel's equation is close to the equation $y'' + y = 0$, whose general solution can be written as $y = R\cos(x - \delta)$. Thus, one might expect solutions to Bessel's equation to oscillate and look roughly

111

like sine waves for large x. We present a result that validates this type of comparison.

The geometric method is based on direction fields, which are not directly applicable to a second order equation. We show, however, how to construct a related first order equation whose direction field yields information about the solutions of the second order equation.

Why should we take such an indirect approach to analyzing a differential equation when we could simply examine the plot of a numerical solution produced by *Mathematica*? We can, of course, get much information from numerical methods and graphics. There is other information, however, that qualitative methods yield more effectively: properties shared by all solutions of a differential equation, the oscillatory nature of solutions of an equation, or the precise rate of decay or growth of solutions.

Comparison Methods

In this section, we discuss the Sturm Comparison Theorem and the relation between the zeros of two linearly independent solutions of a second order linear equation.

The Sturm Comparison Theorem. This theorem, whose proof will be given later, validates the type of comparison mentioned at the beginning of this chapter.

STURM COMPARISON THEOREM. *Let $u(x)$ be a solution to the equation*

$$y'' + q(x)y = 0,$$

and suppose $u(a) = u(b) = 0$ for some $a < b$ (but u is not identically zero). Let $v(x)$ be a solution to the equation

$$y'' + r(x)y = 0,$$

where $r(x) \geq q(x)$ for all $a \leq x \leq b$. Then $v(x) = 0$ for some x in $[a, b]$.

We typically use this result to compare a variable coefficient equation with an appropriate constant coefficient equation. Consider, for example, the equation

$$y'' + \frac{1}{x}y = 0. \tag{3}$$

Let K be a positive number. If $0 < x \leq K$, then $1/x \geq 1/K$. We now apply the Comparison Theorem with $q(x) = 1/K$ and $r(x) = 1/x$. Thus, we compare equation (3) to the constant coefficient equation $y'' + (1/K)y = 0$, whose general solution is $u(x) = R\cos(\sqrt{1/K}x - \delta)$. The zeros of these solutions are spaced $\pi\sqrt{K}$ apart. The Sturm Comparison Theorem implies that adjacent zeros of any solution of (3) in $(0, K]$ cannot be farther apart than $\pi\sqrt{K}$. To see this, suppose two adjacent zeros of a solution v of equation (3) are farther apart that $\pi\sqrt{K}$. Then by choosing δ appropriately, we would have a solution u with two zeros between the adjacent zeros of v. Then the Comparison Theorem would imply that v has a zero between the zeros of u, and hence between the adacent zeros of v; this is a contradiction.

In particular, solutions of (3) must oscillate as $x \to \infty$, though the oscillations may become less frequent as x increases. Indeed, by turning the above comparison around, one concludes that the zeros of solutions of (3) in $[K, \infty)$ must be at least $\pi\sqrt{K}$ apart.

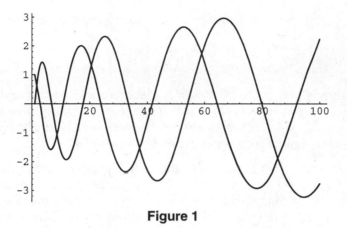

Figure 1

Figure 1 shows two representative solutions of (3) computed with **NDSolve**. As you can see, the predictions of the previous paragraph are confirmed by the graph.

The Sturm Comparison Theorem can also be used to study the zeros of Airy's equation and of Bessel's equation. In the latter case, a substitution is made to eliminate the y' term. See Problems 15 and 16 in Problem Set D.

The Interlacing of Zeros. You may have noticed that the curves in Figure 1 take turns crossing the horizontal axis. We say that the zeros of the two solutions are *interlaced*: between any two zeros of one solution there is a zero of the other. This is a common phenomenon—the property of interlaced zeros holds for any pair of linearly independent solutions of a homogeneous second order linear differential equation

$$y'' + p(x)y' + q(x)y = 0. \tag{4}$$

If $p(x) = 0$, as is the case in equation (1), the proof of the interlacing result follows from an application of the Sturm Comparison Theorem by comparing the equation with itself. For the more general equation (4), the proof is based on the Wronskian. Let $y_1(x)$ and $y_2(x)$ be any two linearly independent solutions of (4). Recall that the Wronskian of $y_1(x)$ and $y_2(x)$ is

$$W(x) = y_1(x)y_2'(x) - y_1'(x)y_2(x).$$

Since y_1 and y_2 are solutions of (4), it follows that W satisfies the differential equation

$$W' = -p(x)W,$$

whose general solution is

$$W(x) = Ce^{-\int p(x)dx}.$$

This formula shows that $W(x)$ does not change sign—it always has the same sign as the constant C, which must be nonzero (or else y_1 and y_2 would be linearly dependent).

Assume $y_1(a) = y_1(b) = 0$, and that there are no zeros of y_1 between a and b. Then

$$W(a) = -y_1'(a)y_2(a),$$
$$W(b) = -y_1'(b)y_2(b).$$

Since y_1 does not change sign between a and b, we know $y_1'(a)$ and $y_1'(b)$ have opposite signs. Then, since $W(a)$ and $W(b)$ have the same sign, $y_2(a)$ and $y_2(b)$ must have opposite signs. Therefore y_2 must be zero somewhere between a and b. Similarly, y_1 must have a zero between any two zeros of y_2.

EXERCISE. The solutions to Airy's equation and Bessel's equation are considered so important that they have been given names in *Mathematica*. The Airy functions $Ai(x)$ and $Bi(x)$ are a fundamental set of solutions for (1), and the Bessel functions $J_0(x)$ and $Y_0(x)$ are a fundamental set of solutions for (2). These functions are built into *Mathematica* as **AiryAi[x]**, **AiryBi[x]**, **BesselJ[0,x]**, and **BesselY[0,x]**. Use *Mathematica* to check that the zeros of the two solutions **AiryAi[x]** and **AiryBi[x]** to Airy's equation are interlaced, and do the same for the Bessel functions **BesselJ[0,x]** and **BesselY[0,x]**.

Proof of the Sturm Comparison Theorem. The proof is based on the Wronskian, as was the proof of the interlacing result. Recall the hypotheses: $u'' + q(x)u = 0$ and $v'' + r(x)v = 0$, with $q(x) \leq r(x)$ between two zeros a and b of u. Since u is not identically zero, we can assume u does not change sign between a and b (if it did it would have a zero between a and b, and we could look at a smaller interval). Assume for instance that $u > 0$ between a and b. Since $u = 0$ at a and b, it follows that $u'(a) > 0$ and $u'(b) < 0$. (Notice that these derivatives cannot be zero because then by the uniqueness theorem u would be identically zero.) We want to prove that v is zero somewhere in $[a, b]$; we suppose it is not, say $v(x) > 0$ throughout $[a, b]$, and argue to obtain a contradiction.

Let $W(x)$ be the Wronskian of u and v,

$$W(x) = u(x)v'(x) - u'(x)v(x);$$

then

$$W(a) = -u'(a)v(a) < 0,$$
$$W(b) = -u'(b)v(b) > 0.$$

Also, since $q(x) \leq r(x)$,

$$W' = uv'' - u''v = u(-r(x)v) - (-q(x)u)v = (q(x) - r(x))uv \leq 0.$$

But this is impossible—the last inequality implies W does not increase between a and b, yet $W(a) < 0 < W(b)$. This contradiction means that v cannot have the same sign throughout $[a, b]$, and therefore v must be zero somewhere in the interval.

A Geometric Method

As mentioned above, direction fields are not directly applicable to second order equations. We now show, however, that with a given second order homogeneous equation, we can associate a first order equation whose direction field yields information about the solutions of the second order equation.

Consider the homogeneous equation

$$y'' + p(x)y' + q(x)y = 0. \tag{5}$$

Let

$$z = \arctan\left(\frac{y}{y'}\right);$$

then

$$z' = \left(1 + \left(\frac{y}{y'}\right)^2\right)^{-1} \frac{d}{dx}\left(\frac{y}{y'}\right) = \frac{y'^2}{y'^2 + y^2}\frac{y'^2 - yy''}{y'^2} = \frac{y'^2 - yy''}{y'^2 + y^2}.$$

Also, since $\tan z = y/y'$, notice that

$$\sin z = \frac{y}{\sqrt{y'^2 + y^2}}, \quad \cos z = \frac{y'}{\sqrt{y'^2 + y^2}}.$$

Then if y satisfies (5), and y is not identically zero, it follows that

$$z' = \frac{y'^2 - yy''}{y'^2 + y^2} = \frac{y'^2 - y(-p(x)y' - q(x)y)}{y'^2 + y^2} = \frac{y'^2 + p(x)yy' + q(x)y^2}{y'^2 + y^2}.$$

In other words,

$$z' = \cos^2 z + p(x)\sin z \cos z + q(x)\sin^2 z. \tag{6}$$

We have shown that for every solution y of (5) that is not identically zero, there is a corresponding solution z of (6). (This is not a one-to-one correspondence—every constant multiple of a solution y corresponds to the same solution z.) Though the solution curves of (6) will be different from the solution curves of (5), we now show that we can learn about the solutions of (5) by studying the solutions of (6); specifically, by considering the direction field of (6).

The Constant Coefficient Case. We begin by considering the equation

$$y'' - y = 0,$$

whose general solution is

$$y = c_1 e^x + c_2 e^{-x}.$$

The corresponding first order equation is

$$z' = \cos^2 z - \sin^2 z.$$

In Figure 2, we show the direction field of this equation, which we produced with the *Mathematica* command

PlotVectorField[{1, Cos[z]^2 − Sin[z]^2}, {x, 0, 10}, {z, −Pi/2, Pi/2},
    PlotPoints −> 20, ScaleFunction −> (1&), Frame −> True,
    Axes −> True, AspectRatio −> 1]

(Recall that we first must type **<<Graphics`PlotField`** to load the *Mathematica* package **PlotField**.)

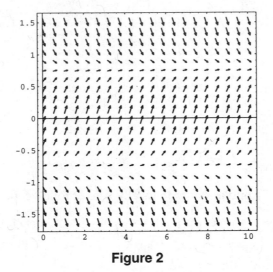

Figure 2

Notice that we plot z from $-\pi/2$ to $\pi/2$; this is the range of values taken on by the arctan function. You may wonder what happens if z goes off the bottom of the graph. The answer is that z "wraps around" to the top of the graph. Recall that $z = \arctan(y/y')$; the points $z = \pm\pi/2$ correspond to $y' = 0$, and when y' changes sign, then so does z by passing from $-\pi/2$ to $\pi/2$ (or vice versa).

Next, observe that there is an unstable equilibrium at $z = -\pi/4$, which corresponds to $y/y' = \tan(-\pi/4) = -1$; this represents solutions of the form $y = ce^{-x}$. Likewise, the stable equilibrium $z = \pi/4$ corresponds to $y/y' = \tan(\pi/4) = 1$, which represents the solutions $y = ce^x$. The fact that most solutions of the equation satisfied by z (those with initial condition other than $-\pi/4$) approach the stable equilibrium $z = \pi/4$ corresponds to the fact that most solutions $y = c_1 e^x + c_2 e^{-x}$ (those with $c_1 \neq 0$) grow like e^x as x increases.

Another basic example is
$$y'' + y = 0,$$
for which the corresponding first order equation is
$$z' = \cos^2 z + \sin^2 z = 1.$$

That is, z simply increases linearly, though every time it reaches $\pi/2$ it wraps around to $-\pi/2$. This corresponds to the oscillation of solutions y, for every time $z = \arctan(y/y')$ passes through zero then so must y, and vice versa.

EXERCISE. Consider the general second order linear homogeneous equation with constant coefficients:
$$ay'' + by' + c = 0.$$

Investigate how the roots of the characteristic equation, if real, correspond to equilibrium solutions for z. Show that if the roots of the characteristic equation are complex, then z' is always positive.

The Variable Coefficient Case. The examples above suggest ways to draw parallels between solutions z of (6) and solutions y of (5). First of all, if z is positive, then y and y' have the same sign. This implies that y is moving away from zero as x increases. We say in this case that y is *growing*, meaning that $|y|$ is increasing. Likewise, if z is negative then y and y' have opposite signs, which implies that y is moving toward zero as x increases—we say in this case that y is *decaying*, meaning that $|y|$ is decreasing. If z changes sign by passing through zero, then so does y, and if z passes through $\pm\pi/2$, then y' changes sign, showing that y has passed through a local maximum or minimum.

In light of these observations, let us summarize what we can predict about the *long-term behavior* of a solution y of (5) in terms of the corresponding solution z of (6).

- If z remains positive as x increases, then y grows away from zero.
- If z remains negative as x increases, then y decays toward zero.
- If z continues to increase from $-\pi/2$ to $\pi/2$ and wraps around to $-\pi/2$ again, then y *oscillates* as x increases.

Notice from (6) that $z' = 1$ whenever $z = 0$, so it is not possible for z to decrease through zero. Thus the long-term behavior of z will usually fall into one of the three categories above.

We can be more precise about the growth or decay rate of y in cases where z approaches a limiting value. If the limiting value is θ, then y/y' approaches $\tan\theta$ as x increases. In other words, $y' \approx (\cot\theta)y$ for large x. Thus
$$y \approx ce^{(\cot\theta)x}$$
for large x, and $\cot\theta$ is the asymptotic exponential growth (or decay) rate of y. If z approaches zero as x increases, then y/y' approaches zero as well. One can show that y grows (if $z > 0$) or decays (if $z < 0$) faster than any exponential function.

Likewise, if z approaches $\pi/2$, then y grows slower than exponentially, and if z approaches $-\pi/2$, then y decays slower than exponentially. Since y'/y approaches zero in these cases, y could grow or decay toward a finite, nonzero value.

Let us now see what the direction field of (6) tells us about solutions of Airy's and Bessel's equations.

Airy's Equation.   For Airy's equation,

$$y'' - xy = 0, \tag{7}$$

the corresponding first order equation is

$$z' = \cos^2 z - x \sin^2 z.$$

Figure 3 shows the direction field of this equation, plotted by a *Mathematica* command similar to the one used for Figure 2.

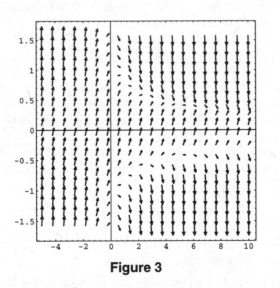

Figure 3

Notice that z is increasing steadily for negative x, so solutions of (7) must oscillate for negative x. For positive x, it is evident that solutions of (7) cannot oscillate; z passes through zero at most once, after which it remains positive. Hence the corresponding solution of (7) grows away from zero as x increases. It appears that once z becomes positive, it decreases to zero, indicating that most solutions of (7) grow faster than exponentially.

We now know there are solutions of (7) that grow very fast as x increases, and there are no oscillating solutions for positive x. Is it possible to have a decaying solution of (7)? Equivalently, is it possible for z to remain negative as x increases?

Figure 3 strongly suggests that there is such a solution z, and hence that there is a solution y to (7) that decays toward zero at a rate faster than exponential.

The Airy function Ai(x) is, by definition, the unique (up to a constant multiple) solution of (7) that decays as x increases. As expected, the other Airy function Bi(x) grows as x increases. You can see what these functions look like by plotting **AiryAi[x]** and **AiryBi[x]** in *Mathematica*. The general solution of (7) is a linear combination of Ai(x) and Bi(x).

Bessel's Equation. For Bessel's equation

$$y'' + \frac{1}{x}y' + y = 0, \tag{8}$$

the corresponding first order equation is

$$z' = \cos^2 z + \frac{1}{x}\sin z \cos z + \sin^2 z.$$

Figure 4 shows the direction field of this equation.

Figure 4

The picture is simpler than the one for Airy's equation. When x is away from zero, z is increasing steadily. So, solutions of (8) oscillate for both positive and negative x. Near $x = 0$, the direction field is irregular because of the $1/x$ term in the differential equation. We can't tell what happens from this picture, but there is reason to expect solutions of (8) will not behave nicely near this singularity in the differential equation.

One question this approach cannot answer easily is whether the amplitude of oscillating solutions grows, decays, or remains steady as x increases. Since the coefficient of the y' term in (8) is positive, we can expect solutions of (8) to behave like a physical oscillator with damping—the amplitude of oscillations should decrease as x increases. Since the damping coefficient goes to zero as x increases, we cannot be sure (without a more refined analysis) whether the amplitude of solutions of (8) must decrease to zero. In fact it does, as you can check by plotting the Bessel functions **BesselJ[0,x]** and **BesselY[0,x]** in *Mathematica*.

Other Equations. Here are some other differential equations for which you can try this method.

- Bessel's equation of order n,

$$y'' + \frac{1}{x}y' + \left(1 - \frac{n^2}{x^2}\right)y = 0,$$

for various n (above we studied the case $n = 0$). You can check your predictions using the *Mathematica* functions **BesselJ[n,x]** and **BesselY[n,x]**.

- The modified Bessel equation of order n,

$$y'' + \frac{1}{x}y' - \left(1 + \frac{n^2}{x^2}\right)y = 0,$$

for various n. The *Mathematica* functions **BesselI[n,x]** and **BesselK[n,x]** are a fundamental set of solutions for this equation.

- The parabolic cylinder equation

$$y'' + \left(n + \frac{1}{2} - \frac{1}{4}x^2\right)y = 0$$

for various n. This equation arises in quantum mechanics, but its solutions are not built into *Mathematica*; you can check your predictions against approximate solutions from **NDSolve** instead. This equation is considered in Problem 17 of Problem Set D.

Problem Set D

Second Order Equations

1. Airy's equation is the linear second order homogeneous equation $y'' = xy$. Although it arises in a number of applications, including quantum mechanics, optics and waves, it cannot be solved exactly by the standard methods. In order to analyze the solution curves, let us reason as follows.

(a) For x close to zero, the equation resembles $y'' = 0$, which has general solution $y = c_1 x + c_2$. We refer to this as a "facsimile" solution. Graph a numerical solution to Airy's equation with initial conditions $y(0) = 0, y'(0) = 1$, and the facsimile solution (with the same initial data) on the interval $(-2, 2)$. How well do they match?

(b) For $x \sim -K^2 << 0$, the equation resembles $y'' = -K^2 y$, and the corresponding facsimile solution is given by $y = c_1 \sin(Kx + c_2)$. Again using the initial conditions $y(0) = 0, y'(0) = 1$, plot a numerical solution of Airy's equation over the interval $(-18, -14)$. Using the value $K = 4$, try to find values of c_1 and c_2 so that the facsimile solution matches well with the actual solution. Why shouldn't we expect the initial conditions for Airy's equation to be the appropriate initial conditions for the facsimile solution?

(c) For $x \sim K^2 >> 0$, Airy's equation resembles $y'' = K^2 y$, which has solution $y = c_1 \sinh(Kx + c_2)$. (The hyperbolic sine function is called **Sinh[x]** in *Mathematica*.) Plot a numerical solution of Airy's equation together with a facsimile solution (with $K = 4$) on the interval $(14, 18)$. In analogy with part (b), you have to choose values for c_1 and c_2 in the facsimile solution. (Try $c_1 = 1, c_2 = 0$.)

(d) Plot the numerical solution of Airy's equation on the interval $(-20, 2)$. What does the graph suggest about the frequency and amplitude of oscillations as $x \to -\infty$? Could any of that information have been predicted from the facsimile analysis?

2. Consider Bessel's equation of order zero

$$x^2 y'' + xy' + x^2 y = 0 \qquad (i)$$

with initial data $y(0) = 1$, $y'(0) = 0$. The solution $J_0(x)$ is usually called the Bessel function of order zero of the first kind. Strictly speaking, this equation has a singularity at $x = 0$. However, this is one instance of a solution to a linear equation that exists outside the expected domain of definition. Still, as you will see below, the presence of the singularity can affect your computations.

(a) For x close to 0, x^2 is very small compared to x. The equation (i) is therefore approximately $xy' = 0$. Solve this equation with the preceding initial data. What does this "facsimile" solution to the original problem suggest to you about the behavior of J_0 near the origin?

(b) For x large and positive, x is small compared to x^2; and so we may approximate (i) by the equation $x^2(y'' + y) = 0$. Solve this equation with the same initial data. (*Hint*: Do it by hand or, if you use **DSolve**, divide by x^2.) What does this suggest about the nature of the function J_0 for large x?

(c) Still thinking of x as large and positive, rewrite (i) in the form

$$y'' + \frac{1}{x}y' + y = 0.$$

If $x \approx K \gg 0$, we might approximate the equation by the constant coefficient equation

$$y'' + \frac{1}{K}y' + y = 0.$$

Solve that equation and see what further information you obtain about J_0. (If need be, choose a specific value for K, say $K = 100$, and examine the solution in order to refine your conclusion from (b).) Now explain why J_0 must be an even function, and so make the same deduction for large negative x.

(d) Throw caution to the winds and try **DSolve** on the original problem. You may be surprised to learn that *Mathematica* can handle it. Graph the solution function and see how well it manifests the qualitative properties you inferred in parts (a)-(c).

(e) Have a crack at the IVP with **NDSolve**. No luck? Why?

3. This and some of the following problems concern models for the motion of a pendulum, which consists of a weight attached to a rigid arm of length L that is free to pivot in a complete circle. Neglecting friction and air resistance, the angle $\theta(t)$ that the arm makes with the vertical direction satisfies the differential equation

$$\theta''(t) + \frac{g}{L}\sin(\theta(t)) = 0, \tag{i}$$

where $g = 32.2$ ft/sec^2 is the gravitational acceleration constant. We will assume the arm has length 32.2 ft, and so replace (i) by the simpler form

$$\theta'' + \sin\theta = 0. \tag{ii}$$

(Alternatively, one can rescale time, replacing t by $\sqrt{g/L}\,t$, to convert (i) to (ii).) For motions with small displacements (θ small), $\sin\theta \approx \theta$, and (ii) can be approximated by the linear equation

$$\theta'' + \theta = 0. \tag{iii}$$

This equation has general solution $\theta(t) = A\cos(t + \delta)$, with *amplitude A* and *phase shift* δ. Since all the solutions to the linear approximation (iii) have period 2π, we expect that, for small displacements, the solutions to the true pendulum (ii) should have period close to 2π. One can see how the period depends on the amplitude A by solving equation (ii) with **NDSolve** using initial conditions $\theta(0) = A, \theta'(0) = 0$, plotting the solution, and then looking for the first time the solution hits zero. The period will be 4 times this amount. Thus for small amplitudes, the solution should first hit zero around $t = \pi/2$. Follow the above procedure and estimate, to within 0.1, the period of the pendulum for the amplitudes $A = 0.1, 0.8$, and 1.6. What is happening to the accuracy of the linear approximation as the initial displacement increases?

4. In this problem, we'll look at what the pendulum does for various initial velocities (*cf.* Problem 3). Define a *Mathematica* function of v that will numerically solve the differential equation $(3.ii)$ using initial conditions $\theta(0) = 0, \theta'(0) = v$. Do likewise for equation $(3.iii)$. Plot the solutions to both the nonlinear equation $(3.ii)$ and the linear equation $(3.iii)$ for each of the following values of the initial velocity v: 1, 1.99, 2, 2.01. Use a time interval from $t = 0$ to $t = 40$. Clearly mark which is the nonlinear solution and which is the linear solution on each plot. Interpret what is happening physically in each case. What is special about the case $v = 2$?

5. In this problem, we'll investigate the effect of damping on the pendulum, using the model

$$\theta'' + b\theta' + \sin\theta = 0$$

(*cf.* Problem 3). Define a *Mathematica* function of b that will find a numerical solution of this differential equation with initial conditions $\theta(0) = 0, \theta'(0) = 4$. Then plot the solution from $t = 0$ to $t = 20$ for the values $b = 0.5$, 1, and 2. Interpret what is happening *physically* in each case, *i.e.*, describe explicitly what the graph says the pendulum is doing. Now do the same for the linear approximation

$$\theta'' + b\theta' + \theta = 0,$$

for the same values of b. Compare the linear and nonlinear behavior in each case.

6. In this problem, we'll look at the effect of a periodic external force on the pendulum, using the model

$$\theta'' + 0.05\theta' + \sin\theta = 0.3\cos\omega t$$

(*cf.* Problems 3–5). We have chosen a value for the damping coefficient that is more typical of air resistance than the values in the previous problem. Write a *Mathematica* function of ω that numerically solves this equation with initial conditions $\theta(0) = 0, \theta'(0) = 0$. Then plot the result from $t = 0$ to $t = 60$ for the following values of the frequency ω: $0.6, 0.8, 1, 1.2$. Which frequency moves the pendulum farthest away from its equilibrium position? Do the same analysis for the linear approximation

$$\theta'' + 0.05\theta' + \theta = 0.3\cos\omega t$$

and answer the same question. For which frequencies do the linear and nonlinear equations have widely different behaviors? Which forcing frequency induces resonance type behavior in the pendulum?

7. In many applications, second order equations come with *boundary conditions* rather than *initial conditions*. For example, consider a cable that is attached at each end to a post, with both ends at the same height (let us call this height $y = 0$). If the posts are located at $x = 0$ and $x = 1$, the height y of the cable as a function of x satisfies the differential equation

$$y'' = c\sqrt{1 + (y')^2}$$

with boundary conditions $y(0) = 0, y(1) = 0$. The constant c depends on the length of the cable; for this problem we'll use $c = 1$. *Mathematica* can't solve the above differential equation with **DSolve**. (However, you may be able to solve it viewing it as a first order equation in y'; or by trying the fortified **DSolve** command in the package **Calculus`DSolve`** in *Mathematica* Version 2.2.) Moreover, **NDSolve** requires initial conditions. Nonetheless we can use **NDSolve** as follows to approximate the solution of the differential equation that satisfies the given boundary conditions. Write a function that, for a given value of s, finds a numerical solution to the above equation (using $c = 1$) with initial conditions $y(0) = 0, y'(0) = s$, and plots the solution from $x = 0$ to $x = 1$. By evaluating this function for various values of s, find to within 0.01 the value of s which leads to a solution satisfying the condition $y(1) = 0$. Graph the solution on $[0, 1]$ and determine the maximum dip in the cable.

8. The problem of finding the function $u(x)$ satisfying

$$\begin{cases} a(x)u''(x) + a'(x)u'(x) = f(x), 0 \le x \le 1 \\ u(0) = u(1) = 0 \end{cases}$$

arises in studying the longitudinal displacements in a longitudinally loaded elastic bar. The bar is of length 1, its left end is at $x = 0$, and its right end at $x = 1$. In the differential equation above, $f(x)$ represents the external force on the bar (which is assumed to be longitudinal, *i.e.*, to be directed along the bar), $a(x)$ represents both the elastic properties and the cross-sectional area of the bar, and $u(x)$ is the longitudinal displacement of the bar at the point x. This problem is an example of a *boundary value problem*; the conditions $u(0) = u(1) = 0$, which specify that the ends of the bar are fixed, are called boundary conditions. The function $a(x)$ may be constant; this is the case if neither the elastic properties nor the cross-sectional area depends on the position x in the rod, *i.e.*, if the rod is uniform. But if the rod is not uniform, then $a(x)$ is not constant, and the equation has variable coefficients. Likewise, $f(x)$ will be constant only if the external force is applied uniformly along the rod.

Now suppose $a(x) = 1 + x^2$ and $f(x) = 50x^4$. Find and plot the corresponding solution $u(x)$. Since the equation has variable coefficients, constant coefficient methods are not applicable, so we will use a numerical method. We cannot apply **NDSolve** directly, since it requires initial conditions. Nonetheless, we can use **NDSolve** as follows to approximate the solution. Write a function that, for a given value of s, finds a numerical solution to the equation with the initial conditions $u(0) = 0, u'(0) = s$ and plots this solution for $0 \le x \le 1$. Note that the first boundary condition is one of our initial conditions. Then by evaluating this function for various values of s you should be able to get a fairly accurate value for the s that leads to a solution satisfying the second boundary condition $u(1) = 0$. Next define a second function (of s) that finds a numerical solution of the equation with the initial conditions $u(0) = 0, u'(0) = s$, and then numerically evaluates $u(1)$. Using this function, you should be able to get an accurate approximation for the desired s. Plot the final (accurate) solution to the boundary value problem.

9. In this problem, we study the effects of air resistance.

(a) A paratrooper steps out of an airplane at a height of 1000 ft., and after 5 seconds opens her parachute. Her weight, with equipment, is 195 lbs. Let $y(t)$ denote her height above the ground after t seconds. Assume that the air resistance is $0.005y'(t)^2$ lbs. in free fall and $0.6y'(t)^2$ lbs. with the chute open. At what height does the chute open? How long does it take to reach the ground? At what velocity does she hit the ground? (This model assumes air resistance is proportional to the *square* of the velocity; and that the parachute opens instantaneously. *Please do not try this at home!*)

(*Hint*: Pay attention to units. Recall that the mass of the paratrooper is 195/32, measured in lb sec^2/ft. Here, 32 is the acceleration due to gravity, measured in ft/sec^2.)

(b) One can view the equation of motion during the second phase of the fall (while the chute is open) as a first order ODE in the velocity. Do this, and then make a qualitative analysis of the first order equation, finding in particular the critical or equilibrium velocity. This velocity is called the terminal velocity. How does the terminal velocity compare with the velocity at the time the chute opens, and with the velocity of impact?

(c) Assume the paratrooper is safe if she strikes the ground at a velocity within 5% of the terminal velocity in (b). What is the lowest height from which she may parachute safely? Except for the initial height, use the parameters in (a).

10. This problem is based on Problems 26 and 27 in Boyce & DiPrima, Section 3.8. Consider the IVP

$$u'' + cu' + u = 0, \quad u(0) = 2, \quad u'(0) = 0.$$

(a) Find the solution. For $c = 0.25$, graph the solution. Determine an approximate time τ at which the solution becomes "negligible." Interpret negligible to mean that no meaningful difference between the curve and the x-axis can be discerned on your plot. Repeat this process for the values $c = 0.25, 0.5, \ldots, 1.75, 2$. Make a list of values (c, τ) corresponding to the eight values of c. Plot the resulting points. (Use **ListPlot** and the **PlotJoined** $\rightarrow$ **True** option.) How does τ depend on c?

(b) Now plot the solution curves for the values $c = 1.75, 1.8, \ldots, 2.2, 2.25$. The issue we would like to resolve is: at what point does the transition from oscillatory to nonoscillatory behavior occur. The characteristic equation tells you it is $c = 2$. Why? By adjusting your domain and range, try to verify that. If you cannot, explain what prevents you from doing so. (*Hint*: For $c = 1.9$ for example, compute where the curve first crosses the x-axis. What is the magnitude at nearby points?)

11. This problem is based on Problems 19 and 20 in Boyce & DiPrima, Section 3.9. Consider the IVP

$$u'' + u = 3\cos(\omega t), \quad u(0) = 0, \quad u'(0) = 0.$$

(a) Find the solution (using **DSolve**). For $\omega = 0.5, 0.6, 0.7, 0.8, 0.9$, plot the solution curves on the interval $0 \le x \le 10$. Note that $\omega_0 = 1$ is the natural frequency of the homogeneous equation. Describe how the solution curves behave as ω gets closer to 1.

(b) Compute and plot the solution curve for $\omega = 1$. What phenomenon is exhibited? Corroborate your conclusion by plotting on a longer interval.

(c) Compare the plots for $\omega = 1$ and $\omega = 0.9$ on a longer interval to see that the behavior for $\omega = 0.9$ is different from that in (b). What phenomenon is exhibited by the curve for $\omega = 0.9$?

(d) Now change the initial data to $u(0) = 1$, $u'(0) = 1$. Redo parts (a)-(c). What effect does the nonzero initial data have on the solution curves?

12. In this problem we study how solutions of the initial value problem

$$\frac{d^2y}{dt^2} + 0.15\frac{dy}{dt} - y + y^3 = 0, \quad y(0) = a, \quad y'(0) = 0$$

depend on the initial value a.

Plot a numerical solution of this equation from $t = 0$ to $t = 40$ for each of the initial values $a = 0.5, 1, 1.5, 2, 2.5$. You may have to increase **MaxSteps** in **NDSolve** (as described in Chapter 7) in order to make some of these plots.

Describe how increasing the initial value of y affects the solutions, both in terms of their limiting behavior and their general appearance. (In making comparisons, be careful to pay attention to the scale on the y-axis. Better still, use the **PlotRange** option to the **Plot** command to force the same scale on all of your plots.)

Finally, plot all five solutions on one graph. Would such a picture be possible for solutions of a first order differential equation? Why or why not?

13. In this problem, we consider the long-term behavior of solutions of the initial value problem

$$\frac{d^2y}{dt^2} + 0.15\frac{dy}{dt} - y + y^3 = 0.3\cos(\omega t), \quad y(0) = 0, \quad y'(0) = 0$$

for various frequencies ω in the forcing term.

Plot a numerical solution of this equation from $t = 0$ to $t = 100$ for each of the 8 frequencies $\omega = 0.8, 0.9, \ldots, 1.4, 1.5$. You may have to increase **MaxSteps** in **NDSolve** (as described in Chapter 7) in order to make these plots. You should also expect *Mathematica* to take more time than usual in making them.

Describe and compare the different long-term behaviors you see. Due to the forcing term, all solutions will oscillate, but pay particular attention to the magnitude of the oscillations, and to whether or not there is a periodic pattern to them. Are there any similarities between your results for this nonlinear system and the phenomenon of resonance for linear systems with periodic forcing?

14. In this problem, we study the zeros of solutions of the second order differential equation

$$y'' + (2 + \sin x)y = 0. \tag{i}$$

(a) Using **NDSolve**, compute and plot several solutions of this equation with different initial conditions: $y(0) = c, y'(0) = d$. To be specific, choose three different values for the pair c, d and plot the corresponding solutions over $[-10, 10]$. By inspecting your plots, find a number L that is an upper bound for the distance between successive zeros of the solutions. Then find a number l that is a lower bound for the distance between successive zeros.

(b) Information on the zeros of solutions of linear second order ODE's can be obtained from the Sturm Comparison Theorem (see Chapter 9). By comparing (i) with the equation $y'' + y = 0$, you should be able to get a value for L, and by comparing (i) with $y'' + 3y = 0$, you should be able to find l. How do these values compare with the values obtained in part (a)? (You will find it useful to note that the general solution of $y'' + ky = 0$, where k is a positive constant, can be written as $y = R\cos(\sqrt{k}x - \delta)$, with $R \geq 0, \delta$ arbitrary. R is called the *amplitude* and δ the *phase shift*.)

(c) Plot a solution of (i) and a solution of $y'' + y = 0$ on the same graph, and verify that between any two zeros of the latter solution, there is at least one zero of the solution of (i).

15. Consider Bessel's equation of order zero

$$x^2 y'' + xy' + x^2 y = 0.$$

(a) Using **NDSolve**, compute and plot several solutions of this equation with different initial conditions: $y(1) = c, y'(1) = d$. To be specific, choose three different values for the pair c, d and plot the corresponding solutions over $[0.1, 20]$. (Why isn't it a good idea to use $x = 0$ in the initial conditions?) By inspecting your plots, find a number L that is an upper bound for the distance between successive zeros of the solutions. Then find a number l that is a lower bound for the distance between successive zeros.

(b) Now confirm your findings with the Sturm Comparison Theorem. It doesn't apply directly, but if we introduce the new function $z(x) = x^{1/2} y(x)$, Bessel's equation becomes

$$z'' + (1 + 1/(4x^2))z = 0,$$

which has the form of the equation in the Comparison Theorem. Since y will have a zero wherever z has a zero, we can study the zeros of y by studying the zeros of z. By comparing the equation for z with the equation $z'' + z = 0$, determine an upper bound L on the distance between successive zeros of any solution of Bessel's equation.

(c) Let a be a positive number. For $x \in [a, \infty)$, the quantity $1 + 1/(4x^2)$ is less than or equal to the constant $1 + 1/(4a^2)$. By making an appropriate comparison, determine a lower bound l on the distance between successive zeros of any solution of Bessel's equation (for $x > a$). What is the limiting value of l as a goes to ∞? Approximately how far apart are the zeros when x is large? Did your graphical study lead to comparable values for l and L?

16. A solution of a second order linear differential equation is called *oscillatory* if its graph crosses the x-axis infinitely many times, and *nonoscillatory* if it crosses only finitely many times. In this problem, we will be interested in determining the oscillatory nature of nonzero solutions to some second order linear ODE's. First consider the equation $y'' + ky = 0$, where k is a constant. If $k > 0$, it has the general solution $y = R\cos(\sqrt{k}x - \delta)$, with $R \geq 0, \delta$ arbitrary. R is called the *amplitude* and δ the *phase shift*. From this formula we see that any solution $y(x)$ has infinitely many zeros and hence crosses the axis infinitely many times, *i.e.*, is oscillatory. If $k < 0$, the general solution is $y(x) = c_1 e^{\sqrt{-k}x} + c_2 e^{-\sqrt{-k}x}$, so

we see that solutions have at most one zero, *i.e.*, are nonoscillatory. If $k = 0$, the general solution is $y(x) = c_1 x + c_2$. These have at most one zero, so are nonoscillatory.

Next consider Airy's equation

$$y'' = xy, \tag{i}$$

which arises in various applications. Since (i) has a variable coefficient, we cannot study it by elementary methods; in particular, we cannot find the general solution as we did above for the constant coefficient equation. We will instead first make a graphical study of the solutions of (i), and then study the solutions using the Sturm Comparison Theorem (see Chapter 9). Compute and plot several numerical solutions of (i) with different initial conditions $y(0) = c, y'(0) = d$. To be specific, choose three different values for the pair (c, d), and graph the corresponding solutions over the interval $[-10, 5]$. What do you observe? Do solutions have zeros on the negative x-axis? A few? Many? Do they get closer together as x becomes more negative? Do solutions have zeros on the positive x-axis? Where are the solutions oscillatory?

Information on the zeros of solutions of linear second order ODE's, and hence information on their oscillatory nature, can also be obtained from the Sturm Comparison Theorem. By comparing (i) with the equation $y'' - by = 0$ for $x \leq b < 0$, what do you learn about negative zeros and their spacing, and hence about the oscillatory nature of solutions of (i) for $x \leq 0$? By comparing (i) with $y'' = 0$ for $0 < x$, what do you learn about the oscillatory nature of solutions for $x > 0$? How many positive zeros could a solution have? Do the graphs you plotted above confirm these results?

17. In this problem, we study solutions of the parabolic cylinder equation

$$y'' + \left(n + \frac{1}{2} - \frac{x^2}{4}\right) y = 0,$$

which arises in the study of quantum-mechanical vibrations. Since the equation is unchanged if x is replaced by $-x$, any solution function will be symmetric with respect to the y-axis. Therefore, we focus our attention on $x \geq 0$.

(a) Find the corresponding first order equation for $z = \arctan(y/y')$, as described in the *Geometric Method* section of Chapter 9.

(b) For $n = 1$, plot the direction field for the z equation from $x = 0$ to $x = 10$. (Remember to use $-\pi/2 \leq z \leq \pi/2$.) Based on the plot, predict what the solutions y to the parabolic cylinder equation look like near $x = 0$, and for larger x. Is there a value of x around which you expect their behavior to change?

(c) Now numerically solve the parabolic cylinder equation for $n = 1$ with two sets of initial conditions $y(0) = 1, y'(0) = 0$ and $y(0) = 0, y'(0) = 1$. Plot the two solutions on the same graph. (It will probably help to use the **PlotRange** option.) Do the solutions behave as you expected?

(d) Repeat parts (b) and (c) for $n = 5$. Point out any differences from the case $n = 1$.

(e) Repeat parts (b) and (c) for $n = 15$. Discuss how the solutions are changing as n increases.

(f) Now consider the three solutions (for $n = 1, 5$, and 15) with $y(0) = 0$. Point out similarities and differences. By drawing an analogy with Airy's equation, argue from the direction fields that, for any n, exactly one solution function decays for large x while all others grow. Do you have enough graphical evidence from the numerical plots to conclude that the solution corresponding to the initial data $y(0) = 0$, $y'(0) = 1$ is that function? Why or why not? (*Hint*: Look to previous discussions of stability of solutions as a guide.)

Chapter 10

Symbolic
Computational Methods

A primary theme of this book is that numerical, geometric, and qualitative methods can be used to study solutions of differential equations, even when we cannot find an exact formula solution. Of course, exact solutions are extremely valuable, and there are many techniques for finding them. For instance, techniques for finding exact solutions of second order linear differential equations include:

- The exponential substitution, which leads to solutions of an arbitrary constant coefficient homogeneous equation;

- The method of *reduction of order,* which produces a second linearly independent solution of a homogeneous equation when one solution is already known;

- The method of *undetermined coefficients,* which solves special kinds of inhomogeneous equations with constant coefficients; and

- The method of *variation of parameters,* which yields the solution of a general inhomogeneous equation, given a fundamental set of solutions to the homogeneous equation.

Each of these techniques reduces the search for a formula solution to a simpler problem in algebra or calculus: finding the root of a polynomial, computing an antiderivative, or solving a pair of simultaneous linear equations.

The process of finding formulas for exact solutions of equations, either by hand or by computer, is called *symbolic computation.* The **DSolve** command, which incorporates some of the techniques listed above, is one method for symbolic computation using a computer. As a tool for symbolic computation, **DSolve** enables us to find exact solutions more rapidly and more reliably than we could by hand.

There are many differential equations that do not yield to the techniques listed above. By using more advanced ideas from calculus, however, we can find exact solutions for a wider class of differential equations. In this chapter, we discuss two such calculus-based techniques for finding exact solutions of differential equations: *Series Solutions* and *Laplace Transforms.* The method of Series Solutions enables us to solve differential equations with variable coefficients. The theory of

Laplace Transforms enables us to solve differential equations with discontinuous inhomogeneous terms. These are sophisticated techniques, which use improper integrals, complex variables, and power series. Consult your text for a more thorough discussion of these techniques. (For example, see Chapters 5 and 6 of Boyce & DiPrima.)

Both techniques are computationally intensive. For each technique, we describe a short *Mathematica* program that automates the process of computing a symbolic solution to a differential equation or to an initial value problem. Using the methods discussed in this chapter is different from using **DSolve**, because they involve a *series* of *Mathematica* commands. As with numerical and graphical methods, computationally intensive symbolic methods become more tractable when applied with the aid of a mathematical software system.

Series Solutions

Consider the second order homogeneous linear differential equation with variable coefficients

$$a(x)y''(x) + b(x)y'(x) + c(x)y(x) = 0. \tag{1}$$

Suppose the coefficient functions a, b, and c are *analytic* (i.e., have convergent power series representations) in a neighborhood of a point $x = x_0$. For simplicity, we shall assume that $x_0 = 0$, but everything we say remains valid in the neighborhood of any point of analyticity. We begin by dividing by $a(x)$ to normalize the equation. This causes no problems as long as $a(0) \neq 0$. In this case, we refer to the origin as an *ordinary point* for the equation. Changing notation, we write

$$y''(x) + p(x)y'(x) + q(x)y(x) = 0. \tag{2}$$

Equations (1) and (2) have the same solutions. We will search for a power series solution of the form

$$y(x) = \sum_{n=0}^{\infty} a_n x^n. \tag{3}$$

If we can find such a solution, then $y(0) = a_0$ and $y'(0) = a_1$. Thus, if we are given initial values, then we can find the first two coefficients of the power series solution.

By substituting the infinite series (3) into equation (2), expanding p and q as power series, and combining terms of the same degree, we obtain a recursion relation for the coefficients a_n. In other words, we obtain algebraic equations for a_n that involve $a_0, a_1, \ldots, a_{n-1}$ and known coefficients of the power series of p and q. Sometimes, we can solve the recursion relation in *closed form* by finding an algebraic formula for a_n. This formula would involve known functions of n (such as $n!$ or powers of n) and a_0 and a_1, but no other coefficients of lower degree. If no initial data is given, then a solution to the recursion relation produces a general solution of the differential equation with arbitrary constants a_0 and a_1.

Solving a recursion relation in closed form is like finding an exact formula solution for a differential equation. In many cases, we cannot solve the recursion relation. Nevertheless, we can still use the recursion relation to compute as many coefficients as we wish. As long as we stay close to the origin, the leading terms should give a good approximation to the full power series solution. One must be careful, however, because the power series solution will be valid only inside its radius of convergence. The radius of convergence will be at least as large as the distance from the origin to the nearest singularity of p or q. When the recursion relation is solvable in closed form, we can use a standard test from calculus to compute the radius of convergence precisely. In general, we can only make an educated guess.

We can use *Mathematica* to automate the process of finding power series solutions. In fact, *Mathematica* can solve some recursion relations in closed form. You can explore that possibility by loading the package **DiscreteMath`RSolve`** and typing **?RSolve**. Here, however, we shall describe a straightforward technique for computing the leading coefficients explicitly.

EXAMPLE.   We begin with Problem 15 in Section 5.2 of Boyce & DiPrima: Find the first four terms in the power series solution of the initial value problem

$$y'' - xy' - y = 0, \qquad y(0) = 2, \qquad y'(0) = 1.$$

The **Series** command generates a power series for an analytic function in a neighborhood of a point to any number of terms. For example, the command

Series[Exp[x], {x, 0, 3}]

gives the first four terms of the Taylor series for e^x, namely

$$1 + x + \frac{x^2}{2} + \frac{x^3}{6} + O(x)^4.$$

The symbol $O(x)^4$ means terms of degree at least 4. We can also work symbolically. For example,

formalseries = Series[y[x], {x, 0, 5}]

yields

$$y(0) + y'(0)\, x + \frac{y''(0)\, x^2}{2} + \frac{y^{(3)}(0)\, x^3}{6} + \frac{y^{(4)}(0)\, x^4}{24} + \frac{y^{(5)}(0)\, x^5}{120} + O(x)^6.$$

Now we can incorporate the differential equation as follows

odeseries = Series[y''[x] − x*y'[x] − y[x], {x, 0, 3}]

The result is

$$\left(-y(0) + y''(0)\right) + \left(-2\,y'(0) + y^{(3)}(0)\right)\,x + \left(\frac{-3\,y''(0)}{2} + \frac{y^{(4)}(0)}{2}\right)\,x^2 +$$

$$\left(\frac{-2\,y^{(3)}(0)}{3} + \frac{y^{(5)}(0)}{6}\right)\,x^3 + \mathrm{O}(x)^4.$$

Next, we insert the initial data

> **twocoeffs = {y[0] –> 2, y'[0] –> 1}**
> **ivpseries = odeseries /. twocoeffs**

We obtain

$$\left(-2 + y''(0)\right) + \left(-2 + y^{(3)}(0)\right)\,x + \left(\frac{-3\,y''(0)}{2} + \frac{y^{(4)}(0)}{2}\right)\,x^2 +$$

$$\left(\frac{-2\,y^{(3)}(0)}{3} + \frac{y^{(5)}(0)}{6}\right)\,x^3 + \mathrm{O}(x)^4.$$

Then we expand and solve for the coefficients:

> **morecoeffs = Solve[ivpseries == 0]**

The result is

$$\{\{y''(0) \rightarrow 2, y^{(3)}(0) \rightarrow 2, y^{(4)}(0) \rightarrow 6, y^{(5)}(0) \rightarrow 8\}\}.$$

The coefficients we desire are the above numbers divided by the appropriate factorials. Thus, the series solution to the IVP computed to degree 5 is:

$$y(x) = 2 + x + x^2 + \frac{1}{3}x^3 + \frac{1}{4}x^4 + \frac{1}{15}x^5.$$

You can even have *Mathematica* automate the last step by the sequence of commands

> **coeffs = Join[twocoeffs, First[morecoeffs]]**
> **answer = Normal[formalseries] /. coeffs**

We have used the *Mathematica* command **Normal** to convert the standard output of the **Series** command into an approximation suitable for use as a function. We also used the **Join** command to combine two lists.

Chapter 5 of Boyce & DiPrima discusses the generalization of this method to the case when one (or both) of p or q has a singularity. The prototype is Euler's equation:

$$ax^2 y'' + bxy' + cy = 0.$$

Dividing by ax^2 introduces a pole of order 1 in the coefficient of y' and a pole of order 2 in the coefficient of y. Such isolated singularities, where the coefficient of $y^{(k)}$ is a pole of order no worse than $2 - k$, are called *regular singular points*. In fact, **DSolve** can handle Euler's equation. For general equations with regular singular points, one needs to adopt a method analogous to the one above.

EXAMPLE. Consider Problem 1 in Section 5.6 of Boyce & DiPrima

$$2xy'' + y' + xy = 0.$$

The origin is a regular singular point and the indicial equation has roots $r = 0$ and $r = 1/2$. Hence, the differential equation should have a Frobenius series solution of the form

$$x^{1/2} \sum_{n=0}^{\infty} a_n x^n.$$

We will adapt the method above (developed for ordinary points) to compute the leading terms of the Frobenius series. We set up the mechanism by defining $y(x) = \sqrt{x}u(x)$ and expanding both y and the differential equation. We have to be more careful with the derivatives; in particular, we must use **D[y[x], x]** rather than **y'[x]** in the series. Here is the program:

```
y[x_] := Sqrt[x] u[x]
frobseries = Series[y[x], {x, 0, 5}]
odeseries = Series[2 x*D[y[x], {x, 2}] + D[y[x], x] + x*y[x], {x, 0, 5}]
leadcoeff = {u[0] -> 1}
ivpseries = odeseries /. leadcoeff
morecoeffs = Solve[ivpseries == 0]
coeffs = Join[leadcoeff, First[morecoeffs]]
answer = Normal[frobseries] /. coeffs
```

The final result is

$$\sqrt{x} - \frac{x^{5/2}}{10} + \frac{x^{9/2}}{360}.$$

EXERCISE. Compute two more terms in each of the examples presented in this section.

If the singular point is not regular, then we cannot expect a Frobenius series solution to be valid, and other techniques (numerical or qualitative) must be brought to bear. Some of those techniques are addressed in Problem Set E.

Laplace Transforms

Transform techniques provide another method for finding exact solutions of differential equations. Common to all transform techniques is an invertible process that converts functions of one type into functions of another type. The process is designed to convert the derivative of a function f into a function that is algebraically related to f. In this way, each differential equation is converted into an algebraic equation. After solving the algebraic equation, one tries to invert the transform to recover a solution to the differential equation.

Recall that the Laplace Transform of a piecewise continuous function $y(t)$ of exponential growth on the positive half-line $t \geq 0$ is defined by

$$Y(s) = \mathcal{L}(y)(s) = \int_0^\infty e^{-st} y(t) \, dt.$$

The key property that enables one to transform a differential equation into an algebraic equation is the relation

$$\mathcal{L}(y')(s) = sY(s) - y(0).$$

Because of this relation, a second order constant coefficient inhomogeneous linear initial value problem

$$ay''(t) + by'(t) + cy(t) = f(t), \qquad y(0) = y_0, \qquad y'(0) = y_0'$$

is transformed into the single algebraic equation

$$(as^2 + bs + c)Y(s) - asy_0 - ay_0' - by_0 = F(s),$$

where $F(s)$ is the Laplace Transform of $f(t)$. One solves the algebraic equation for $Y(s)$, and then computes the inverse transform. In an elementary ODE course, this procedure is usually carried out by reading tables. In more advanced courses, contour integrals are employed to compute the inverse transform analytically.

You can use *Mathematica* to compute Laplace Transforms automatically. Here is the syntax. First, you must load the Laplace Transform package via

   <<Calculus ` LaplaceTransform `

The Laplace Transform of a function $y(t)$ is computed by

   LaplaceTransform[y[t], t, s]

and the inverse transform of a function $U(s)$ is computed by

   InverseLaplaceTransform[U[s],s,t]

The elementary functions of calculus can be treated with these commands. In addition, *Mathematica* Versions 2.1 and later recognize the unit step function $u_0(t)$ and the Dirac delta function $\delta_0(t)$. These built-in *Mathematica* functions are called **UnitStep** and **DiracDelta**, respectively. Because these functions are available, you can use *Mathematica* to deal with discontinuous inhomogeneous terms.

With these tools, you can solve most of the problems in Chapter 6 of Boyce & DiPrima. To illustrate, here is a program to solve the above IVP. We will use the *Mathematica* variables **y0** to represent y_0 and **yp0** to represent y_0'.

   F := LaplaceTransform[f[t], t, s]
   Y[s_] := (a*s^2 + b*s + c)^(−1) ((a*s + b) y0 + a*yp0 + F)
   y[t_] := InverseLaplaceTransform[Y[s], s, t]

This program concisely expresses the essential structure of a transform method: transform the differential equation into an algebraic equation, solve that equation, and then transform back. The program focuses on the algebraic form of the equation; you never enter the original differential equation directly. Instead, you define the variables that encode the data for a particular problem, and then type **y[t]**. For example, to solve

$$y'' + y = \sin 2t, \qquad y(0) = 1, \qquad y'(0) = -1,$$

you would type

a = 1; b = 0; c = 1; y0 = 1; yp0 = −1; f[t_] := Sin[2 t];

and then **y[t]** on a separate line.

EXAMPLE. The initial value problem

$$y'' + 4y = g(t), \qquad y(0) = 0, \qquad y'(0) = 0,$$

where

$$g(t) = \begin{cases} t, & \text{if } 0 \leq t \leq \pi/2 \\ \pi/2, & \text{if } t \geq \pi/2 \end{cases}$$

is discussed in Example 2 of Section 6.4 of Boyce & DiPrima. We observe that

$$g(t) = t - u_{\pi/2}(t)(t - \pi/2).$$

Therefore all we have to do is enter the program, then type

a = 1; b = 0; c = 4; y0 = 0; yp0 = 0;
f[t_] := t − UnitStep[t − Pi/2](t − Pi/2);

and finally type **y[t]** on a separate line. The result is

$$\frac{t - (-\pi/2 + t)\, \text{UnitStep}(-\pi/2 + t)}{4} + \frac{-\frac{\sin(2t)}{2} + \frac{\sin(2\,(-\pi/2+t))\,\text{UnitStep}(-\pi/2+t)}{2}}{4}.$$

The program above focuses on the algebraic form of the equation. Here is an alternative method that allows you to work directly with the original differential equation. Type in succession:

Y[s_] := LaplaceTransform[y[t], t, s]
eqn = LaplaceTransform[y''[t] + y[t] == Sin[2t], t, s]
tran = Solve[eqn /. {y[0] −> 1, y'[0] −> −1}, Y[s]]
InverseLaplaceTransform[Y[s] /. tran, s, t]

The result is the solution to the first IVP, namely

$$\{\frac{3\cos t - \sin t}{3} - \frac{\sin(2t)}{3}\}.$$

Problem Set E

Series Solutions
and Laplace Transforms

1. Use the program in the *Series Solutions* section of Chapter 10 to compute the terms of degree 10 or less in the Taylor series expansion of the solution $y(x)$ to Airy's equation $y'' - xy = 0$ that satisfies $y(0) = 1$, $y'(0) = 0$. On the interval $(-20, 2)$, graph the solution you obtained, together with the precise Airy function that satisfies the given initial data. (*Hint*: You will have to find a suitable linear combination of the two built-in Airy functions **AiryAi** and **AiryBi**. Either solve two linear equations, or use **DSolve**.) Where is the approximation accurate?

2. Use the *Series Solutions* program in Chapter 10 to compute the terms of degree 10 or less in the Taylor series expansion of the solution to Problem 23 in Section 5.2 of Boyce & DiPrima:

$$y'' - xy' - y = 0, \quad y(0) = 1, \quad y'(0) = 0.$$

   (a) Graph the solution.

   (b) What is the long-term behavior of the solution (as $x \to \pm\infty$)?

   (c) Is y an even function? odd? neither?

   (d) Does the solution have any singularities?

   (e) Explain purely from the IVP itself why each of your three conclusions above is to be expected. (*Hints*: In (b), you will have to do a little qualitative analysis— approximate x by a constant; in (c), consider $y_1(x) = y(-x)$; in (d), use Theorem 5.3.1 in Boyce & DiPrima.)

3. Use the *Series Solutions* program to compute the terms of degree 10 or less in the Taylor series expansion of the solution to Problem 18 in Section 5.2 of Boyce & DiPrima:

$$(1 - x)y'' + xy' - y = 0, \quad y(0) = -3, \quad y'(0) = 2.$$

   The theory suggests the true solution may have a singularity at $x = 1$. Graph the solution you obtained. Do you see any signs of the singularity? Observe that $y = x$ is a solution of the differential equation. Use reduction of order to find the other. Now explain your answer to the question about the singularity.

4. Use **DSolve** to solve the following Euler equations in Section 5.5 of Boyce & DiPrima (Probs. 3, 6, 8, 13):

   (a) $x^2 y'' - 3xy' + 4y = 0$

   (b) $(x - 1)^2 y'' + 8(x - 1)y' + 12y = 0$

   (c) $2x^2 y'' - 4xy' + 6y = 0$

   (d) $2x^2 y'' + xy' - 3y = 0, \quad y(1) = 1, \quad y'(1) = 4.$

5. Use the program for a Frobenius series expansion in Chapter 10 to compute the terms of degree 10 or less in the Frobenius series expansion of the solution to the following problems in Section 5.6 of Boyce & DiPrima (Probs. 2, 5, 8):

   (a) $x^2 y'' + xy' + (x^2 - \frac{1}{9})y = 0, \quad r = -\frac{1}{3}$

   (b) $3x^2 y'' + 2xy' + x^2 y = 0, \quad r = \frac{1}{3}$

   (c) $2x^2 y'' + 3xy' + (2x^2 - 1)y = 0, \quad r = \frac{1}{2}.$

6. This problem concerns Bessel's equation, which arises in many physical problems with circular symmetry, such as the study of water waves in a circular pond, vibrations of a circular drum, or the diffraction of light by the circular aperture of a telescope. The Bessel function $J_n(x)$ (where the parameter n is an arbitrary integer) is defined to be the coefficient of t^n in the power series expansion of the function

$$\exp\left(\frac{1}{2}x\left(t - \frac{1}{t}\right)\right).$$

(It follows easily that $J_{-n}(x) = J_n(x)$ for n even and $J_{-n}(x) = -J_n(x)$ for n odd.) $J_n(x)$ is also a solution to *Bessel's equation of order n*,

$$x^2 y'' + xy' + (x^2 - n^2)y = 0.$$

We note that the Taylor series expansion for J_0 is derived in Section 5.9 of Boyce & DiPrima:

$$J_0(x) = \sum_{j=0}^{\infty} (-1)^j \frac{1}{2^{2j}} \frac{x^{2j}}{(j!)^2}.$$

(a) *Mathematica* has a built-in function for $J_n(x)$, called **BesselJ[n, x]**. Use it to plot $J_0(x)$ for $0 \le x \le 10$. (You don't need to graph the function for negative x since J_0 is an even function.) On the same axes, draw the graphs of the 4th order, 10th order, and 20th order Taylor polynomials of J_0. (In other words, the sum of the terms in the above series out to the desired power of x. Remember that the jth term in the series involves x^{2j}, not x^j, so you don't need very many terms of the series.) How well do the Taylor polynomials approximate the function?

(b) An interesting equality satisfied by the Bessel functions is

$$J_n'(x) = \frac{1}{2}\left(J_{n-1}(x) - J_{n+1}(x)\right).$$

In particular,

$$J_0'(x) = \frac{1}{2}\left(J_{-1}(x) - J_1(x)\right) = \frac{1}{2}\left(-J_1(x) - J_1(x)\right) = -J_1(x).$$

Thus the maxima and minima of J_0 occur at the zeros of J_1. Using **FindRoot** to solve the equations $J_0(x) = 0$ and $J_1(x) = 0$ numerically (you will need lots of different starting values—use your graph for guidance), find the first five zeros and the locations of the first five relative extreme points of J_0, starting at $x = 0$. Compute the differences between successive zeros. Can you make a guess about the periods of the oscillations as $x \to \infty$?

(c) From the general theory (*cf.* Boyce & DiPrima, Chapter 5), one knows that Bessel's equation of order n has another linearly independent solution $Y_n(x)$, with a logarithmic singularity as $x \to 0^+$. *Mathematica* also has a built-in function for computing $Y_n(x)$, **BesselY[n, x]**. Graph the function $Y_0(x)$ on the interval $0 < x \le 10$. Then compute the limit $\lim_{x\to 0^+} Y_0(x)/\ln x$. Graph the function

$$Y_0(x) - c \ln x$$

(on the same interval), where c is the value of the limit you obtained, and observe that it is smooth in a neighborhood of $x = 0$. Thus the "singular part" of $Y_0(x)$ behaves like $c \ln x$.

7. The first order homogeneous linear differential equation

$$x^2 y' + y = 0$$

has an irregular singular point at $x = 0$ (why?); however, it happens to be an equation that is easy to solve exactly. Find the general solution of the equation (for $x > 0$ and for $x < 0$). How do the solutions behave as $x \to 0^+$? as $x \to 0^-$? Use *Mathematica* to graph a solution for $0 < x < 2$ and a solution for $-2 < x < 0$. Why is it hard to fit solutions for $x > 0$ and for $x < 0$ on the same set of axes?

Now find (for $x > 0$ and for $x < 0$) the general solution of the Euler equation

$$xy' + ry = 0,$$

that has a regular singular point at $x = 0$ if $r \ne 0$. How do the solutions behave as $x \to 0^+$? as $x \to 0^-$? Use *Mathematica* to graph a solution for each of the cases $r = 0.5, r = 1, r = -0.5, r = -1$. What difference do you notice between the behavior of solutions near a regular singular point and the behavior near an irregular singular point?

8. Consider the equation
$$x^3 y'' - y = 0, \qquad (i)$$
which has an irregular singular point at $x = 0$. In contrast to the preceding problem, this equation cannot be solved exactly. Let's examine what happens when one studies such an equation using numerical methods.

(a) Try solving (i) in the interval $(0.0000001, 1)$ using **NDSolve**, with what would appear to be innocuous initial conditions near 0:
$$y(0.0001) = 1, \quad y'(0.0001) = 0.$$
What error message do you get? Why do you get two messages? Try increasing the number of steps to 1000. (Be patient!) Does that help? On both problems? Graph the solution on the interval for which *Mathematica* is able to generate an interpolating function (with number of steps equal to 1000). Explain why that graph is misleading given the expected behavior of $y(x)$ as $x \to 0^+$. Now graph the solution on a tiny interval near the left endpoint and compare to the previous graph.

(b) Now let's study equation (i) by another method. First observe that if $u(x) = \ln y(x)$, then
$$u'(x) = \frac{y'(x)}{y(x)}, \qquad u''(x) = \frac{y(x)y''(x) - y'(x)^2}{y(x)^2} = \frac{y''(x)}{y(x)} - u'(x)^2.$$
Thus if $v(x) = u'(x)$, we obtain from (i) a first order differential equation for v:
$$v' + v^2 = \frac{1}{x^3}. \qquad (ii)$$
Try to solve (ii) numerically with the initial condition $v(0.0001) = 0$ in the interval $(0.00001, 1)$. What happens? Are your results different if you replace x^3 by x^2 in (ii) (the case of a regular singularity)? Graph v in the latter case.

9. Nonlinear differential equations can sometimes be solved by series methods. Consider, for example, the equation
$$y' = y^2 + x, \qquad (i)$$
mentioned in Chapter 7 as an example of an equation that cannot be solved in terms of elementary functions. Consider this equation with the initial condition $y(0) = 0$, and let's look for a solution of the form
$$y(x) = \sum_{i=1}^{\infty} a_i x^i. \qquad (ii)$$
(We know there is no constant term in the Taylor series for y at $x = 0$, because of the initial condition.) Substituting (ii) into (i) and expanding the right-hand side gives a sequence of simultaneous quadratic equations for the coefficients a_i that become increasingly complicated as $i \to \infty$. However, we can solve

inductively for the coefficients, by first equating the terms in x, then the terms in x^2, etc. *Mathematica* can assist us in this task.

(a) Explain why y'_0 must be 0.

(b) Now employ the scheme in the program from Chapter 10 to compute a Taylor series expansion of the solution to (i). (Don't be concerned about the term **y[x]^2** in the **Series** command. *Mathematica* can manipulate algebraic combinations of series.) Make sure you go far enough to get the 11th degree monomial. What pattern do you see?

(c) Plot the 11th degree Taylor approximation for y on the same axes with a numerical solution of (i) obtained using **NDSolve** on the interval $-1 < x < 1$. How close are the graphs? Now note that $y(x) > x^2/2$, for $0 < x < 1$, as you can see, for example, from the series. Thus $y(1) > 0.5$. But for $x > 1$, the right-hand side of (i) is greater than $y(x)^2 + 1$, so the solution grows faster than the solution to the IVP $y' = y^2 + 1$, $y(1) = 0.5$, which is of the form $y(x) = \tan(x - C)$, where $C \approx 0.54$. Since the tangent function blows up when its argument reaches $\frac{\pi}{2}$, this analysis shows that the solution of (i) must become infinite somewhere between $x = 1$ and $x = 2.2$. Is there any way of seeing this from the series solution? Use **NDSolve** to locate the point P where the solution blows up. Graph the two solutions (that is, the series solution out to degree 11 and the numerical solution on the interval $(-1, P)$). What do you observe?

10. Consider the following IVP:

$$y'' + y' + y = t^2 e^{-t} \cos t, \qquad y(0) = 1, \qquad y'(0) = 0.$$

This problem could be solved by the method of undetermined coefficients—but it would not be a pleasant chore.

(a) Try to solve the IVP using **DSolve**. What is the result?

(b) Now use the program in the *Laplace Transforms* section of Chapter 10 to solve the problem.

(c) Define a new function $g(t)$ to be the output from part (b). Verify that g is a solution to the differential equation. (Don't forget **Simplify**.)

(d) Clear the value of $y0$ and use the program. You should get an answer in terms of the parameter $y0$. What does that illustrate about *Mathematica's* symbolic capabilities?

11. This problem requires Version 2.1 or later of *Mathematica*. Use the Laplace Transform program to solve the following IVP's from Sections 6.4 (Probs. 2, 6, 10) and 6.5 (Probs. 7, 11) of Boyce & DiPrima:

(a) $y'' + 2y' + 2y = h(t)$, $\quad y(0) = 0, y'(0) = 1$, $\quad h(t) = \begin{cases} 1, & \text{if } \pi \le t < 2\pi \\ 0, & \text{otherwise} \end{cases}$

(b) $y'' + 3y' + 2y = u_2(t)$, $\quad y(0) = 0, \quad y'(0) = 1$

(c) $y'' + y' + \dfrac{5}{4}y = g(t)$, $\quad y(0) = 0$, $\quad y'(0) = 0$, $\quad g(t) = \begin{cases} \sin t, & \text{if } 0 \leq t < \pi \\ 0, & \text{if } t \geq \pi \end{cases}$

(d) $y'' + y = \delta(t - \pi)\cos t$, $\quad y(0) = 0$, $\quad y'(0) = 1$

(e) $y'' + 2y' + 2y = \cos t + \delta(t - \pi/2)$, $\quad y(0) = 0$, $\quad y'(0) = 0$.

12. This problem is based on Problem 35 in Section 6.2 of Boyce & DiPrima. Consider Bessel's equation

$$ty'' + y' + ty = 0.$$

We will use the Laplace Transform to find some leading terms of the power series expansion of the Bessel function of order zero that is continuous at the origin. Let $y(t)$ be such a solution of the equation, and suppose $Y(s)$ is its transform.

(a) Show that $Y(s)$ satisfies the equation

$$(1 + s^2)Y'(s) + sY(s) = 0.$$

(b) Solve the equation in part (a) using **DSolve**. (Use $Y(0) = 1$.)

(c) Use the **Series** command to expand the solution in part (b) in negative powers of s out to terms of degree 10. (*Hint*: Do not expand around $s = 0$.)

(d) Apply the inverse Laplace Transform to part (c) to obtain the power series expansion of y up to degree 10.

Chapter 11

Higher Order Equations and Systems of First Order Equations

First and second order differential equations arise naturally in many applications. For example, first order differential equations occur in models of population growth and radioactive decay, and second order equations in the study of the motion of a falling body or the motion of a pendulum. There are several techniques for solving special classes of first and second order equations. These techniques produce symbolic solutions, expressed by a formula. For equations that cannot be solved by any of these techniques, we use numerical, geometric, or qualitative methods to investigate solutions.

Equations of higher order, and systems of first order equations, also arise naturally. For example, third order equations come up in fluid dynamics; fourth order equations, in elasticity; and systems of first order equations, in the study of spring–mass systems with several springs and masses. For general higher order equations and systems, there are hardly any techniques for obtaining explicit formula solutions, and numerical, geometric, or qualitative techniques must be used. Nevertheless, for the special class of constant coefficient linear equations and first order linear systems, there are techniques for producing explicit solutions.

In this chapter, we consider higher order equations and first order systems. We outline the basic theory in the linear case. We show how to solve linear first order systems, first by using *Mathematica* to compute eigenpairs of the coefficient matrix, and then by using **DSolve**. In addition, we discuss the the plotting of phase portraits using *Mathematica*.

Higher Order Linear Equations

Consider the linear equation

$$y^{(n)} + p_1(x)y^{(n-1)} + \cdots + p_n(x)y = g(x), \tag{1}$$

and assume the coefficient functions are continuous on the interval $a < x < b$. Then the following are true:

- If $y_1(x), y_2(x), \ldots, y_n(x)$ are n linearly independent solutions of the corresponding homogeneous equation,

$$y^{(n)} + p_1(x)y^{(n-1)} + \cdots + p_n(x)y = 0, \tag{2}$$

and if y_p is *any* particular solution of the inhomogeneous equation (1), then the general solutions of the equations (1), (2) are, respectively,

$$y = \sum_{i=1}^{n} C_i y_i(x) + y_p(x)$$

and

$$y = \sum_{i=1}^{n} C_i y_i(x).$$

- Given a point $x_0 \in (a, b)$ and initial values $y(x_0) = y_0$, $y'(x_0) = y_0'$, $\ldots$, $y^{(n-1)}(x_0) = y_0^{(n-1)}$, there is a unique solution to equation (1) that satisfies the initial data; the solution has n continuous derivatives and exists on the entire interval (a, b).

- A set of n solutions $y_1(x), y_2(x), \ldots, y_n(x)$ of (2) is linearly independent if and only if the Wronskian

$$W(y_1, y_2, \ldots, y_n) = \det \begin{pmatrix} y_1 & y_2 & \cdots & y_n \\ y_1' & y_2' & \cdots & y_n' \\ \vdots & \vdots & \ddots & \vdots \\ y_1^{(n-1)} & y_2^{(n-1)} & \cdots & y_n^{(n-1)} \end{pmatrix}$$

is nonzero at some point in (a, b); the collection $y_1, \ldots, y_n$ is called a *fundamental set* of solutions of (2).

We see that the general theory of higher order linear equations parallels that of first and second order equations. We note, however, that solutions may be difficult to construct. In practice, we can construct fundamental sets of solutions only for constant coefficient and Euler equations. In these cases, solutions can be constructed by considering trial solutions e^{rx} and x^r, as in the second order case. There is a difficulty even for these equations if n is large, since it is difficult to compute the roots of the characteristic polynomial. We can, however, use *Mathematica* to find good approximations to the roots.

The **DSolve** command can solve many homogeneous constant coefficient and Euler equations. You can confirm this by solving several linear equations of higher order from your text.

Systems of First Order Equations

Consider the general system of first order equations,

$$\begin{aligned}
x_1' &= F_1(t, x_1, x_2, \ldots, x_n) \\
x_2' &= F_2(t, x_1, x_2, \ldots, x_n) \\
&\ \ \vdots \\
x_n' &= F_n(t, x_1, x_2, \ldots, x_n).
\end{aligned} \tag{3}$$

Such systems arise in the study of spring–mass systems with many springs and masses, and in many other applications. Systems of first order equations also arise in the study of higher order equations. A single higher order differential equation

$$y^{(n)} = F(t, y, y', \ldots, y^{(n-1)}),$$

can be converted into a system of first order equations, simply by setting

$$x_1 = y, x_2 = y', \ldots, x_n = y^{(n-1)}.$$

The resulting system is

$$\begin{aligned}
x_1' &= x_2 \\
x_2' &= x_3 \\
&\ \ \vdots \\
x_{n-1}' &= x_n \\
x_n' &= F(t, x_1, x_2, \ldots, x_n).
\end{aligned}$$

It is not surprising that the problem of analyzing the general system (3) is quite formidable. Generally, the techniques we can bring to bear will be numerical, geometric, or qualitative. We shall discuss the application of these techniques to nonlinear equations in Chapter 12. For now, we merely observe that we can expect to make some progress toward a formula solution for *linear systems*. So, consider a linear system

$$\begin{aligned}
x_1' &= a_{11}(t)x_1 + \ldots + a_{1n}(t)x_n + b_1(t) \\
x_2' &= a_{21}(t)x_1 + \ldots + a_{2n}(t)x_n + b_2(t) \\
&\ \ \vdots \qquad \vdots \\
x_n' &= a_{n1}(t)x_1 + \ldots + a_{nn}(t)x_n + b_n(t).
\end{aligned}$$

We can write this system in matrix notation:

$$\mathbf{X}' = \mathbf{A}(t)\mathbf{X} + \mathbf{B}(t),$$

where

$$\mathbf{X} = \begin{pmatrix} x_1(t) \\ x_2(t) \\ \vdots \\ x_n(t) \end{pmatrix}, \qquad \mathbf{B} = \begin{pmatrix} b_1(t) \\ b_2(t) \\ \vdots \\ b_n(t) \end{pmatrix},$$

and

$$\mathbf{A} = \begin{pmatrix} a_{11}(t) & a_{12}(t) & \cdots & a_{1n}(t) \\ \vdots & \vdots & \ddots & \vdots \\ a_{n1}(t) & a_{n2}(t) & \cdots & a_{nn}(t) \end{pmatrix}.$$

There is a general theory for linear systems, which is completely parallel to the theory for linear differential equations. If $\mathbf{X}^{(1)}, \mathbf{X}^{(2)}, \ldots, \mathbf{X}^{(n)}$ is a family of linearly independent solutions, *i.e.*, a *fundamental set* of solutions, of the homogeneous equation (with $\mathbf{B} = 0$), and if $\mathbf{X}_p$ is a particular solution of the inhomogeneous equation, then the general solutions of these equations are, respectively,

$$\mathbf{X} = \sum_{i=1}^{n} C_i \mathbf{X}^{(i)}$$

and

$$\mathbf{X} = \sum_{i=1}^{n} C_i \mathbf{X}^{(i)} + \mathbf{X}_p.$$

The test for linear independence of n solutions is

$$\det(\mathbf{X}^{(1)} \ldots \mathbf{X}^{(n)}) \neq 0.$$

For linear systems, the constant coefficient case is the easiest to handle, just as it was for single linear equations. Consider the homogeneous linear system

$$\mathbf{X}' = \mathbf{A}\mathbf{X}, \tag{4}$$

where

$$\mathbf{A} = \begin{pmatrix} a_{11} & a_{12} & \cdots & a_{1n} \\ \vdots & \vdots & \ddots & \vdots \\ a_{n1} & a_{n2} \cdots & \cdots & a_{nn} \end{pmatrix}$$

is an $n \times n$ matrix of constants. We seek solutions of the form $\mathbf{X}(t) = \boldsymbol{\xi} e^{rt}$; note the similarity to the case of a single linear eqation. We find that $\mathbf{X}(t)$ is a nonzero solution of (4) if and only if

$$\mathbf{A}\boldsymbol{\xi} = r\boldsymbol{\xi},$$

i.e., if and only if r is an eigenvalue of $\mathbf{A}$ and $\boldsymbol{\xi}$ is a corresponding eigenvector. We call the pair $r, \boldsymbol{\xi}$ an eigenpair. In order to explain how to construct a fundamental set of solutions, we have to consider three separate cases.

Case I. A has distinct real eigenvalues.

Let $r_1, r_2, \ldots, r_n$ be the distinct eigenvalues of A, and let $\boldsymbol{\xi}^{(1)}, \boldsymbol{\xi}^{(2)}, \ldots, \boldsymbol{\xi}^{(n)}$ be corresponding eigenvectors. Then

$$\mathbf{X}^{(1)}(t) = \boldsymbol{\xi}^{(1)} e^{r_1 t}, \ldots, \mathbf{X}^{(n)}(t) = \boldsymbol{\xi}^{(n)} e^{r_n t}$$

is a fundamental set of solutions for (4), and

$$\mathbf{X}(t) = c_1 \boldsymbol{\xi}^{(1)} e^{r_1 t} + \cdots + c_n \boldsymbol{\xi}^{(n)} e^{r_n t}$$

is the general solution.

Case II. A has distinct eigenvalues, some of which are complex.

Since A is real, if $r, \boldsymbol{\xi}$ is a complex eigenpair, then the complex conjugate $\bar{r}, \bar{\boldsymbol{\xi}}$ is also an eigenpair. Thus the corresponding solutions

$$\mathbf{X}^{(1)}(t) = \boldsymbol{\xi}^{(1)} e^{r_1 t}, \quad \mathbf{X}^{(2)}(t) = \bar{\boldsymbol{\xi}}^{(1)} e^{\bar{r}_1 t}$$

are conjugate. Therefore, we can find two real solutions of (4) corresponding to r_1 and r_2 by taking the real and imaginary parts of $\mathbf{X}_1(t)$ or $\mathbf{X}_2(t)$. Writing $\boldsymbol{\xi}^{(1)} = \mathbf{a} + i\mathbf{b}$, where a and b are real, and $r_1 = \lambda + i\mu$, where λ and μ are real, we have

$$\begin{aligned} X^{(1)}(t) &= (\mathbf{a} + i\mathbf{b})e^{(\lambda + i\mu)t} \\ &= (\mathbf{a} + i\mathbf{b})e^{\lambda t}(\cos \mu t + i \sin \mu t) \\ &= e^{\lambda t}(\mathbf{a} \cos \mu t - \mathbf{b} \sin \mu t) + i e^{\lambda t}(\mathbf{a} \sin \mu t + \mathbf{b} \cos \mu t). \end{aligned}$$

Thus the vector functions

$$\mathbf{u}(t) = e^{\lambda t}(\mathbf{a} \cos \mu t - \mathbf{b} \sin \mu t)$$

$$\mathbf{v}(t) = e^{\lambda t}(\mathbf{a} \sin \mu t + \mathbf{b} \cos \mu t)$$

are real solutions to (4).

To keep the discussion simple, assume that $r_1 = \lambda + i\mu, r_2 = \lambda - i\mu$ are complex, and that $r_3, \ldots, r_n$ are real and distinct. Let the corresponding eigenvectors be $\boldsymbol{\xi}^{(1)} = \mathbf{a} + i\mathbf{b}, \boldsymbol{\xi}^{(2)} = \mathbf{a} - i\mathbf{b}, \boldsymbol{\xi}^{(3)}, \ldots, \boldsymbol{\xi}^{(n)}$. Then

$$\mathbf{u}(t), \mathbf{v}(t), \boldsymbol{\xi}^{(3)} e^{r_3 t}, \ldots, \boldsymbol{\xi}^{(n)} e^{r_n t}$$

is a fundamental set of solutions for (4). The general situation should now be clear.

Case III. A has repeated eigenvalues.

We restrict our discussion to the case $n = 2$. Suppose $r = \rho$ is an eigenvalue of A of multiplicity 2, meaning that ρ is a double root of the characteristic polynomial $Z(r) = \det(\mathbf{A} - r\mathbf{I})$. There are still two possibilities. If we can find two linearly independent eigenvectors $\boldsymbol{\xi}^{(1)}$ and $\boldsymbol{\xi}^{(2)}$ corresponding to ρ, then the solutions $\mathbf{X}^{(1)}(t) = \boldsymbol{\xi}^{(1)} e^{\rho t}$ and $\mathbf{X}^{(2)}(t) = \boldsymbol{\xi}^{(2)} e^{\rho t}$ form a fundamental set. The other possibility is that there is only one (linearly independent) eigenvector $\boldsymbol{\xi}$ with eigenvalue ρ. Then one solution of (4) is given by

$$\mathbf{X}^{(1)}(t) = \boldsymbol{\xi} e^{\rho t},$$

and a second by

$$\mathbf{X}^{(2)}(t) = \boldsymbol{\xi} t e^{\rho t} + \boldsymbol{\eta} e^{\rho t},$$

where $\boldsymbol{\eta}$ satisfies

$$(\mathbf{A} - r\mathbf{I})\boldsymbol{\eta} = \boldsymbol{\xi}.$$

The vector $\boldsymbol{\eta}$ is called a generalized eigenvector of $\mathbf{A}$ for the eigenvalue ρ.

Using *Mathematica* to Solve Linear Systems

We now show how to use *Mathematica* to find the eigenpairs of a matrix, and thus to find fundamental sets of solutions and the general solution of a system of linear differential equations with constant coefficients.

EXAMPLE 1.   Consider the system

$$\mathbf{x}' = \begin{pmatrix} 3 & -2 & 0 \\ 2 & -2 & 0 \\ 0 & 1 & 1 \end{pmatrix} \mathbf{x}.$$

We enter the coefficient matrix in *Mathematica* as a list of lists:

A = {{3, −2, 0},{2, −2, 0}, {0, 1, 1}}

We can display **A** in standard matrix form using the command **MatrixForm[A]**, which produces

$$\begin{matrix} 3 & -2 & 0 \\ 2 & -2 & 0 \\ 0 & 1 & 1 \end{matrix}$$

We find the eigenpairs of **A** with the command **Eigensystem[A]**, which produces

$$\{\{-1, 1, 2\}, \{\{-1, -2, 1\}, \{0, 0, 1\}, \{2, 1, 1\}\}\}$$

The output of this command is a list containing first a list of the eigenvalues, and then a list of the corresponding eigenvectors. In this example, the eigenpairs are

$$r_1 = -1, \; \boldsymbol{\xi}^{(1)} = \begin{pmatrix} -1 \\ -2 \\ 1 \end{pmatrix}$$

$$r_2 = 1, \; \boldsymbol{\xi}^{(2)} = \begin{pmatrix} 0 \\ 0 \\ 1 \end{pmatrix}$$

$$r_3 = 2, \; \boldsymbol{\xi}^{(3)} = \begin{pmatrix} 2 \\ 1 \\ 1 \end{pmatrix}.$$

Thus, a fundamental set of solutions is

$$\mathbf{X}^{(1)}(t) = \begin{pmatrix} -1 \\ -2 \\ 1 \end{pmatrix} e^{-t}, \quad \mathbf{X}^{(2)}(t) = \begin{pmatrix} 0 \\ 0 \\ 1 \end{pmatrix} e^{t}, \quad \mathbf{X}^{(3)}(t) = \begin{pmatrix} 2 \\ 1 \\ 1 \end{pmatrix} e^{2t},$$

and the general solution is

$$\mathbf{x}(t) = c_1 \begin{pmatrix} -1 \\ -2 \\ 1 \end{pmatrix} e^{-t} + c_2 \begin{pmatrix} 0 \\ 0 \\ 1 \end{pmatrix} e^{t} + c_3 \begin{pmatrix} 2 \\ 1 \\ 1 \end{pmatrix} e^{2t}.$$

Suppose we are seeking the specific solution with initial value

$$\mathbf{x}(0) = \begin{pmatrix} 3 \\ 5 \\ 0 \end{pmatrix}.$$

The constants c_1, c_2, and c_3 must satisfy

$$c_1 \begin{pmatrix} -1 \\ -2 \\ 1 \end{pmatrix} + c_2 \begin{pmatrix} 0 \\ 0 \\ 1 \end{pmatrix} + c_3 \begin{pmatrix} 2 \\ 1 \\ 1 \end{pmatrix} = \begin{pmatrix} -1 & 0 & 2 \\ -2 & 0 & 1 \\ 1 & 1 & 1 \end{pmatrix} \begin{pmatrix} c_1 \\ c_2 \\ c_3 \end{pmatrix} = \begin{pmatrix} 3 \\ 5 \\ 0 \end{pmatrix}.$$

To solve this linear system, we use the command **LinearSolve**. Let **m** be the coefficient matrix and let **b** be the right-hand side:

m = {{−1, 0, 2}, {−2, 0, 1}, {1, 1, 1}};   b = {3, 5, 0}

(Note that the columns of the matrix **m** are the eigenvectors of **A**, so an easy way to define the matrix **m** is to type **m = Transpose[Last[Eigensystem[A]]]**.) Then to solve the system we type **LinearSolve[m,b]**, which produces $\{-\frac{7}{3}, 2, \frac{1}{3}\}$. Thus the solution of the linear system is $c_1 = -\frac{7}{3}$, $c_2 = 2$, $c_3 = \frac{1}{3}$, and the solution to our initial value problem is

$$\mathbf{x}(t) = -\frac{7}{3} \begin{pmatrix} -1 \\ -2 \\ 1 \end{pmatrix} e^{-t} + 2 \begin{pmatrix} 0 \\ 0 \\ 1 \end{pmatrix} e^{t} + \frac{1}{3} \begin{pmatrix} 2 \\ 1 \\ 1 \end{pmatrix} e^{2t}.$$

EXAMPLE 2.   Consider the system

$$\mathbf{x}' = \begin{pmatrix} 3 & -2 \\ 4 & -1 \end{pmatrix} \mathbf{x} \qquad \text{(Boyce \& DiPrima, Sect. 7.6, Prob. 1).}$$

We set **B = {{3, −2}, {4, −1}}**, and find the eigenpairs with **Eigensystem[B]**, which produces

$$\{\{1 - 2\mathbf{I}, 1 + 2\mathbf{I}\}, \{\{\frac{1}{2} - \frac{1}{2}\mathbf{I}, 1\}, \{\frac{1}{2} + \frac{1}{2}\mathbf{I}, 1\}\}\}$$

So the eigenpairs are

$$1 - 2i, \quad \begin{pmatrix} \frac{1}{2} - \frac{1}{2}i \\ 1 \end{pmatrix}$$

and

$$1 + 2i, \quad \begin{pmatrix} \frac{1}{2} + \frac{1}{2}i \\ 1 \end{pmatrix}.$$

Note that the second pair is the complex conjugate of the first. Thus a complex fundamental set is

$$\mathbf{X}^{(1)}(t) = \begin{pmatrix} \frac{1}{2} - \frac{1}{2}i \\ 1 \end{pmatrix} e^{(1-2i)t}, \quad \mathbf{X}^{(2)}(t) = \begin{pmatrix} \frac{1}{2} + \frac{1}{2}i \\ 1 \end{pmatrix} e^{(1+2i)t}.$$

The real and imaginary parts of the solution can be extracted by hand, or by using the *Mathematica* commands **ComplexExpand, Re,** and **Im,** as in

ComplexExpand[Re[{1/2 − 1/2*I, 1}* Exp[(1 − 2*I)t]]]
ComplexExpand[Im[{1/2 − 1/2*I, 1}* Exp[(1 − 2*I)t]]]

Either way, we see that a fundamental set of real solutions is

$$\mathbf{u}(t) = e^t \left[\begin{pmatrix} \frac{1}{2} \\ 1 \end{pmatrix} \cos 2t + \begin{pmatrix} -\frac{1}{2} \\ 0 \end{pmatrix} \sin 2t \right]$$

$$\mathbf{v}(t) = e^t \left[- \begin{pmatrix} \frac{1}{2} \\ 1 \end{pmatrix} \sin 2t + \begin{pmatrix} -\frac{1}{2} \\ 0 \end{pmatrix} \cos 2t \right].$$

EXAMPLE 3. Consider the system

$$\mathbf{x}' = \begin{pmatrix} 3 & -4 \\ 1 & -1 \end{pmatrix} \mathbf{x} \qquad \text{(Boyce \& DiPrima, Sect. 7.7, Prob. 1).}$$

We set **A = {{3,−4},{1,−1}}**. The command **Eigensystem[A]** produces

$$\{\{1, 1\}, \{\{2, 1\}, \{0, 0\}\}\}$$

The number 1 is listed twice as an eigenvalue and $\{0, 0\}$ is listed as an eigenvector (although it really isn't one because eigenvectors must be nonzero). This is *Mathematica*'s way of reporting that 1 is an eigenvalue of multiplicity 2 and that $\{2, 1\}$ is the only corresponding eigenvector. Thus $\rho = 1$ and $\boldsymbol{\xi} = \begin{pmatrix} 2 \\ 1 \end{pmatrix}$, and

$$\mathbf{X}^{(1)}(t) = \begin{pmatrix} 2 \\ 1 \end{pmatrix} e^t$$

is one solution. To find a second solution we solve

$$(\mathbf{A} - \rho\mathbf{I})\boldsymbol{\eta} = \begin{pmatrix} 2 & -4 \\ 1 & -2 \end{pmatrix} \boldsymbol{\eta} = \boldsymbol{\xi} = \begin{pmatrix} 2 \\ 1 \end{pmatrix}.$$

Let **m = {{2,−4},{1,−2}}** be the coefficient matrix and let **b = {2,1}** be the right-hand side. Then **LinearSolve[m,b]** produces $\{1, 0\}$, so

$$\boldsymbol{\eta} = \begin{pmatrix} 1 \\ 0 \end{pmatrix}.$$

(This system actually has an infinite number of solutions; **LinearSolve** returns one of them.) Thus a second solution is

$$\mathbf{X}^{(2)}(t) = \xi t e^{\rho t} + \eta e^{\rho t} = \begin{pmatrix} 2 \\ 1 \end{pmatrix} t e^t + \begin{pmatrix} 1 \\ 0 \end{pmatrix} e^t.$$

The general solution is

$$\mathbf{X}(t) = c_1 \begin{pmatrix} 2 \\ 1 \end{pmatrix} e^t + c_2 \left[\begin{pmatrix} 2 \\ 1 \end{pmatrix} t e^t + \begin{pmatrix} 1 \\ 0 \end{pmatrix} e^t \right].$$

We have shown how to use *Mathematica*'s linear algebra commands to find eigenpairs, and thus solutions, for linear systems of differential equations with constant coefficients. The solutions to systems of linear equations can also be found with a direct application of **DSolve**.

EXAMPLE. Consider the system $x' = y$, $y' = -x$. To find its general solution, you would type

DSolve[{x′[t] == y[t], y′[t] == −x[t]}, {x[t], y[t]}, t]

The result is

$$x(t) = e^{-it}[c_1 + c_1 e^{2it} + c_2 i - c_2 i e^{2it}]/2$$
$$y(t) = e^{-it}[-c_1 i + c_1 i e^{2it} + c_2 + c_2 e^{2it}]/2.$$

To solve the same system with initial conditions $x(0) = 1$, $y(0) = 0$, you would type

DSolve[{x′[t] == y[t], y′[t] == −x[t], x[0] == 1, y[0] == 0}, {x[t], y[t]}, t]

Both methods for solving linear systems are useful. Solving in terms of the eigenpairs of the coefficient matrix is somewhat involved, but yields a simple and useful formula for the solution. The eigenpairs contain valuable information about the solution, which we will exploit further in Problem Set F. On the other hand, it is simpler to use **DSolve**, and for many purposes the solutions generated by **DSolve** are completely satisfactory. We note, however, that **DSolve** sometimes presents the solution in a rather complicated form, as in the example above.

Here are some examples on which you can practice:

(a) $x' = -3x + 2y$, $\quad y' = -x$
(b) $x' = x - 2y$, $\quad y' = -x$
(c) $x' = x + 2y$, $\quad y' = -x$.

Phase Portraits

A solution of a 2×2 linear system is a pair of funtions $x(t)$, $y(t)$. The plot of a solution as a function of t would be a curve in (t, x, y)-space. Generally, such 3-dimensional plots are too complicated to be illuminating. Therefore, we project the curve from 3-dimensional space into the x-y-plane. This plane is called the *phase plane*, and the resulting curve in the phase plane is called a *trajectory*. A trajectory is drawn by plotting $(x(t), y(t))$ as the parameter t varies. A plot of a family of trajectories is called a *phase portrait* of the system.

A trajectory is an example of a *parametrized curve*. The basic *Mathematica* command for plotting a parametrized curve is **ParametricPlot**. In this section, we describe how to use *Mathematica* to (1) solve an initial value problem consisting of a linear system and an initial condition, and plot the corresponding trajectory; (2) solve a linear system using **DSolve** and draw a phase portrait; (3) solve a system using **NDSolve** and draw a phase portrait.

Plotting a Single Trajectory.   Consider the linear system in Example (a) above, with initial condition $x(0) = 1$, $y(0) = 0$. We want to plot the trajectory with this initial condition. First we enter the initial value problem.

> ivp = {x′[t] == −3x[t] + 2y[t], y′[t] == −x[t], x[0]==1, y[0]==0}

Then we type in the following:

> solivp[t_] = {x[t], y[t]} /. DSolve[ivp, {x[t], y[t]}, t]
> traj[t0_, t1_] := ParametricPlot[Evaluate[solivp[t]], {t, t0, t1},
>   AspectRatio −> Automatic]

This program does two things. First, it produces the solution, **solivp**, of the initial value problem; this solution can be evaluated or plotted. Second, it defines a function **traj** that plots the trajectory corresponding to **solivp**. The function **traj** takes two arguments, $t0$ and $t1$, the endpoints of the time interval for the trajectory. Figure 1 contains the picture generated by the command **traj[−5, 5]**. To use this program to plot the solution of a different initial value problem, all you have to do is modify the definition of **ivp** appropriately.

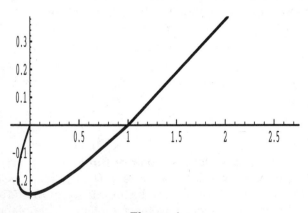

Figure 1

Plotting Several Trajectories.   Consider the linear system in Example (b) above. We want to plot trajectories of this system with various initial conditions $x(0) = a$, $y(0) = b$. We first define a function **sol** that solves this system with initial conditions $x(0) = a, y(0) = b$.

> **sol[t_,a_,b_] = {x[t], y[t]} /. DSolve[{x'[t] == x[t] − 2y[t],**
> **y'[t] == −x[t], x[0] == a, y[0] == b}, {x[t], y[t]}, t]**

The function **sol** can be evaluated for a particular choice of initial conditions $x(0) = a$, $y(0) = b$, at a particular value of t. Next we define a function **phase** that plots a phase portrait of the linear system. We do this by creating a table of functions consisting of solutions with different initial conditions, and then using **ParametricPlot** to plot this table of solution functions.

> **phase[t0_,t1_] := ParametricPlot[Evaluate[Flatten[Table[sol[t,a,b],**
> **{a, −2, 2}, {b, −2, 2}], 2]],{t, t0, t1}, AspectRatio –> Automatic]**

The **Table** command embedded in this definition produces a list with two levels of braces; we used the **Flatten[. . . , 2]** command to remove the unnecessary braces. Note that **sol** was defined with =, but := was used in the definition of **phase** to suppress plotting until a time interval is specified. Note also that we have chosen a rectangular grid of 25 initial conditions, with a ranging from −2 to 2 and b ranging from −2 to 2 (both in integer increments).

To use the function **phase**, simply enter **phase[t0, t1]**, where $t0$ and $t1$ are the endpoints of the time interval $[t0, t1]$ for which you wish to plot the trajectories. This will plot 25 trajectories corresponding to the 25 different initial conditions. The time interval $[t0, t1]$ must be chosen somewhat carefully: a small time interval could result in solution curves that are too short to get an idea of where they're headed; while a large time interval could cause the scale of the graph to get very large, resulting in solution curves that are squeezed together. Moreover, the larger the time interval, the longer it will take for *Mathematica* to produce the plot. You should start with a small time interval like $[−3, 3]$, and then adjust the interval to get a satisfactory picture. The command **phase[−3, 3]** generated the phase portrait shown in Figure 2.

You should be able to plot the phase portraits for any linear system using the procedure above, replacing the differential equations in the definition of **sol**, and choosing, by trial and error, an appropriate time interval to use with the function **phase**. By combining the phase portrait with a plot of the vector field (see Chapter 12), you should be able to determine the direction of increasing t on the curves. Also, in each case you should be able to decide whether the origin is a *sink* (all solutions approach the origin as t increases), *source* (all solutions move away from the origin), *saddle point* (solutions approach the origin along one direction, then move away from the origin in another direction), or *center* (solutions follow closed curves around the origin).

Figure 2

The procedure for plotting a phase portrait must be modified slightly if you wish to vary only one parameter in the initial data. For example, the program

sol[t_,a_] = {x[t], y[t]} /. DSolve[{x′[t] == x[t] + 2y[t],
   y′[t] == −x[t], x[0] == a, y[0] == 0}, {x[t], y[t]}, t]
phase[t0_,t1_] := ParametricPlot[Evaluate[Flatten[Table[sol[t,a],
   {a, −4, 4}], 1]],{t, t0, t1}, AspectRatio −> Automatic]

will yield (upon entering **phase[−3,3]**) the nine curves shown in Figure 3 as a phase portrait for Example (c). (Count the curves! One of the solutions is the equilibrium solution $x(t) = 0$, $y(t) = 0$.) Note that in this program the **Table** command produces only one level of braces, and we use the **Flatten[. . . ,1]** command to strip off these braces.

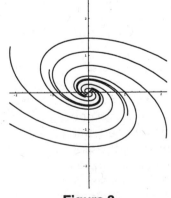

Figure 3

Plotting Trajectories of Solutions Generated by NDSolve. The symbolic solver **DSolve** should be able to solve any homogeneous linear system with constant coefficients. For inhomogeneous linear systems, linear systems with variable coefficients, and nonlinear systems, **DSolve** will generally not do the job. In these situations, we turn to the numerical solver **NDSolve**.

A naive approach to using **NDSolve** would be to simply replace **DSolve** with **NDSolve** in the programs above. This will not work, in part because the syntax of **NDSolve** is different from that of **DSolve**, but more importantly, because **NDSolve** must have numerical values for the initial conditions before it is evaluated. To circumvent this problem you could define the numerical solution using (:=). Here is an example that uses **NDSolve** on the linear system in Example (b) above.

> nsol[t_, a_, b_] := {x[t], y[t]} /. NDSolve[{x'[t] == x[t] −2y[t],
>   y'[t] == −x[t], x[0] == a, y[0] == b}, {x[t], y[t]}, {t, −3, 3}]

Then you could incorporate the function **nsol** into the **phase** function defined above (replacing **sol** by **nsol**), and then enter **phase[−3,3]** to plot the trajectories.

Note that in the definition of **nsol**, the time interval on which **NDSolve** will compute the solution is built into the definition (in this case, {**t**, −3, 3}), and therefore must be fixed in advance. A more flexible scheme, useful for some of the problems in Problem Set F, is given by

> nsol[t_, a_, b_, t1_] := {x[t], y[t]} /. NDSolve[{x'[t] == x[t] − 2y[t],
>   y'[t] == −x[t], x[0] == a, y[0] == b}, {x[t], y[t]}, {t, 0, t1}]
> nphase[t1_] := ParametricPlot[Evaluate[Flatten[Table[nsol[t, a, b, t1],
>   {a,−3, 3}, {b,−3, 3}], 2]],{t, 0, t1}, AspectRatio −> Automatic]

This program starts the solution curves at time $t = 0$ and gives you the freedom to choose the final time. You could, of course, define a slightly more complicated function that would allow you to vary both endpoints of the time interval.

One limitation of these two schemes is that the solutions cannot be directly evaluated at various values of the initial condition and time variable (see the section on **NDSolve** in Chapter 8 for an indirect way of evaluating them). If you wish to evaluate a numerical solution at specific values of t, you could use the following program:

> nsoleval[a_, b_, t1_] := (v[t_] = {x[t], y[t]} /.
>   NDSolve[{x'[t] == x[t] − 2y[t], y'[t] == −x[t], x[0] == a, y[0] == b},
>   {x[t], y[t]}, {t, 0, t1}])

This program, when evaluated for particular values of a, b, and $t1$, defines a function **v**, which is a numerical solution of the system, with initial conditions $x(0) = a$ and $y(0) = b$, on the interval $[0, t1]$. The function **v** can then be evaluated at various values of t. For example, the input

> nsoleval[0.1, 0.1, 10]; v[1]

will yield the values at $t = 1$ of the solution functions $x(t)$, $y(t)$ corresponding to initial data $x(0) = 0.1$, $y(0) = 0.1$. Note that **nsoleval** need only be evaluated once for each new set of initial conditions. Thus we could simply type **v[8]**, for example, to get the value of the previously defined solution at $t = 8$.

Chapter 12

Qualitative Theory for Systems of Differential Equations

In this chapter, we extend the qualitative theory of autonomous differential equations from single equations to systems of two equations. Thus, consider a system of the form

$$\begin{cases} x' = F(x, y) \\ y' = G(x, y). \end{cases} \tag{1}$$

We assume the functions F and G have continuous partial derivatives everywhere in the plane, and the critical points—the common zeros of F and G—are isolated.

We know from the fundamental existence and uniqueness theorems that, corresponding to any choice of initial data (x_0, y_0), there is a unique pair of functions $x(t)$, $y(t)$ that satisfy the system (1) of differential equations and the initial conditions $x(0) = x_0$, $y(0) = y_0$. Taken together, this pair of functions parametrizes a curve, or trajectory, in the *phase plane* that passes through the point (x_0, y_0). Since we are dealing with autonomous systems (*i.e.*, the variable t does not appear on the right side of (1)), the solution curves are *independent of the starting time*. That is, if we consider initial conditions $x(t_0) = x_0$, $y(t_0) = y_0$, then we get the same solution curve with a time delay of t_0 units. Moreover, we also know that two distinct trajectories cannot intersect. Thus, the plane is covered by the family of trajectories; the plot of these curves is the *phase portrait* of (1).

As we know, we can find explicit formula solutions $x(t)$, $y(t)$ only for simple systems. Thus, we are forced to turn to qualitative and numerical methods. It is our purpose here to discuss qualitative techniques for studying the solutions of (1).

In most cases of physical interest, every solution curve behaves in one of the following ways:

   (i) The curve consists of a single critical point;
  (ii) The curve tends to a critical point as $t \to \infty$;
 (iii) The curve is unbounded: the distance from $(x(t), y(t))$ to the origin becomes arbitrarily large as $t \to \infty$, or as $t \to t^*$, for some finite t^*;
  (iv) The curve is periodic: the parametric functions satisfy $x(t + t_p) = x(t)$, $y(t + t_p) = y(t)$ for some fixed t_p;
   (v) The curve approaches a periodic solution, *e.g.*, spiraling in on a circle.

159

Qualitative techniques may be able to identify the kinds of solutions that appear. In order to keep matters simple, we try to answer the following specific questions:

(1) What can we say about the critical points? Can we make a qualitative guess about their nature and stability? Can we deduce anything about the solution curves that start out close to the critical points?

(2) Can we predict anything about the long-term behavior of the solution curves? This includes those near critical points as well as the solution curves in general.

This list of possible limiting behaviors of solution curves is based on the Poincaré-Bendixson Theorem (Theorem 9.7.3 in Boyce & DiPrima), which is valid for autonomous systems of two equations. Systems of three or more equations can have much more complicated limiting behavior. For example, solution curves can remain bounded yet fail to approach any equilibrium or periodic state as $t \to \infty$. This phenomenon, called "chaos" by mathematicians, was anticipated by Poincaré (and perhaps even earlier by the physicist Maxwell), but most scientists did not appreciate how widespread chaos is until the arrival of computers. See Section 9.8 in Boyce & DiPrima for a more detailed discussion. See also Problem 13 in Problem Set F.

There are two qualitative methods for analyzing systems of equations: one based on the idea of a *vector field*; and the other based on the principle of *linearized stability*. The latter method is treated in detail in Sections 9.3–9.5 of Boyce & DiPrima; it provides information about the stability of critical points of a nonlinear system by studying associated linear systems. In this chapter, we discuss the use of vector fields in qualitative analysis.

Here is the basic idea. For any solution curve $(x(t), y(t))$, and any point t, we have the differential equations

$$\begin{cases} x'(t) = F(x(t), y(t)) \\ y'(t) = G(x(t), y(t)). \end{cases}$$

If we employ vector notation

$$\mathbf{x}(t) = \begin{pmatrix} x(t) \\ y(t) \end{pmatrix}, \quad \mathbf{f}(\mathbf{x}) = \begin{pmatrix} F(\mathbf{x}) \\ G(\mathbf{x}) \end{pmatrix},$$

then the system is written

$$\mathbf{x}' = \mathbf{f}(\mathbf{x}).$$

Moreover, the vector $\mathbf{x}'(t) = \mathbf{f}(\mathbf{x}(t))$ is just the tangent vector to the curve $\mathbf{x}(t)$. Since knowledge of the collection of tangent vectors to the solution curves would give a good idea of the curves themselves, it would be useful to have a plot of these vectors. Thus, corresponding to any vector $\mathbf{x}$, we draw the vector $\mathbf{f}(\mathbf{x})$, translated so that its foot is at the point $\mathbf{x}$. This plot is called the vector field of the system (1). Since we cannot do this at every point of the phase plane, we only draw the vectors at a set of regularly chosen points. Then we step back and look at the resulting vector field. We do not have the solution curves sketched, but we do have a representative collection of their tangent vectors. From the tangent vectors, we can get a good idea of the curves themselves. Indeed, we can often answer the questions above by a careful examination of the vector field.

Vector fields can be drawn by hand for simple systems, but the command **PlotVectorField**, which you have been using to plot direction fields of single first order differential equations, can draw vector fields of any first order system of two equations. We illustrate the use of this command by examining two specific systems, namely

$$\begin{cases} x' = x(1 - x - y) \\ y' = y(0.75 - 0.5x - y); \end{cases} \tag{2}$$

and

$$\begin{cases} x' = x(5 - x - y) \\ y' = y(-2 + x). \end{cases} \tag{3}$$

System (2) is a competing species model that is discussed in Boyce & DiPrima in Section 9.4, Example 1. System (3) is a predator-prey model that can be found on p. 614 of *Elementary Differential Equations with Applications*, by Edwards & Penney, Prentice-Hall, Inc., 1985.

The **PlotVectorField** command is in the package **Graphics`PlotField`**, and is loaded by typing << **Graphics`PlotField`**. The syntax of the command is

PlotVectorField[{F[x, y], G[x, y]}, {x, x0, x1}, {y, y0, y1}, (options)]

We first consider system (2). To draw the vector field we enter

PlotVectorField[{x(1 − x − y), y(0.75 − 0.5x − y)}, {x, −1, 1},
   {y, −1, 1}, Frame −> True]

The result is shown in Figure 1.

In a vector field, the vector at the point $x = (x, y)$ is $f(x)$, indicating both the direction and length of $f(x)$. The vector at x drawn by **PlotVectorField** faithfully represents the direction of $f(x)$ but, for the sake of visual effectiveness, its length is only proportional to the length of $f(x)$. The critical, or equilibrium, points are those points at which the vector field vanishes, *i.e.*, those points where $F(x, y) = G(x, y) = 0$. Thus the vectors are very short near the critical points. In the plot above we can approximately identify the critical points, but it is difficult to see the directions of the very short vectors near the critical points.

We can improve the picture in this regard by rescaling the sizes of the vectors. One way to do this would be to make the vectors a constant length. This can be done with the option **ScaleFunction −>(1&)** (the "&" indicates to *Mathematica* that the constant "1" is to be interpreted as a pure function.) A better way to do it is to use a scaling function that lengthens the vectors near the critical points enough that their directions are clearly indicated, but not so much that the critical points cannot be located. For example, we could use a scaling function such as $h(r) = \log(50r + 1)$. This causes a vector of length proportional to r to be replaced by a vector of length proportional to $h(r)$. It is a good choice because $h(0) = 0$, and $h(r)$ rises sharply near 0 and then levels off.

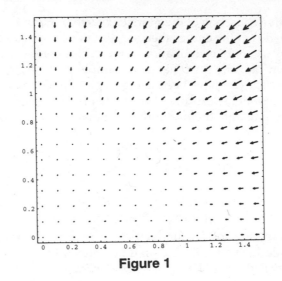

Figure 1

Here is the command we use to plot the "improved" vector field.

PlotVectorField[{x(1 − x − y), y(0.75 − 0.5x − y)}, {y, 0, 1.5},
    {x, 0, 1.5}, Frame −> True, ScaleFunction −> (Log[50 # +1]&),
    PlotPoints −> 18]

The result is shown in Figure 2. (The option **PlotPoints−> 18** increases the number of vectors plotted. The symbol "#" refers to the argument of the scaling function.)

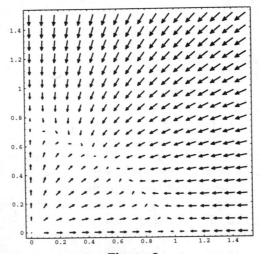

Figure 2

This picture gives us a much clearer indication of what's going on, but it still doesn't allow us to identify the critical points precisely. To do this we actually have to solve the equations $x' = 0$ and $y' = 0$ simultaneously. We can do this with the **Solve** command,

Solve[{x(1 − x − y) == 0, y(0.75 − 0.5 x − y) == 0}, {x, y}]

which produces the answer

$$\{\{x \rightarrow 0, y \rightarrow 0.75\}, \{x \rightarrow 0, y \rightarrow 0\}, \{x \rightarrow 0.5, y \rightarrow 0.5\}, \{x \rightarrow 1, y \rightarrow 0\}\}$$

(This is an instance where the **Solve** command in Version 2.2 misses some solutions; see the remark in the *Software Considerations* subsection of Chapter 1. This difficulty can be circumvented by entering the decimal numbers as fractions.)

Thus, the critical points are $(0,0)$, $(0, 0.75)$, $(1, 0)$, and $(0.5, 0.5)$. Knowing the critical points, we can deduce from the vector field that $(0,0)$ is an unstable node, $(0, 0.75)$ and $(1, 0)$ are unstable saddle points, and $(0.5, 0.5)$ is an asymptotically stable node. Solutions starting near the saddle points (but not on the axes) tend away from them, and those starting near the point $(0.5, 0.5)$ tend toward it. In fact, the vector field strongly suggests that every solution curve starting in the first quadrant (but not on the axes) tends toward $(0.5, 0.5)$. Hence $(0.5, 0.5)$, which corresponds to equal populations, is apparently the limiting state that all positive solutions approach as t increases. We have thus answered both questions (1) and (2) on the basis of the vector field.

Figure 3 provides a closer look at the vector field near the point $(0.5, 0.5)$.

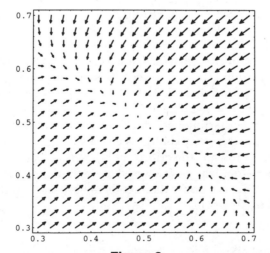

Figure 3

Now consider the predator-prey system (3). Here $x(t)$ represents the population of prey, and $y(t)$ the population of predators. The critical points of this system are $(0,0), (5,0), (2,3)$. As in system (2), our goal is to use the vector field to answer questions (1) and (2). Here is the appropriate *Mathematica* command (we have used a slightly different scaling function to make the graph look better):

PlotVectorField[{x(5 − x − y), y(−2 + x)}, {x, 0, 6}, {y, 0, 5},
   Frame −> True, ScaleFunction −> (Log[2 # + 1]&),
   PlotPoints −> 18]

The output is shown in Figure 4.

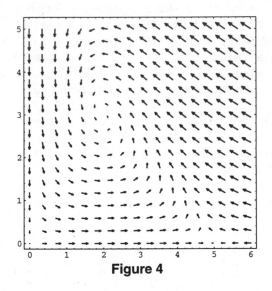

Figure 4

It is evident from the portrait that $(0,0)$ and $(5,0)$ are unstable saddle points; and that solutions spiral around $(2,3)$. The vectors near $(2,3)$ strongly suggest that the solutions spiral into $(2,3)$, so that $(2,3)$ is an asymptotically stable spiral point. In particular, solutions starting near the first two critical points tend away from them, whereas solution curves starting near the latter tend toward it. In fact, the vector field suggests strongly that every solution curve starting in the first quadrant (but not on the axes) tends toward the critical point $(2,3)$. This is the strongest kind of stable equilibrium—namely, no matter what the initial populations are, as long as they are both positive, the population tends toward the equilibrium position of 40% predators and 60% prey.

REMARKS.

- We indicated above that vector fields could be drawn by hand. It would be difficult, however, to draw as satisfactory a vector field as we have produced with *Mathematica*. On the other hand, we note that a careful study of the signs of F and G can lead to a good understanding of the nature of the vector field. This is done for Example (2) in Section 9.4 in Boyce & DiPrima. See in particular Figures 9.4.1 and 9.4.2 there.

- The essential idea in Chapter 6 for a single autonomous first order equation

$$x' = f(x)$$

is to determine the qualitative nature of the solutions purely on the basis of the sign of $f(x)$ for various x's. Actually, we have done the same thing here: namely, determine the qualitative nature of the solutions (trajectories) of a system from information on the signs of F and G.

- You used the command

PlotVectorField[{1, h[x,y]}, {x, x0, x1}, {y, y0, y1}, (options)]

to plot the direction field of the single first order differential equation

$$\frac{dy}{dx} = h(x, y).$$

This corresponds to plotting the vector field of the system

$$\begin{cases} x' = 1 \\ y' = h(x, y). \end{cases}$$

The "1" here explains the "1" that was used in the command for plotting direction fields.

- As mentioned above, according to the principle of linearized stability, the nature of critical points for nonlinear systems can be deduced from the associated linear systems. If the point is asymptotically stable for the associated linear system (the case if the eigenvalues are negative, or have negative real parts), then the point is asymptotically stable for the original nonlinear system. If it is unstable for the linear system, it is unstable for the nonlinear system. Centers are ambiguous. This analysis is valid in exactly the same way for a single equation. Suppose $\bar{x}$ is a critical point for $x' = f(x)$. Then letting $u(t) = x(t) - \bar{x}$, we see that

$$u' = f(u + \bar{x}) \approx f(\bar{x}) + f'(\bar{x})u = f'(\bar{x})u,$$

so the associated linear equation is $u' = f'(\bar{x})u$. The solutions are $u(t) = ce^{\lambda t}$, where $\lambda = f'(\bar{x})$. Therefore, $x(t) = \bar{x} + ce^{\lambda t}$. It is clear that $\bar{x}$ is asymptotically stable if $\lambda < 0$ and unstable if $\lambda > 0$. The same is true of the nonlinear system (with the situation for $\lambda = 0$ being ambiguous). Thus we see that this assessment of stability parallels the situation for systems.

Conclusion. Solutions of systems can be calculated with **NDSolve** and their trajectories plotted. Suggestions on convenient ways to do this are made in Chapter 11. Taken together, the information provided by a vector field, by a plot of the trajectories, and by linearized stability analyses, gives a complete understanding of the behavior of the solutions of a system of two first order equations. The information provided by these three approaches is similar, but each approach yields information the other approaches don't provide. For example, a vector field provides a good global indication of what the phase portrait will look like, as well as indicating the approximate location of the critical points and their type; a plot of the trajectories gives a precise indication of the solution curves; and a linearized stability analysis determines the type of the critical points.

In using these approaches to study a system, it is almost always best to start with a vector field plot or with linearized stability analyses. Typically, it takes a long time to plot trajectories of nonlinear systems. But by using the information from a vector field plot or from linearized stablility analyses you can choose appropriate initial data points to use with **NDSolve**. A vector field plot will also help you choose an appropriate time interval (*e.g.*, positive or negative time).

Problem Set F

Systems of Equations

A number of suggestions for using *Mathematica* to solve these problems may be found in Chapter 11. The parameters in those suggestions may need to be modified according to the problem at hand. In particular, you may have to change the time interval or the table of initial conditions.

1. In this problem, you will study three systems of equations taken from Boyce & DiPrima:

$$\mathbf{x}' = \begin{pmatrix} 2 & -1 \\ 3 & -2 \end{pmatrix} \mathbf{x} \qquad \text{(Prob. 3, Sect. 7.5)} \qquad (i)$$

$$\mathbf{x}' = \begin{pmatrix} 1 & -1 \\ 5 & -3 \end{pmatrix} \mathbf{x} \qquad \text{(Prob. 5, Sect. 7.6)} \qquad (ii)$$

$$\mathbf{x}' = \begin{pmatrix} -3 & 5/2 \\ -5/2 & 2 \end{pmatrix} \mathbf{x} \qquad \text{(Prob. 4, Sect. 7.7).} \qquad (iii)$$

(a) Use *Mathematica* to find the eigenvalues and eigenvectors of each linear system. Use the eigenvectors and eigenvalues to write down the general solution of the system.

(b) Use **DSolve** to compute the solution of system (i). Compare the general solution you obtained in part (a) with the solution generated by **DSolve**. Are they the same? If not, explain how they are related (that is, match up the constants).

(c) Using the solution formulas obtained in (a) or (b), plot several trajectories of each system. On your graphs, identify the eigenvectors (if relevant), the direction of increasing time on the trajectories, and the type and stability of the origin as a critical point. You may find that the quality of your portraits can be enhanced by modifying the t-interval or the range of values assumed by the initial data. (A word of caution: If you request too many curves, you may find that *Mathematica* will take a long time to generate the plot.)

2. Do Problem 1 but replace the three systems listed there by the following three from Boyce & DiPrima:

$$x' = \begin{pmatrix} 5/4 & 3/4 \\ 3/4 & 5/4 \end{pmatrix} x \qquad \text{(Prob. 6, Sect. 7.5)} \qquad (i)$$

$$x' = \begin{pmatrix} 2 & -5/2 \\ 9/5 & -1 \end{pmatrix} x \qquad \text{(Prob. 4, Sect. 7.6)} \qquad (ii)$$

$$x' = \begin{pmatrix} -3/2 & 1 \\ -1/4 & -1/2 \end{pmatrix} x \qquad \text{(Prob. 3, Sect. 7.7).} \qquad (iii)$$

3. Use the command **Eigensystem** to find the eigenvalues and eigenvectors of the following systems. Use the eigenvalues and eigenvectors to write down the general solutions.

(a)

$$x' = \begin{pmatrix} 2 & -1 \\ 1 & -2 \end{pmatrix} x.$$

Determine the possible limiting behavior of $x(t)$, of $y(t)$, and of $x(t)/y(t)$ as t approaches $+\infty$.

(b)

$$x' = \begin{pmatrix} -3 & 5/2 \\ -5/2 & 2 \end{pmatrix} x \qquad \text{(Prob. 4, Sect. 7.7, Boyce & DiPrima).}$$

(c)

$$x' = \begin{pmatrix} 0 & 0 & -1 \\ 2 & 0 & 0 \\ -1 & 2 & 4 \end{pmatrix} x \qquad \text{(Prob. 19, Sect. 7.5, Boyce & DiPrima).}$$

Find the solution with initial condition

$$x(0) = \begin{pmatrix} 7 \\ 5 \\ 5 \end{pmatrix}.$$

(d) Now solve the initial value problem in (c) with **DSolve** and compare the answer with the solution you obtained in (c).

4. *Mathematica* can solve some inhomogeneous linear systems. Here are three such systems (taken from Boyce & DiPrima, Sect. 7.9, Problems 1, 3, & 10).

$$x' = \begin{pmatrix} 2 & -1 \\ 3 & -2 \end{pmatrix} x + \begin{pmatrix} e^t \\ t \end{pmatrix} \qquad (i)$$

$$x' = \begin{pmatrix} 2 & -5 \\ 1 & -2 \end{pmatrix} x + \begin{pmatrix} -\cos t \\ \sin t \end{pmatrix} \qquad (ii)$$

$$\mathbf{x}' = \begin{pmatrix} -3 & \sqrt{2} \\ \sqrt{2} & -2 \end{pmatrix} \mathbf{x} + \begin{pmatrix} e^{-t} \\ -e^{-t} \end{pmatrix}. \tag{iii}$$

(a) Solve the three systems using **DSolve**.

(b) Now impose the initial data

$$\mathbf{x}(0) = \begin{pmatrix} 1 \\ 1 \end{pmatrix}$$

on each system. For each of (*i*)–(*iii*), draw the solution curve using a time interval $-1 \le t \le 1$. Based on the differential equation, indicate the direction of motion through the initial value. Then expand the time interval and, purely on the graphical evidence, venture a guess as to the behavior of the solution curve as $t \to -\infty$ and as $t \to \infty$.

5. Here we reconsider the pendulum models examined in Problems 3–6 of Problem Set D. (See also the discussion in Section 9.3 of Boyce & DiPrima.)

(a) Consider first the undamped pendulum

$$\theta'' + \sin\theta = 0, \quad \theta(0) = 0, \quad \theta'(0) = b.$$

Let $x = \theta$ and $y = \theta'$; then x and y satisfy the system

$$\begin{cases} x' = y \\ y' = -\sin x \end{cases} \qquad \begin{cases} x(0) = 0 \\ y(0) = b. \end{cases}$$

Use **NDSolve** to solve this system. Then plot, on a single graph, the resulting trajectories for the initial conditions $x(0) = 0$, and $y(0) = 0.5, 1, 1.5, 2, 2.5$. Use a positive time range (*e.g.*, {**t, 0, 20**}) and the option **AspectRatio -> Automatic** to improve your pictures.

(b) Based on your pictures in part (a), describe physically what the pendulum is doing in the three cases $\theta'(0) = 1.5, 2$, and 2.5. What is special about the case $\theta'(0) = 2$?

(c) The energy of the pendulum is defined as the sum of kinetic energy $(\theta')^2/2$ and potential energy $1 - \cos\theta$, so

$$E = \frac{1}{2}(\theta')^2 + 1 - \cos\theta = \frac{1}{2}y^2 + 1 - \cos x.$$

Show, by taking the derivative dE/dt, that E is constant when $\theta(t)$ is a solution to the pendulum equation. What basic physical principle does this represent?

(d) Use **ContourPlot** (with the options **PlotPoints -> 60, ContourShading -> False, AspectRatio -> Automatic, AxesOrigin -> {0,0}**) to plot the contour lines for the energy. Explain how your picture is related to the trajectory plot from part (a).

(e) Now consider the damped pendulum

$$\theta'' + 0.5\theta' + \sin\theta = 0, \quad \theta(0) = 0, \quad \theta'(0) = b.$$

Use **NDSolve** to solve the corresponding first order system (which you need to determine) and plot the resulting trajectories for the initial velocities $b = 0, 0.5, 1, \ldots, 6$. You will notice that all the trajectories in your graph tend toward the critical points $(0,0)$ or $(2\pi, 0)$. Explain what this means physically. There is a value b_0 for which the trajectory tends toward the critical point $(\pi, 0)$. Estimate, up to two decimal accuracy, the value of b_0. What would this correspond to physically?

(f) For one of your trajectories that tends to $(0,0)$, plot the energy E as a function of t, and interpret. Show, by computing E', that the rate of decay of the energy is proportional to the square of the angular velocity. Why is the energy decaying at a varying rate?

6. Consider the *competing species* model (from Boyce & DiPrima)

$$\begin{cases} \dfrac{dx}{dt} = x(1.5 - x - 0.5y) \\ \dfrac{dy}{dt} = y(2 - 1.5x - 0.5y) \end{cases} \quad \text{(Prob. 2, Sect. 9.4).}$$

(a) Find all critical points of the system. At each critical point, calculate the corresponding linear system and find the eigenvalues of the coefficient matrix; then identify the type and stability of the critical point. (*Note:* In Version 2.2 of *Mathematica*, you must enter the decimal numbers as fractions in the **Solve** command; see the comment on the use of **Solve** in the discussion of the competing species model in Chapter 12.)

(b) Plot the vector field.

(c) Use several initial data points (x_0, y_0) in the first quadrant to draw a phase portrait for the system. Identify the direction of increasing t on the trajectories you obtain. Use your vector field plot from part (b) to choose a representative sample of initial conditions.

(d) Suppose the initial state of the population is given by

$$x(0) = 2.5, \ y(0) = 2.$$

Find the state of the population at $t = 1, 2, 3, 4, 5, \ldots, 20$.

(e) Explain why practically speaking there is no "peaceful coexistence", *i.e.*, with the exception of a *degenerate* set of starting populations (the *separatrix* curve), one or the other population must die out. For which nonzero initial populations is there no change? Sketch (by hand) on your plot the separatrices; *i.e.*, the solution curves that approach the unstable equilibrium point where both populations are positive and form the boundary between the solution curves that approach each of the two stable points where only one population survives. (In Problem 11, we investigate how to approximate the separatrix using *Mathematica*.)

(f) The vertical line $x = 1.5$ cuts the separatrix. By experimenting with the long-term behavior of solutions emanating from several points on this line, find an approximation to two decimal point accuracy of the value $\bar{y}$ such that $(1.5, \bar{y})$ is on the separatrix. Could you actually verify numerically whether the point is in fact on the separatrix? Why or why not?

7. Consider the *competing species* model (from Boyce & DiPrima)

$$
\begin{cases}
\dfrac{dx}{dt} = x(1.5 - 0.5x - y) \\[2mm]
\dfrac{dy}{dt} = y(0.75 - 0.125x - y)
\end{cases}
\qquad \text{(Prob. 4, Sect. 9.4).}
$$

(a) Find all critical points of the system. At each critical point, calculate the corresponding linear system and find the eigenvalues of the coefficient matrix; then identify the type and stability of the critical point. (*Note*: In Version 2.2 of *Mathematica*, you must enter the decimal numbers as fractions in the **Solve** command; see the comment on the use of **Solve** in the discussion of the competing species model in Chapter 12.)

(b) Plot the vector field.

(c) Use several initial data points (x_0, y_0) in the first quadrant to draw a phase portrait for the system. Identify the direction of increasing t on the trajectories you obtain. Use your vector field plot from part (b) to choose a representative sample of initial conditions.

(d) Suppose the initial state of the population is given by

$$x(0) = 0.1, \; y(0) = 0.1.$$

Find the state of the population at $t = 1, 2, 3, 4, 5, \ldots, 20$.

(e) Explain why, practically speaking, "peaceful coexistence" is the only outcome — *i.e.*, with the exception of the situation in which one or both species starts out without any population, the population distributions always tend toward a certain equilibrium point. Sketch (by hand) on your plot the separatrices that connect the stable equilibrium point to the two unstable points at which one population is zero; these separatrices divide the solution curves that tend toward the origin as $t \to -\infty$ from those that are unbounded as $t \to -\infty$. (In Problem 11, we investigate how to approximate the separatrix using *Mathematica*.)

(f) The vertical line $x = 2.5$ cuts that separatrix. By experimenting with the behavior of solutions for *negative* time emanating from several points on this line, find an approximation to two decimal point accuracy of the value $\bar{y}$ such that $(2.5, \bar{y})$ is on the separatrix. (*Hint*: $-3 \le t \le 0$ should suffice.) Could you actually verify numerically whether the point is in fact on the separatrix? Why or why not?

8. Consider the *predator-prey* model

$$\begin{cases} \dfrac{dx}{dt} = x(2 - y) \\[2mm] \dfrac{dy}{dt} = y(x - 1) \end{cases}$$

in which x represents the population of the prey, and y represents the population of the predators.

(a) Find all critical points of the system. At each critical point, calculate the corresponding linear system and find the eigenvalues of the coefficient matrix; then identify the type and stability of the critical point.

(b) Plot the vector field.

(c) Use several initial data points (x_0, y_0) in the first quadrant to draw a phase portrait for the system. Identify the direction of increasing t on the trajectories you obtain. Use your vector field plot from part (b) to choose a representative sample of initial conditions.

(d) Explain from your phase portrait how the populations vary for initial data close to the equilibrium point $(\bar{x}_0, \bar{y}_0)$ (the unique critical point inside the first quadrant). What about initial data far from the critical point?

(e) Suppose the initial state of the population is given by

$$x(0) = 1, \; y(0) = 1.$$

Find the state of the population at $t = 1, 2, 3, 4, 5$.

(f) Estimate the period of the solution curve with initial data $(1, 1)$.

9. Consider a *predator-prey* model where the behavior of the prey is governed by a logistic equation (in the absence of the predator). Such a model is typified by the following system from Boyce & DiPrima:

$$\begin{cases} \dfrac{dx}{dt} = x(1 - 0.5x - 0.5y) \\[2mm] \dfrac{dy}{dt} = y(0.5x - 0.25) \end{cases} \qquad \text{(Prob. 3, Sect. 9.5),}$$

where x represents the population of the prey, and y represents the population of the predators.

(a) Find all critical points of the system. At each critical point, calculate the corresponding linear system and find the eigenvalues of the coefficient matrix; then identify the type and stability of the critical point.

(b) Plot the vector field.

(c) Use several initial data points (x_0, y_0) in the first quadrant to draw a phase portrait for the system. Identify the direction of increasing t on the trajectories you obtain. Use your vector field plot from part (b) to choose a representative sample of initial conditions.

(d) Explain from your phase portrait how the populations vary over time for initial data near the equilibrium point $(\bar{x}_0, \bar{y}_0)$ (the unique critical point inside the first quadrant, not on the axes). What happens when the initial condition is far from the equilibrium point?

(e) Suppose the initial state of the population is given by

$$x(0) = 1, \ y(0) = 1.$$

Find the state of the population at $t = 1, 2, 3, 4, 5$.

(f) Estimate how long it takes for both populations to come within 0.01 of their equilibrium values if we start on the solution curve with initial data $(1, 1)$.

10. Consider a modified predator-prey system where the behavior of the prey is governed by a logistic/threshold equation (in the absence of the predator). Such a model is typified by the following system from Boyce & DiPrima:

$$\begin{cases} \dfrac{dx}{dt} = x(-1 + 2.5x - 0.3y - x^2) \\ \dfrac{dy}{dt} = y(-1.5 + x) \end{cases} \quad \text{(Prob. 5, Sect. 9.5),}$$

where x represents the population of the prey, and y represents the population of the predators.

(a) Find all critical points of the system. At each critical point, calculate the corresponding linear system and find the eigenvalues and eigenvectors of the coefficient matrix; then identify the critical points as to type and stability.

(b) Plot the vector field.

(c) Use several initial data points (x_0, y_0) in the first quadrant to draw a phase portrait for the system. Use your vector field plot from part (b) to choose a representative sample of initial conditions.

(d) In parts (a), (b), and (c), you obtained information about the solutions of the system using three different approaches. Combine all of this information by combining the plots from parts (b) and (c) with the **Show** command, and then drawing in by hand the critical points, the eigenvectors from part (a), and any separatrices. What information does the graph part (a) provide that is not provided by the other approaches? Answer the same question for parts (b) and (c).

(e) Interpret your conclusions in terms of the populations of the two species.

11. Some of the nonlinear systems of differential equations we have studied have more than one asymptotically stable equilibrium point. In such cases, it can be difficult to predict which (if any) equilibrium point the solution with a given initial condition will approach as time increases. Generally, the solution curves which approach one stable equilibrium will be separated from the solutions which approach another stable equilibrium by a separatrix curve. The separatrix is itself a solution curve which does not approach either stable equilibrium— often it approaches a saddle point instead. (See, for example, Figure 9.4.8 in Section 9.4 of Boyce & DiPrima.)

Having located a relevant saddle point, one can approximate the separatrix by choosing an initial condition very close to the saddle point and solving the differential equation *backwards* in time. The reason for going "back in time" is to find (approximately) a solution curve that approaches very close to the saddle point as time increases. For two population dynamics models, we will use this idea to get a fairly precise map of which initial conditions go to which equilibria.

(a) Consider the system

$$\begin{cases} \dfrac{dx}{dt} = x(1.5 - x - 0.5y) \\ \dfrac{dy}{dt} = y(2 - 1.5x - 0.5y) \end{cases}$$

studied in Problem 6 above. There are two asymptotically stable equilibria, $(1.5, 0)$ and $(0, 4)$, a saddle point at $(1, 1)$, and an unstable node at $(0, 0)$. Plot a family of solution curves in the first quadrant (positive x and y) on the same graph; use a time interval from $t = 0$ to a positive time large enough that you can clearly see where the solutions curves are headed, but not so large that your plot takes forever to compute. (We suggest a set of initial values between 0.5 and 4.5. It also may be useful to adjust the range of the plot until you get a reasonably square graph.) Observe where the solution curves seem to be heading and where the separatrix seems to be.

(b) Draw an approximate separatrix by plotting a solution curve with initial values for x and y very close to the saddle point (1,1), using a *negative* range of values for t. This should give you a good picture of the separatrix on one side of the saddle point; to approximate the rest of the separatrix you will need to choose a set of initial conditions on the other side of (but still very close to) the saddle point. In each case, you may need to fine-tune the time interval, since a time interval that is too small will only show you a small part of the separatrix, while too large an interval may cause the solution to blow up. Finally, show all of your plots on one graph, and make sure the separatrix really does separate the different asymptotic properties of the solution curves found in part (a). Discuss how the possible limiting values of the species depend on the initial values of the species.

(c) Repeat part (a) using the system

$$\begin{cases} \dfrac{dx}{dt} = x(-1 + 2.5x - 0.3y - x^2) \\ \dfrac{dy}{dt} = y(-1.5 + x) \end{cases}$$

from Problem 10 above. This time there are asymptotically stable equilibria at the origin and $(3/2, 5/3)$, and saddle points at $(0.5, 0)$ and $(2, 0)$.

(d) Repeat part (b) for the system in part (c). It is up to you to decide whether one or both of the saddle points are relevant to drawing the separatrix or separatrices that divide those solution curves which approach one equilibrium from those which approach the other as time increases; your picture from part (c) may be helpful. Also, keep in mind that since the saddle points are on the x-axis in this case, you need only consider nearby initial conditions above the x-axis because we are only interested in solutions in the first quadrant.

12. This problem is based on Problems 34 & 35 on page 601 of the book *Elementary Differential Equations with Applications*, by Edwards and Penney, Prentice-Hall, Inc., 1985. (See also Boyce & DiPrima, Problem 17, Section 9.3.)

(a) Consider the linear system

$$\begin{cases} \dfrac{dx}{dt} = -x + hy \\ \dfrac{dy}{dt} = x - y. \end{cases}$$

Draw phase portraits for the system for the values $h = 0$, 0.5, and -0.5. What can you deduce about the change in the type and/or stability of the equilibrium point $(0,0)$ corresponding to relatively small perturbations of the system?

(b) Now consider the system

$$\begin{cases} \dfrac{dx}{dt} = y + hx(x^2 + y^2) \\ \dfrac{dy}{dt} = -x + hy(x^2 + y^2). \end{cases}$$

Draw phase portraits (using **NDSolve** this time) for $h = 0$, 1, and -1. (*Note:* For $h = 1$, you may have to keep the initial data close to the origin and keep the time interval very short. Even with $t = 1$ *Mathematica* complains; but be patient, you will get a nice picture eventually.) Illustrate how the linear approximation method (*cf.* Chapter 9 of Boyce & DiPrima) is inconclusive in the case of a *center* by citing the evidence in your portraits. (In fact, you need to decide which way the solution curves are going for $h \neq 0$. To do that, examine the signs of dx/dt and dy/dt at the point $x = 1$, $y = 0$.)

13. In Chapter 5 we investigated the sensitivity to initial values of solutions of a single differential equation. In this problem, we investigate the same issue for two systems of equations. The systems we study are said to be *chaotic* because the solutions are sensitive to initial values, but in contrast to the examples in Chapter 5 and Problems 14 and 15 of Problem Set C, the solutions remain bounded.

Since we do not know the exact solutions for the systems we will study, in order to judge the time it takes for a small perturbation of the system to become large we will compare pairs of numerical solutions whose initial conditions are close, but still relatively far apart compared with the local error (*cf.* Chapter 7) of our numerical method. Since **NDSolve** tries to keep its errors within 10^{-6}, to be safe we only consider perturbations as small as 10^{-4}.

(a) Consider the Lorenz system

$$x' = 10(y - x)$$
$$y' = 28x - y - xz$$
$$z' = -(8/3)z + xy$$

studied in Section 9.8 of Boyce & DiPrima. We investigate the idea illustrated in Figure 9.8.3, that small changes in the initial conditions can lead to large changes in the solution after a relatively short period of time. For $a = 0.1$, plot on the same graph the first coordinate $x(t)$ of the solutions corresponding to the initial conditions $(5, 5, 5)$ and $(5 + a, 5, 5)$ from $t = 0$ to $t = 20$. (It may be useful in distinguishing between the two curves to make one of them black and the other gray—you can do this with a **Plot** option like **PlotStyle** -> {{}, **GrayLevel[0.5]**}. You may also have to increase **PlotPoints**.) Observe the time at which the solutions start to differ noticeably. Repeat for $a = 0.01, 0.001, 0.0001$. (The criterion for a "noticeable" difference between the two solutions is up to you, just try to be consistent from one observation to the next.)

(b) Make a table or graph of the number of decimal places in which the initial condition was perturbed (that is, 1, 2, 3, and 4 for the four given values of a) versus the amount of time the solutions stayed close to each other. This graph shows roughly how long we should trust a numerical solution to be close to the actual solution for a given number of digits of accuracy in each step of our numerical method. Describe how the amount of time we can trust a numerical solution seems to depend on the number of digits of accuracy per time step, judging from your data. If a numerical method has 16 digits of accuracy, about how long do you think the numerical solution can be trusted? What if the accuracy were 100 digits?

(c) Repeat part (a) for the Rössler system

$$x' = -y - z$$
$$y' = x + 0.36y$$
$$z' = 0.4x - 4.5z + xz.$$

This time plot from $t = 0$ to $t = 100$, and use $(2, 2, 2)$ as the initial condition.

(d) Repeat part (b) for the Rössler system. Judging from the results of parts (b) and (d), is there a common priniciple you can draw for systems of differential equations of this type?

Complex Systems. In the following three problems, we consider a special class of 2×2 systems, namely those that may be represented as a differential equation involving a single complex variable z. Consider, for example, the equation

$$z' = z(e^{i\phi} + z\bar{z}). \tag{1}$$

Here $z(t) = x(t) + iy(t)$ is a complex-valued function of the independent variable t, ϕ is a a real parameter, and $\bar{z}$ is the complex conjugate of z. If we compute the real and imaginary parts of (1), we obtain the equivalent nonlinear 2×2 system

$$\begin{cases} x' = x \cos \phi - y \sin \phi + x^3 - xy^2 \\ y' = x \sin \phi + y \cos \phi + x^2 y - y^3. \end{cases} \tag{2}$$

In spite of the fact that these are equivalent, the expression (1) offers several advantages over (2). First, (1) is "one-dimensional" in the sense that there is only one dependent variable z. Second, there are certain properties of the equation (1) that are apparent in the complex form, but obscure in the 2×2 form. For example, (1) is invariant by rotations through any angle (see the following problem), and therefore its set of solutions is rotationally symmetric. Symmetry plays a large role in the theory of differential equations, and complex-valued equations like (1) are the simplest kind of differential equations displaying rotational symmetry. Third, equations like (1) exhibit a phenomenon called *bifurcation* when the parameter ϕ varies. A parametrized family of differential equations is said to *bifurcate* at a parameter value ϕ_0 if the qualitative behavior of the differential equation changes as the parameter passes through ϕ_0. Examples of bifurcations are: loss of stability of a critical point; and creation or annihilation of limit cycles, or periodic solutions.

You may have noticed that for certain real-valued differential equations **DSolve** returns complex-valued solutions. In fact, many *Mathematica* commands do not distinguish between real and complex numbers. This is true of the commands **DSolve** and **NDSolve**. In particular, we can use these commands on equations like (1) without worrying about the fact that these equations are complex-valued. *Mathematica* will report its solutions in exactly the same form as for real-valued differential equations, except that now the solutions will almost always be complex-valued (whereas in the case of real-valued equations, complex-valued solutions were rarely reported).

Unfortunately, the *Mathematica* command **ParametricPlot** *does* distinguish between complex- and real-valued functions, so if we want to draw the phase portraits of the solutions in the complex plane, we have to first extract the real and imaginary parts of the complex solutions, and then use **ParametricPlot** on the real and imaginary parts. In order to save you a considerable amount of trouble figuring out exactly how to do this, we give you the following program:

```
complexsystem[phi_, t0_, t1_] := (Clear[csol, cvar, g];
    csol[t_, r_, theta_] := z[t] /.
      NDSolve[{z'[t] == z[t]*(Exp[I*phi] + z[t]*Conjugate[z[t]]),
          z[0] == r*Exp[I*theta]}, z, {t, t0, t1}];
    coords[cvar_] = {Re[cvar], Im[cvar]};
    g[t_] = Map[coords, Flatten[Table[csol[t, 0.25i, 2Pi*j/6],
        {i, 1, 3, 2}, {j, 0, 5}]]];
    ParametricPlot[Evaluate[g[t]], {t, t0, t1},
        PlotRange -> {{-2, 2}, {-2, 2}}, AspectRatio -> Automatic];)
```

This program is designed to solve equation (1) numerically and plot solutions for various values of the parameter ϕ. It is this ϕ that appears as an argument of the function **complexsystem[phi_, t0_, t1_]**. Note that multiplication by $e^{i\phi}$ corresponds in the complex plane to counterclockwise rotation by angle ϕ. The other arguments of the function are the endpoints of the time interval on which to solve the differential equation.

In order to use and modify this program you should note the following features:

- The differential equation appears in the **NDSolve** command in exactly the same way that an ordinary real-valued equation would. Note that **I** is *Mathematica*'s notation for $\sqrt{-1}$.

- We have included an initial condition **z[0] == r*Exp[I*theta]**, which is a complex number given in polar coordinates. The reason for this will become clear below. In this particular example, the initial conditions consist of points on the circles of radius 0.25 and 0.75, spaced evenly at angles $2\pi j/6$, for $j = 0, \ldots, 5$.

- The syntax we have used in **NDSolve** is slightly different from what you are used to. In particular, when **z** appears as the second argument of **NDSolve**, it appears as **z** and not **z[t]**. This is a technical modification that makes things a little simpler, and has nothing to do with the fact that we're solving a complex-valued rather than a real-valued equation.

- The *Mathematica* command **Map** is used to apply the function **coords** to the table of complex-valued numerical solutions of the differential equation. The end result is a table of real and imaginary parts of the complex solutions.

- When you evaluate the program you will encounter a deluge of warning messages from *Mathematica* concerning stepsize, maximum number of steps, etc. Once you have determined that things are working correctly you may want to turn these messages off (see Chapter 8). For example, you might type **Off[NDSolve::mxst]** to turn off warning messages about maximum number of steps. At the very least, you should delete the warning messages from the Notebook before you print it.

To summarize, the only things you'll have to modify to use this program in other problems are:

- The actual differential equation.
- The list of initial conditions inside the **Table** command.
- Possibly the parameters of the **PlotRange** option.

14. This exercise concerns the equation mentioned above,

$$z' = z(e^{i\phi} + z\bar{z}). \tag{i}$$

(a) Show that equation (i) is rotationally invariant in the following sense: If we let $w = e^{i\theta}z$, for any angle θ, then w satisfies the same differential equation as z; that is, $w' = w(e^{i\phi} + w\bar{w})$. You may show this by hand or by using *Mathematica* (but it's easier to do it by hand).

(b) Plot the trajectories of the differential equation for parameter values $\phi = 0, \pi/4, \pi/3, 2\pi/3$. Determine the direction of the trajectories by evaluating the right-hand side at various values of z. (We suggest plotting the trajectories on the time interval $[-3, 2]$.) What kind of symmetries can you see in the plots?

(c) Examine the results of (b). Can you detect whether the parameter has passed through a bifurcation value? What exactly is the qualitative change in the behavior of the solutions?

(d) Plot the trajectories of the system for the two parameter values $\phi = \pi/2 \pm 0.2$. (You should also change the time interval to $[-5, 3]$.) Estimate the bifurcation value of the parameter.

(e) Let $\rho = z\bar{z}$. Note that ρ is the square of the distance from the origin to z. In particular, ρ is a real-valued positive function of t. Moreover, one can show that ρ satisfies the differential equation $\rho' = 2\rho(\mathrm{Re}(e^{i\phi}) + \rho)$. Note that a critical point of this differential equation corresponds to a solution of (i) that stays a fixed distance from the origin. By finding the critical points of the differential equation for ρ, explain the results of (c) and (d).

15. Consider the complex-valued differential equation

$$z' = e^{i\phi}z + \bar{z}^2. \tag{i}$$

Refer to the text preceding Problem 14 for general remarks concerning complex-valued differential equations.

(a) Show that equation (i) is rotationally invariant through an angle of $2\pi/3$ in the following sense: If we let $w = e^{2\pi i/3}z$, then w also satisfies the differential equation (*i*), *i.e.*, $w' = e^{i\phi}w + \bar{w}^2$. You may show this by hand or by using *Mathematica*.

(b) Plot the trajectories of the differential equation for parameter values $\phi = 0, \pi/4, \pi/2$. You should use a set of initial conditions consisting of 12 evenly spaced points on each of the circles of radius 0.5 and 1.5. Determine the direction of the trajectories by evaluating the right-hand side at various values of z. (We suggest plotting the trajectories on the time interval $[-3, 2]$.) What symmetries can you detect in the plot? (*Note*: These plots may take five minutes or longer to draw.)

(c) Look at the results of (b). On which interval does the parameter pass through a bifurcation value? What exactly is the qualitative change in the behavior of the solutions?

(d) Set $z = x + iy$ in equation (*i*), expand the equation in terms of x and y, and take the real and imaginary parts to obtain an equivalent real-valued 2×2 system.

(e) Using the result of (d), for each of the parameter values $0, \pi/4, \pi/2$, find the critical points of the system (there are 4 in each case). Indicate these critical points on your plots in (b).

16. Consider the complex-valued differential equation

$$z' = 0.3e^{i\phi}z - (1 + i)z^3\bar{z}^2 + \bar{z}^4. \qquad (i)$$

Refer to the text preceding Problem 14 for general remarks concerning complex-valued differential equations.

(a) Show that equation (*i*) is rotationally invariant through an angle of $2\pi/5$ in the following sense: If we let $w = e^{2\pi i/5}z$, then w also satisfies the differential equation (*i*).

(b) Plot the trajectories of the differential equation for parameter values $\phi = 0, \pi/4, \pi/2$. You should use a set of initial conditions consisting of 20 evenly spaced points on the each of the circles of radius 0.25 and 0.75. Determine the direction of the trajectories by plotting the vector field associated to this equation. (We suggest plotting the trajectories on the time interval $[-8, 10]$, with **PlotRange** $\rightarrow \{\{-1, 1\}, \{-1, 1\}\}$.) What symmetries can you detect in the plots?

(c) Examine the results of (b). On which interval or intervals does the parameter pass through a bifurcation value? What exactly is the qualitative change in the behavior of the solutions? Using the **Show** command, plot the vector fields and integral curves on the same graph for each parameter value. By examining these plots try to figure out how many critical points there are inside the unit square. (*Note*: The stable critical points are easy to find. The unstable ones are not so obvious.)

Glossary

We list here the *Mathematica* objects that arise in the various input statements encountered in this course. We list them according to four types: commands, options, built-in functions, and constants. The distinction between the first and third is somewhat artificial, as *Mathematica* makes no distinction between them. However, for the purposes of this course, it is convenient to think of a *Mathematica* built-in function as we normally think of functions, in particular as something that can be evaluated or plotted; while a command is something that manipulates data or expressions, or initiates a process.

Each command and option is followed by a brief description of its effect, and then one or more examples. To find the full syntax of a command you can type **?command** or **??command** in a Notebook.

Mathematica Commands

Clear   Clears values and definitions for variables and functions.
   Clear[x]
   Clear[f, g]

Conjugate   Gives the complex conjugate of a complex number.
   Conjugate[2 + 3I]

ContourPlot   Plots the level curves of a function of two variables.
   ContourPlot[x^2 + y^2, {x, −2, 2}, {y, −2, 2}]

D   Differentiation operator.
   D[f[x], x]
   D[x^3 − 3x, x]
   D[Cos[x], {x, 2}]

DSolve   Symbolic ODE solver.
   DSolve[y''[x] − x*y[x] == 0, y[x], x]
   DSolve[{y'[x] + y[x]^2 == 0, y[0] == 1}, y[x], x]
   DSolve[{x'[t] == 2x[t] + y[t], y'[t] == −x[t]}, {x[t], y[t]}, t]

Eigensystem   Computes eigenvalues and eigenvectors of a matrix.
  Eigensystem[{{a, b}, {c, d}}]
  Eigensystem[{{1, 0, 0}, {1, 1, 1}, {1, 2, 4}}]

Evaluate   Causes an expression to be evaluated; especially useful in **Plot** commands.
  Plot[Evaluate[Table[i*x, {i, 0, 10}]], {x, 0, 1}]

Expand   Expands products and powers in an algebraic expression.
  Expand[(x + y)^3]

Factor   Factors a polynomial.
  Factor[x^4 − y^4]

FindRoot   Finds a numerical solution to an equation; looks for a single solution near a given starting point.
  FindRoot[Cos[x] == x, {x, 1}]

First   Selects the first element in a list.
  First[{2, 4, 6}]
  First[Solve[x^2 − 4 == 0, x]]

Flatten   Removes extra levels of braces in a nested list.
  Flatten[{{1, 2}, 3, {4, 5, 6, {7}}}, 1]
  Flatten[Table[f[a, b], {a, 1, 2}, {b, 1, 3}]]

Function   Specifies a pure function.
  f = Function[x, 3x^3 − x]

If   Introduces a conditional.
  f[x_] := If[x < 0, 4x, −4x]

Integrate   Integration operator for both definite and indefinite integrals.
  Integrate[1/(1 + x^2), x]
  Integrate[Exp[−x], {x, 0, Infinity}]

InverseLaplaceTransform   Computes the inverse Laplace Transform.
  InverseLaplaceTransform[Exp[−s]/s, s, t]

Join   Combines two lists.
  Join[{1, 2, 3}, {4, 5}]

LaplaceTransform   Computes the Laplace Transform.
  LaplaceTransform[f[t], t, s]

Last   Selects the last element in a list.
  Last[{3, 4, 5}]

Limit   Finds a limit.
  Limit[Sin[x]/x, x −> 0]

LinearSolve   Solves a matrix equation.
  LinearSolve[{{1, 2}, {3, 4}}, {6, 7}]

ListPlot   Plots a list of points.
   ListPlot[{{1, 1}, {2, 4}, {3, 10}}]

Map   Applies a function to each element of a list.
   Map[Sqrt, {1, 2, 3}]

N   Evaluates numerically; gives a decimal approximation of a number.
   N[Pi, 15]
   N[Solve[x^2 − 4x + 9 == 0, x]]

NDSolve   Numeric ODE solver.
   NDSolve[{y″[x] − x*y[x] == 0, y[0] == 1, y′[0] == 0}, y[x], {x, 0, 10}]

NestList   Applies a function iteratively.
   NestList[f, x, 3]

NIntegrate   Numerical integration.
   NIntegrate[f[x], {x, 0, 5}]
   NIntegrate[Sin[x]/x, {x, 0, Infinity}]

NSolve   Solves an equation (or list of equations) numerically; equivalent to **N[Solve[. . .]]**.
   NSolve[x^5 − x^2 + 4x − 9 == 0, x]

Off   Suspends printing of an error or warning message.
   Off[NDSolve::mxst]
   Off[General::spell1]

ParametricPlot   Draws a curve (or curves) given by parametric coordinates.
   ParametricPlot[{Cos[t], Sin[t]}, {t, 0, 2Pi}]
   ParametricPlot[Evaluate[Table[f[t, j], {j, 10}]], {t, 0, 5}]

Plot   Basic plot command for a function (or list of functions) of one variable.
   Plot[f[x], {x, 0, 1}]
   Plot[{x^2, x^3}, {x, −2, 2}]

PlotVectorField   Draws a vector field plot given a pair of functions of two variables.
   PlotVectorField[{y, −x}, {x, −1, 1}, {y, −1, 1}]
   PlotVectorField[{f[x, y], g[x, y]}, {x, 0, 2}, {y, 0, 5}, AspectRatio −> 1]

Remove   Removes definitions; useful for removing definitions of names accidentally invoked before a package is loaded.
   Remove[PlotVectorField]

Series   Generates terms of a power series expansion about a point.
   Series[Exp[−x], {x, 0, 10}]

Show   Combines and displays several previously generated graphics.
   Show[graph1, graph2]

Simplify   Simplifies an expression.
  Simplify[1/(1 + x)^2 − 1/(1 − x)^2]

Solve   Solves an equation or list of equations; works best on polynomials.
  Solve[2x^2 − 3x + 6 == 0, x]
  Solve[{x + 3y == 4, −x − 5y == 3}, {x, y}]

Sum   Sums a sequence.
  Sum[(i − 1)/(i + 1), {i, 1, 10}]
  Sum[g[j], {j, 2, 3, 0.1}]

Table   Generates a list.
  Table[1/k, {k, 1, 5}]
  Table[{f[k], g[k]}, {k, 0, −100, −1}]

TableForm   Places data in tabular form.
  Table[{3t, 6t^2}, {t, 1, 50}]//TableForm

Options to *Mathematica* Commands

AccuracyGoal   Specifies digits of accuracy in a numerical procedure.
  NDSolve[{y′[x] == Sin[y[x]], y[0] == 1}, y[x], {x, 0, 2}, AccuracyGoal −> 20]

AspectRatio   Specifies ratio of height to width in a plot; the **Automatic** setting allows *Mathematica* to choose the ratio depending on the coordinates of the plot under consideration.
  ParametricPlot[{Cos[t], Sin[t]}, {t, 0, 2Pi}, AspectRatio −> Automatic]

Axes   Specifies whether axes should be drawn in a plot.
  Plot[g[x], {x, 0, 3}, Axes −> False]

AxesLabel   Specifies labels for axes in a plot.
  Plot[Cos[x], {x, 0, 2Pi}, AxesLabel −> {"x", "y"}]

Contours   Specifies which contour to use in a contour plot.
  ContourPlot[f[x, y], {x, 0, 1}, {y, 0, 2}, Contours −> {f[0, 0]}]

ContourShading   Specifies whether regions between contours are shaded.
  ContourPlot[x*y, {x, 0, 3}, {y, 0, 3}, ContourShading −> False]

Dashing   Indicates that curves or lines should be drawn dashed.
  Plot[{Sin[x], Cos[x]}, {x, 0, 2Pi}, PlotStyle −> {{}, Dashing[{0.03}]}]

Direction   Specifies direction in a one-sided limit.
  Limit[1/x, x −> 0, Direction −> 1]

Frame   Specifies whether a frame should be drawn around a plot. Useful for direction field plots.
  PlotVectorField[{f[x, y], g[x, y]}, {x, −1, 1}, {y, −2, 2}, Frame −> True]

GrayLevel   Allows for shading of curves in a plot.
   Plot[{Sin[x], Cos[x]}, {x, 0, 2Pi}, PlotStyle –> {{}, GrayLevel[0.7]}]

MaxIterations   Specifies number of iterations in **FindRoot**; default is 15.
   FindRoot[−100 + 400 Exp[0.04(t − 1960)] == 3000, {t, 0}, MaxIterations –> 40]

MaxSteps   Specifies number of iterations allowed in a numerical procedure; default is 500.
   NDSolve[{y''[x] − y'[x] + x*y[x] == 0, y[0] == 0, y'[0] == 1}, y[x], {x, 0, 40}, MaxSteps –> 2000]

PlotJoined   Specifies whether to connect the points in a **ListPlot**.
   ListPlot[{{1, 3}, {2, 5}}, PlotJoined –> True]

PlotPoints   Specifies the number of points to sample in drawing a plot; default is 25.
   Plot[Sin[1/x], {x, 0.001, 1}, PlotPoints –> 50]

PlotRange   Specifies the range of the dependent variable in a plot.
   Plot[Tan[x], {x, 0, Pi}, PlotRange –> {0, 10}]
   ParametricPlot[{t^3, t^5}, {t, −10, 10}, PlotRange –> {{−5, 5}, {−10, 10}}]

PlotStyle   Specifies style of curves or points; *cf.* **GrayLevel** or **Dashing**.

PrecisionGoal   A numerical precision option; see **AccuracyGoal** and Chapter 7.

ScaleFunction   Option for scaling vectors in vector field plots; the argument is a pure function.
   PlotVectorField[{f[x, y], g[x, y]}, {x, −1, 1}, {y, −2, 2}, ScaleFunction –> (1&)]

Ticks   Specifies tick marks for the axes in a plot; in the following example, we set the ticks on the x-axis and allow *Mathematica* to set them on the y-axis.
   Plot[Sin[x], {x, 0, Pi}, Ticks –> {{0, Pi/4, Pi/2, 3Pi/4, Pi}, Automatic}]

WorkingPrecision   Another numerical precision option; see **AccuracyGoal** and Chapter 7.

Built-in Functions

Abs $|x|$.

AiryAi   The solution $\text{Ai}(x)$ to Airy's equation $y'' - xy = 0$.

AiryBi   The solution $\text{Bi}(x)$ to Airy's equation.

ArcSin $\arcsin x$.

BesselJ[0, ·]   The solution $J_0(x)$ to Bessel's equation of order zero $x^2 y'' + xy' + x^2 y = 0$.

BesselY[0, ·]   The solution $Y_0(x)$ to Bessel's equation of order zero.

Cos $\cos x$.

Cosh $\cosh x$.

Erf The *error function* $\mathrm{erf}(x) = (2/\sqrt{\pi}) \int_0^x e^{-t^2} \, dt$.

Erfi $-i \, \mathrm{erf}(ix)$.

Exp e^x.

Im $\mathrm{Im}(z)$, the imaginary part of a complex number.

Log The natural logarithm $\ln x = \log_e x$.

Re $\mathrm{Re}(z)$, the real part of a complex number.

Sin $\sin x$.

Sinh $\sinh x$.

SinIntegral The *sine integral* $\mathrm{Si}(x) = \int_0^x (\sin t/t) \, dt$.

Sqrt $\sqrt{x}$.

Tan $\tan x$.

Built-in Constants

E $e = \ln^{-1}(1)$.

I $i = \sqrt{-1}$.

Infinity ∞.

Pi π.

Sample Notebook Solutions

■ Problem Set B, Problem 1

We are interested in the differential equation $xy' + 2y = \sin x$, with initial condition $y(\pi/2) = c$. Here is the general solution.

```
Clear[y,x,c,sol];
sol = DSolve[{x y'[x] + 2y[x] == Sin[x],
    y[Pi/2] == c}, y[x], x]
```

$$\{\{y[x] \;\rightarrow\; \frac{-4 + c\ Pi^2}{4\ x^2} + \frac{-(x\ Cos[x]) + Sin[x]}{x^2}\}\}$$

Here is a function of two variables x and c that gives, for fixed c, the solution of the IVP with initial condition $y(\pi/2) = c$.

```
y[x_, c_] = y[x]/.First[sol]
```

$$\frac{-4 + c\ Pi^2}{4\ x^2} + \frac{-(x\ Cos[x]) + Sin[x]}{x^2}$$

The solution with initial condition $y(\pi/2) = 1$ is given by:

```
y[x,1]
```

$$\frac{-4 + Pi^2}{4\ x^2} + \frac{-(x\ Cos[x]) + Sin[x]}{x^2}$$

□ (a)

Here is a table of values for the solution of the IVP with c = 1.

```
Table[{x, N[y[x,1]]},{x,0.5,5,0.5}] //TableForm
```

```
0.5    6.03214
1.     1.76857
1.5    1.04835
2.     0.802248
2.5    0.650997
3.     0.508722
3.5    0.358712
4.     0.207823
4.5    0.0710347
5.     -0.0363934
```

□ **(b)**

We graph the solution y[x, 1] on several intervals.

```
Plot[y[x,1], {x,0.00000001,2}];
```

```
Plot[y[x,1], {x,1,10}, PlotRange->{-0.15,1}];
```

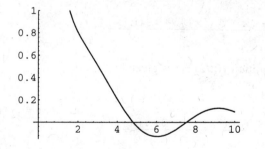

```
Plot [y[x,1], {x,10,100}];
```

By inspecting the function y[x, 1], we see that the solution approaches positive infinity as x goes to 0, and approaches 0 as x goes to infinity. This is borne out by the graphs above.

□ **(c)**

Here is a table of the solutions of the IVP with initial conditions y(π/2) = 0.2j, for j = 1,...,5, and a plot of these solutions over two different intervals. Note that the index j = 1 corresponds to the lowest solution, and the index j = 5 corresponds to the topmost.

```
Table[{j,y[x,0.2 j]}, {j,1,5}] //TableForm
```

$$1 \quad \frac{-4 + 0.2 \ Pi^2}{4 \ x^2} + \frac{-(x \ Cos[x]) + Sin[x]}{x^2}$$

$$2 \quad \frac{-4 + 0.4 \ Pi^2}{4 \ x^2} + \frac{-(x \ Cos[x]) + Sin[x]}{x^2}$$

$$3 \quad \frac{-4 + 0.6 \ Pi^2}{4 \ x^2} + \frac{-(x \ Cos[x]) + Sin[x]}{x^2}$$

$$4 \quad \frac{-4 + 0.8 \ Pi^2}{4 \ x^2} + \frac{-(x \ Cos[x]) + Sin[x]}{x^2}$$

$$5 \quad \frac{-4 + 1. \ Pi^2}{4 \ x^2} + \frac{-(x \ Cos[x]) + Sin[x]}{x^2}$$

```
Plot[Evaluate[Table[y[x,0.2 j], {j,1,5}]],
    {x,0.1,0.2}];
```

```
Plot[Evaluate[Table[y[x,0.2 j], {j,1,5}]],
    {x,0.2,10}];
```

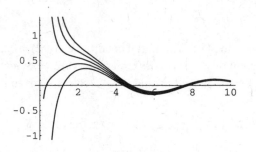

☐ **(d)**

The solutions in (c) approach either ∞ or -∞ as x approaches 0 from the right, and approach 0 as x approaches ∞. Can we find a solution that has no singularity at x = 0? The general solution is given at the beginning of this problem. The only way that solution could possibly be nonsingular at x = 0 is if $c = 4/\pi^2$. We can check using L'Hopital's rule that in this case the function is continuous at 0. Here is a graph of this solution.

```
Plot[y[x,4/Pi^2], {x,-5,5}];
```

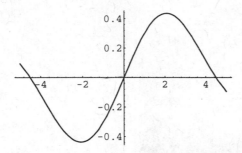

■ Problem Set B, Problem 4

We are interested in the solutions to $y' = (x - e^{-x})/(y + e^y)$, particularly the solution satisfying $y(1.5) = 0.5$.

```
Clear[y];
DSolve[y'[x] == (x - Exp[-x])/(y[x] + Exp[y[x]]),
    y[x], x]
```

Solve::tdep:
    The equations appear to involve transcendental
        functions of the variables in an essentially
        non-algebraic way.

$$\text{Solve}[-E^{-x} + E^{y[x]} - \frac{x^2}{2} + \frac{y[x]^2}{2} == C[1], y[x]]$$

(Note that Version 2.1 of *Mathematica* cannot solve this equation.) The solutions of the equation are implicit, and the warning message indicates that *Mathematica* cannot find an explicit solution. To use the implicit solution, we define a function f(x, y) equal to the left hand side of the equation reported by *Mathematica*. The solution of the IVP is obtained by setting this function equal to f(1.5, 0.5).

```
Clear[f,y,c];
f[x_,y_]= y^2/2+Exp[y]-x^2/2-Exp[-x]
```

$$-E^{-x} + E^{y} - \frac{x^2}{2} + \frac{y^2}{2}$$

```
c=f[1.5, 0.5]
```

0.425591

We can use **ContourPlot** to plot some of the solution curves.

```
ContourPlot[f[x,y], {x,-1,3}, {y,-2,2}];
```

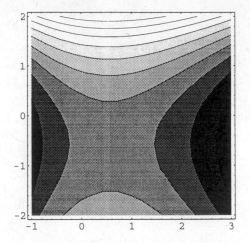

Here are the values of the solution of the IVP at the points   x = 0, 1, 1.8, 2.1.

```
FindRoot[f[0,y] == c, {y,0.5}]
```
{y -> 0.318386}

```
FindRoot[f[1,y] == c, {y,0.5}]
```
{y -> 0.235633}

```
FindRoot[f[1.8,y] == c, {y,0.5}]
```
{y -> 0.682187}

```
FindRoot[f[2.1,y] == c, {y,0.5}]
```
{y -> 0.866212}

The following graph shows the contour corresponding to the value f(1.5, 0.5). The top curve corresponds to the solution of the IVP because it passes through the point (1.5, 0.5). We have marked the points with x-coordinates 0, 1, 1.8, 2.1. (The input that follows actually generates two graphs; we have deleted one.)

```
ContourPlot[f[x,y], {x,-1,3}, {y,-2,2},
    ContourShading->False, Contours->{f[1.5,0.5]}];
Show[%, Graphics[{PointSize[0.03],Point[{0,0.32}],
    Point[{1,0.24}],Point[{1.8,0.68}],
    Point[{2.1,0.87}]}]];
```

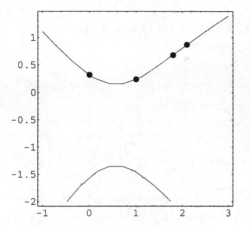

■ Problem Set C, Problem 3

We are going to investigate the IVP $y' = (y - x)(1 - y^3)$, $y(0) = b$, for various choices
of the initial value b. In the next cell the first line clears previous definitions; the
second line creates a function (with delayed evaluation) representing the solution of
the IVP for a given value of the initial condition $y(0) = b$; and the last line makes a list
of solutions for b = 0, .5, 1, 1.5, and 2. We create this list so that *Mathematica* does
not have to run **NDSolve** every time we use the function y(x, b).

```
Clear[y];
y[x_,b_] := y[x] /.
    First[NDSolve[{y'[x] == (y[x] - x)(1 - y[x]^3),
    y[0] == b}, y[x], {x,0,100}]];
sollist = Table[y[x,0.5i], {i,0,4}]
```

NDSolve::ndsz:
  At x = 1.18795, step size is effectively zero;
    singularity suspected.

NDSolve::ndsz:
  At x = 2.11966, step size is effectively zero;
    singularity suspected.

```
{InterpolatingFunction[{0., 1.18795}, <>][x],
  InterpolatingFunction[{0., 2.11966}, <>][x],
  InterpolatingFunction[{0., 100.}, <>][x],
  InterpolatingFunction[{0., 100.}, <>][x],
  InterpolatingFunction[{0., 100.}, <>][x]}
```

Note that with the first two solutions, *Mathematica* stops before it reaches x = 100. As we shall see from the graphs, this is because these solutions have singularities near the indicated values.

□ **(a)**

Here is a plot of the five numerical solutions. The lowest curve corresponds to b = 0 and the highest to b = 2. When we execute this plot command we get a slew of warning messages because we are trying to plot beyond the domain of the first two solutions (which are defined up to 1.19 and 2.12, respectively). We have deleted these warning messages. (Note: We are definitely not suggesting that you ignore warning messages. You should look carefully at any warning messages that *Mathematica* supplies and try to understand why they occur.)

Plot[Evaluate[sollist], {x,0,3}, PlotRange->{-3,3}];

□ **(b)**

The plot indicates that $y = 1$ is a solution. This can be verified by plugging $y = 1$ into the differential equation. It also appears that for values of b less than 1, the solutions have a vertical asymptotes at finite values of x. It is not clear what is happening for values of b greater than 1, so here is a plot of the top three solutions over a longer interval:

```
Plot[Evaluate[sollist[[{3,4,5}]]], {x,0,100}];
```

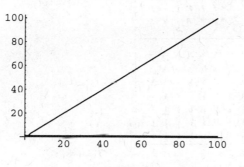

□ **(c)**

Now it appears that for $b > 1$, the solutions are asymptotic to the line $y = x$. To understand this, note that along the line $y = x$, y' is zero; above this line y' is negative; and below the line y' is positive. Thus the solutions are pushed toward the line $y = x$. Here is a plot of the direction field for the differential equation, which confirms the observations we have made about the solutions.

```
<<Graphics`PlotField`
PlotVectorField[{1, (y - x)(1 - y^3)}, {x,0,4},
    {y,-3,5}, ScaleFunction->(1&), Ticks->None,
    Frame->True, AspectRatio->1];
```

■ Problem Set D, Problem 1

We consider Airy's equation

$$y'' = x\,y$$

with initial conditions $y(0) = 0$, $y'(0) = 1$. We first generate a numerical solution.

```
Clear[y,ya];
ya[x_] = y[x] /. First[NDSolve[{y''[x] == x*y[x],
        y[0] == 0, y'[0] == 1}, y[x], {x,-20,20}]]
```

```
InterpolatingFunction[{-20., 20.}, <>][x]
```

□ (a)

For x close to 0, we want to compare the solution of Airy's equation with the solution
to the IVP: $y'' = 0$, $y(0) = 0$, $y'(0) = 1$. The solution of this IVP is $y = x$. Here is a
plot of the numerical solution to Airy's equation and the facsimile solution $y = x$.
The facsimile solution is plotted in gray.

```
Plot[{ya[x],x}, {x,-2,2},
    PlotStyle->{{},{GrayLevel[0.4]}}];
```

The facsimile solution does indeed agree quite well with the actual solution in a neighborhood of the origin.

☐ **(b)**

Now for x close to $-16 = -(4^2)$, we want to compare the solution of Airy's equation to a facsimile solution of the form $c_1 \sin(4x + c_2)$. We plot the numerical solution of Airy's equation on the interval (-18, -14).

```
Plot[ya[x], {x,-18,-14}];
```

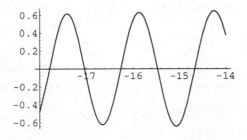

This certainly looks like a sine wave. Let's see how well it matches up with an appropriate sine wave. We have to choose constants c_1 and c_2 in the facsimile solution to make it match up. Note first that c_1 is the amplitude of the facsimile solution, and we can see from the graph that the amplitude of the solution to Airy's equation is about 0.61 on this interval (see the *Graphics* section of Chapter 8 for instruction on finding coordinates of points in *Mathematica* plots). The constant c_2 determines the phase shift, and can be read off from the zeros of the solution. In particular, the solution of Airy's equation has a zero at about -16.3, so we should choose c_2 so that $4*(-16.3) + c_2 = 0$; that is, $c_2 = 65.2$. Here is the plot.

```
Plot[{ya[x], 0.61Sin[4x+65.2]}, {x,-18,-14},
    PlotStyle->{{},{GrayLevel[0.4]}}];
```

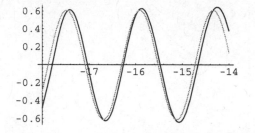

The plots match up very well. Why did we have to choose the values of c_1 and c_2 by hand? Our analysis suggests that the facsimile solution should approximate the actual solution near $x = -K^2$. But the initial condition we've used for Airy's equation is at the point $x = 0$, where the sinusoidal facsimile solutions do not approximate the solution of Airy's equation. Thus the undetermined constants in the facsimile solution do not really have anything to do with the initial conditions in Airy's equation, so we had to choose them by hand to make the solutions match up. Nevertheless, the *frequency* of the facsimile solution is determined by K, and is independent of the undetermined constants. Thus we can conclude at least that the frequency of the solutions of Airy's equation in a neighborhood of $x = -K^2$ will be proportional to K.

□ **(c)**

Now for x close to $16 = (4^2)$, we want to compare the solution of Airy's equation to a facsimile solution of the form $c_1 \sinh(4x + c_2)$. As in (b), we first plot the numerical solution of Airy's equation on the interval (14, 18).

```
Plot[ya[x], {x,14,18}];
```

We'd like to compare this graph to that of the hyperbolic sine function. Again, we have to choose c_1 and c_2. Let's make an arbitrary choice this time: $c_1 = 1, c_2 = 0$.

Plot[Sinh[4x], {x,14,18}];

The graphs are remarkably similar. Note, however, that the values in the second graph are about 10^9 greater than in the first, which means we should have chosen c_1 to be about 10^{-9}.

☐ **(d)**

Plot[ya[x],{x,-20,2}];

It appears from the graph that the frequency increases and the amplitude decreases as x goes to -∞. The increasing frequency was predicted by our facsimile analysis. The decreasing amplitude is harder to account for.

■ Problem Set E, Problem 1

In this problem, we use the program in Chapter 10 to compute the terms up to order 10 of the series solution of Airy's equation.

```
Clear[y];
formalseries = Series[y[x], {x,0,10}]
```

$$y[0] + y'[0] \ x + \frac{y''[0] \ x^2}{2} + \frac{y^{(3)}[0] \ x^3}{6} +$$

$$\frac{y^{(4)}[0] \ x^4}{24} + \frac{y^{(5)}[0] \ x^5}{120} + \frac{y^{(6)}[0] \ x^6}{720} +$$

$$\frac{y^{(7)}[0] \ x^7}{5040} + \frac{y^{(8)}[0] \ x^8}{40320} + \frac{y^{(9)}[0] \ x^9}{362880} +$$

$$\frac{y^{(10)}[0] \ x^{10}}{3628800} + O[x]^{11}$$

```
odeseries = Series[y''[x] - x y[x], {x,0,10}]
```

$$y''[0] + (-y[0] + y^{(3)}[0]) \ x +$$

$$(-y'[0] + \frac{y^{(4)}[0]}{2}) \ x^2 +$$

$$(\frac{-y''[0]}{2} + \frac{y^{(5)}[0]}{6}) \ x^3 +$$

$$(\frac{-y^{(3)}[0]}{6} + \frac{y^{(6)}[0]}{24}) \ x^4 +$$

$$(\frac{-y^{(4)}[0]}{24} + \frac{y^{(7)}[0]}{120}) \ x^5 +$$

$$(\frac{-y^{(5)}[0]}{120} + \frac{y^{(8)}[0]}{720}) \ x^6 +$$

$$(\frac{-y^{(6)}[0]}{720} + \frac{y^{(9)}[0]}{5040}) \ x^7 +$$

$$(\frac{-y^{(7)}[0]}{5040} + \frac{y^{(10)}[0]}{40320}) \ x^8 +$$

$$(\frac{-y^{(8)}[0]}{40320} + \frac{y^{(11)}[0]}{362880}) \ x^9 +$$

$$(\frac{-y^{(9)}[0]}{362880} + \frac{y^{(12)}[0]}{3628800}) \ x^{10} + O[x]^{11}$$

```
twocoeffs = {y[0]->1, y'[0]->0}
```

$$\{y[0] \rightarrow 1, \ y'[0] \rightarrow 0\}$$

ivpseries = odeseries /. twocoeffs

$$y''[0] + (-1 + y^{(3)}[0]) x + \frac{y^{(4)}[0] x^2}{2} +$$

$$(\frac{-y''[0]}{2} + \frac{y^{(5)}[0]}{6}) x^3 +$$

$$(\frac{-y^{(3)}[0]}{6} + \frac{y^{(6)}[0]}{24}) x^4 +$$

$$(\frac{-y^{(4)}[0]}{24} + \frac{y^{(7)}[0]}{120}) x^5 +$$

$$(\frac{-y^{(5)}[0]}{120} + \frac{y^{(8)}[0]}{720}) x^6 +$$

$$(\frac{-y^{(6)}[0]}{720} + \frac{y^{(9)}[0]}{5040}) x^7 +$$

$$(\frac{-y^{(7)}[0]}{5040} + \frac{y^{(10)}[0]}{40320}) x^8 +$$

$$(\frac{-y^{(8)}[0]}{40320} + \frac{y^{(11)}[0]}{362880}) x^9 +$$

$$(\frac{-y^{(9)}[0]}{362880} + \frac{y^{(12)}[0]}{3628800}) x^{10} + O[x]^{11}$$

morecoeffs = Solve[ivpseries == 0]

$\{\{y^{(10)}[0] \to 0, y^{(11)}[0] \to 0, y^{(12)}[0] \to 280,$
$\quad y''[0] \to 0, y^{(3)}[0] \to 1, y^{(4)}[0] \to 0,$
$\quad y^{(5)}[0] \to 0, y^{(6)}[0] \to 4, y^{(7)}[0] \to 0,$
$\quad y^{(8)}[0] \to 0, y^{(9)}[0] \to 28\}\}$

coeffs = Join[twocoeffs, First[morecoeffs]]

$\{y[0] \to 1, y'[0] \to 0, y^{(10)}[0] \to 0,$
$\quad y^{(11)}[0] \to 0, y^{(12)}[0] \to 280, y''[0] \to 0,$
$\quad y^{(3)}[0] \to 1, y^{(4)}[0] \to 0, y^{(5)}[0] \to 0,$
$\quad y^{(6)}[0] \to 4, y^{(7)}[0] \to 0, y^{(8)}[0] \to 0,$
$\quad y^{(9)}[0] \to 28\}$

answer = Normal[formalseries] /. coeffs

$$1 + \frac{x^3}{6} + \frac{x^6}{180} + \frac{x^9}{12960}$$

Now we compute the precise Airy function that satisfies the given initial data. The built-in Airy functions are AiryAi[x] and AiryBi[x]. We could solve the simultaneous equations, c_1AiryAi[0] + c_2AiryBi[0] = 1 and c_1AiryAi'[0] + c_2AiryBi'[0] = 0, but we can also obtain the solution directly using **DSolve**.

```
Clear[w];
airy = DSolve[{w''[x] - x*w[x] == 0, w[0] == 1,
    w'[0] == 0}, w[x], x]
```

$$\left\{\left\{w[x] \rightarrow \frac{3^{2/3}\ \text{AiryAi}[x]\ \text{Gamma}[\frac{2}{3}]}{2} + \frac{3^{1/6}\ \text{AiryBi}[x]\ \text{Gamma}[\frac{2}{3}]}{2}\right\}\right\}$$

```
a[x_] = w[x] /. First[airy]
```

$$\frac{3^{2/3}\ \text{AiryAi}[x]\ \text{Gamma}[\frac{2}{3}]}{2} + \frac{3^{1/6}\ \text{AiryBi}[x]\ \text{Gamma}[\frac{2}{3}]}{2}$$

Now we compare the series approximation to the solution produced by **DSolve**.

```
Plot[{answer,a[x]}, {x,-20,2},
    PlotStyle->{GrayLevel[0.4],{}}];
```

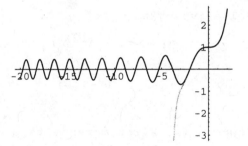

The approximation is accurate on the interval (-3, 2).

■ Problem Set F, Problem 6

□ (a)

First we find the critical points of the system.

```
Clear[x,y];
crit = Solve[{x((3/2) - x - y/2) == 0,
    y(2 - (3/2)x - y/2) == 0}, {x,y}]
```

$$\{\{x \rightarrow 0,\ y \rightarrow 0\},\ \{x \rightarrow 1,\ y \rightarrow 1\},$$
$$\{x \rightarrow \frac{3}{2},\ y \rightarrow 0\},\ \{y \rightarrow 4,\ x \rightarrow 0\}\}$$

We want to analyze the critical points of the system. To do this, we compute the matrix of partials of the system, and then evaluate this matrix and find its eigenvalues at the critical points.

```
sys1 = x((3/2) - x - y/2);
sys2 = y(2 - (3/2)x - y/2);
A = {{D[sys1,x], D[sys1,y]}, {D[sys2,x], D[sys2,y]}}
```

$$\{\{\tfrac{3}{2} - 2\,x - \tfrac{y}{2}, \tfrac{-x}{2}\}, \{\tfrac{-3\,y}{2}, 2 - \tfrac{3\,x}{2} - y\}\}$$

```
Eigensystem[A /. crit[[1]] ]
```

$$\{\{\tfrac{3}{2}, 2\}, \{\{1, 0\}, \{0, 1\}\}\}$$

```
Eigensystem[A /. crit[[2]] ]
```

$$\{\{\tfrac{-3 - \text{Sqrt}[13]}{4}, \tfrac{-3 + \text{Sqrt}[13]}{4}\},$$
$$\{\{\tfrac{1 + \text{Sqrt}[13]}{6}, 1\}, \{\tfrac{1 - \text{Sqrt}[13]}{6}, 1\}\}\}$$

```
Eigensystem[A /. crit[[3]] ]
```

$$\{\{-(\tfrac{3}{2}), -(\tfrac{1}{4})\}, \{\{1, 0\}, \{-(\tfrac{3}{5}), 1\}\}\}$$

```
Eigensystem[A /. crit[[4]] ]
```

$$\{\{-2, -(\tfrac{1}{2})\}, \{\{0, 1\}, \{-(\tfrac{1}{4}), 1\}\}\}$$

By inspecting the eigenvalues at the four critical points, we can classify the critical points as follows:

(0,0)   unstable node
(1,1)   unstable saddle point
(1.5,0)   asymptotically stable node
(0,4)   asymptotically stable node

□ **(b)**

Here is a plot of the vector field of the system.

```
<<Graphics`PlotField`
csvf = PlotVectorField[{x(1.5 - x - 0.5y),
    y(2 - 1.5x - 0.5y)}, {x,0,3}, {y,0,5},
    ScaleFunction->(Log[50#+1]&),
    Frame->True, AspectRatio->1];
```

The vector field confirms what we found in part (a).

□ (c)

To plot the phase portrait of the system, we use the approach described at the end of Chapter 11. We use a rectangular grid of 42 different initial conditions.

```
Clear[t,x0,y0];
cspop[t_,x0_,y0_] := ({x[t], y[t]} /. First[
  NDSolve[{x'[t] == x[t](1.5 - x[t] - 0.5y[t]),
  y'[t] == y[t](2 - 1.5x[t] - 0.5y[t]),
  x[0] == x0, y[0] == y0}, {x[t],y[t]}, {t,0,20}]]);
cs[t_] = Flatten[Table[cspop[t,i,j],
  {i,0,3,0.5}, {j,0,5}], 1];
ParametricPlot[Evaluate[cs[t]], {t,0,20},
  PlotRange->{{0,2},{0,5}}];
```

This graph is not ideal. The problem is that a rectangular grid of initial conditions is not the best choice for this system. We can see from the graph that a better choice of initial conditions would be a collection of evenly spaced points along lines parallel to and above and below the line from (0,4) to (1.5, 0). Since that line has slope about -2.5, we redefine the function **cs** as follows:

```
Clear[cs];
cs[t_] = Flatten[Table[cspop[t,j*x0,j(2.5 - 2.5x0)],
    {x0,0,1,0.1}, {j,0.6,2.6,2}], 1];
csplot = ParametricPlot[Evaluate[cs[t]],
    {t,0,20}, PlotRange->{{0,2},{0,5}}];
```

Much better! By putting the parametric plot and the vector field plot together, we can see the direction of the trajectories.

```
Show[csplot, csvf];
```

□ **(d)**

Here is a table of values of the populations. We use the option **TableDepth->2** to prevent the **TableForm** command from stripping off all levels of braces.

```
TableForm[Table[Evaluate[{t,cspop[t,2.5,2]}],
   {t,1,20}], TableHeadings->{None,
   {"Time", "Populations"}}, TableDepth->2]
```

Time	Populations
1	{1.29443, 0.761069}
2	{1.20257, 0.629452}
3	{1.20352, 0.569923}
4	{1.2221, 0.520469}
5	{1.24499, 0.471821}
6	{1.2692, 0.422989}
7	{1.29376, 0.374567}
8	{1.31806, 0.327472}
9	{1.34158, 0.282627}
10	{1.36383, 0.240847}
11	{1.38442, 0.202758}
12	{1.40307, 0.168753}
13	{1.41961, 0.13899}
14	{1.434, 0.113408}
15	{1.4463, 0.0917786}
16	{1.45665, 0.0737513}
17	{1.46524, 0.0589121}
18	{1.47228, 0.0468244}
19	{1.478, 0.0370648}
20	{1.4826, 0.0292416}

☐ **(e)**

There is no peaceful coexistence because almost all the trajectories tend toward an equilibrium point representing a positive population of one species and a zero population of the other. For example, in (d) we saw that the population of x tends to 1.5 and the population of y tends to 0. The only nonzero initial population distribution which results in no change is x = 1, y = 1.

To approximate the separatrices, we solve the system for negative time for initial conditions near the unstable equilibrium point (1,1). From the portrait in (c), we expect one separatrix running from the origin to (1,1); and another running from (1,1) out toward infinity. To find the first we choose an initial data point just to the left and below (1,1) and solve backwards in time; and to find the second we do the same thing with an initial data point above and to the right of (1,1).

```
Clear[cspop,cs];
cspop[t_,x0_,y0_] := ({x[t], y[t]} /. First[
    NDSolve[{x'[t] == x[t](1.5 - x[t] - 0.5y[t]),
    y'[t] == y[t](2 - 1.5x[t] - 0.5y[t]),
    x[0] == x0, y[0] == y0}, {x[t],y[t]},
    {t,-10,20}]]);
```

If you try the command **cspop** you'll see that it generates a lot of warning messages regarding maximum number of steps in **NDSolve**, and plotting outside the domain of definition in **ParametricPlot**. We'll turn these warning messages off before we proceed.

```
Off[ParametricPlot::pptr];
Off[NDSolve::mxst];
Off[InterpolatingFunction::dmval];
```

Now we can try to plot the separatrix.

```
separatrixplot = ParametricPlot[
Evaluate[{cspop[t,0.95,0.95], cspop[t,1.05,1.05]}],
    {t,-10,0}, PlotStyle->GrayLevel[0.4]];
```

```
Show[csplot, separatrixplot];
```

□ **(f)**

To find a numerical approximation to where the vertical line x = 1.5 cuts the separatrix we delineated above, we first observe that the value is between 1.5 and 2.0. So we plot trajectories beginning at x = 1.5 and y = 1.5, 1.6, ..., 2.0.

```
Clear[cspop,cs];
cspop[t_,x0_,y0_] := ({x[t], y[t]} /. First[
   NDSolve[{x'[t] == x[t](1.5 - x[t] - 0.5y[t]),
   y'[t] == y[t](2 - 1.5x[t] - 0.5y[t]),
   x[0] == x0, y[0] == y0}, {x[t],y[t]},
   {t,-10,20}]]);
cs[t_] = Table[cspop[t,1.5,y0], {y0,1.5,2.0,0.1}];
ParametricPlot[Evaluate[cs[t]],
   {t,0,10}, PlotRange->{{0.5,2},{0.5,2}}];
```

It appears that the desired y-value is very close to 1.7. We now refine the picture using the same strategy. We use the **PlotRange** option to clarify the portrait.

```
cs[t_] = Table[cspop[t,1.5,y0],
   {y0,1.68,1.72,0.01}];
ParametricPlot[Evaluate[cs[t]], {t,0,10},
   PlotRange->{{0.95,1.05},{0.95,1.05}}];
```

The desired value is between 1.69 and 1.70. One more iteration will settle the matter!

```
cs[t_] = Table[cspop[t,1.5,y0],
    {y0,1.69,1.70,0.002}];
ParametricPlot[Evaluate[cs[t]], {t,0,10},
    PlotRange->{{0.995,1.01},{0.995,1.01}}];
```

Voila. The answer is 1.69.

We could, of course, continue this process and obtain greater and greater accuracy, but it is not possible to find the value exactly. Even if we were given the exact value, it would not be possible to verify its correctness. This is because **NDSolve** is an approximate method and errors inevitably occur -- errors that cause the trajectory to fall off the separatrix, and then to tend toward one of the stable equilibria.

Index

The index uses the same conventions for fonts that are used throughout the book. *Mathematica* commands, such as **DSolve**, are printed in boldface. Menu options, such as `File`, are printed in a monospaced typewriter font. Trademarked names, such as *NeXT*, are printed in a slanted font. Everything else is printed in a standard font.